INTERNATIONAL DEVELOPMENT IN FOCUS

Enhancing Skills in Sri Lanka for Inclusion, Recovery, and Resilience

SHOBHANA SOSALE, SEO YEON HONG,
SHALIKA SUBASINGHE, AND HIRAN HERAT

WORLD BANK GROUP

Contents

Boxes

Exhibits

Figures

Tables

Acknowledgments

Enhancing Skills in Sri Lanka for Inclusion, Recovery, and Resilience is part of the ongoing advisory services and analytical work that the World Bank team for education is undertaking in Sri Lanka. The report presents findings from the background analytical study intended to inform the National Planning Department of the Government of Sri Lanka (GoSL) about the status of the skills sector service delivery in the country. It makes the case for strengthening Sri Lanka's institutional framework, governance, and financing to inform the preparation of the GoSL's 21st-century skills strategy. The report provides the analytical basis for investments in skills development by assessing the current institutional setup, the challenges, and the potential for skilling, reskilling, and upskilling of Sri Lanka's workforce.

This study was prepared under the general direction of Chiyo Kanda, World Bank country manager, and Keiko Inoue, education practice manager for the South Asia Region. The authors of the report are Shobhana Sosale (team leader), Seo Yeon Hong (consultant economist), Shalika Subasinghe (consultant technical and vocational education and training specialist), and Hiran Herat (consultant implementation expert). Priyal Mukesh Gala was consultant research analyst. The team is grateful to the GoSL Ministry of Skills Development, Tertiary Vocational Education Commission, and Department of National Planning officials for collaboration, discussions, and comments on the initial drafts of the report. In addition, the team appreciates the comments received from participants at a workshop, including government officials from the Ministry of Skills Development, Department of Census and Statistics, National Education Commission, Sri Lanka Foreign Employment Bureau, Department of Technical Education and Training, Vocational Training Authority of Sri Lanka, National Apprentice Industrial Training Authority, Asian Development Bank, Deutsche Gesellschaft für Internationale Zusammenarbeit GmbH, Department of Foreign Affairs and Trade (Australia), and Korean International Cooperation Agency.

The authors thank Harsha Aturupane, René Antonio Leon Solano, Adelle Pushparatnam, and peer reviewers Diego Angel-Urdilona, James Gresham, and Kirill Vasiliev for their review and useful comments. The authors thank Siddhartha Raja and Junko Narimatsu from the Digital Development Team of the World Bank South Asia Region for engaging with them to address the digital development and skilling aspects. The authors also thank Elizabeth Ruppert Bulmer (lead economist) for sharing information from the 2020 Sri Lanka jobs diagnostic, which has informed analysis. Paul Holtz (Next Partners) edited the report. Caroline Polk coordinated the production of the book.

The following advisory services and analytical works comprise the background research to inform the Skills Development for Inclusion, Recovery, and Resilience project:

- Amarasekera, C. L. 2019. "Background Review on English Language Curriculum." World Bank Country Office, Colombo.
- Ranathunga, L. 2021. "Sri Lanka: Skills Development Background Review on Information and Communications Technology (ICT) Curriculum." World Bank Country Office, Colombo.

About the Authors

Hiran Herat is a consultant with the World Bank. He has more than 45 years of experience in World Bank operations and is an implementation expert. His areas of specialization are in project and program management and evaluation, supplemented by a strong background in finance, accounting, and procurement. He is a consultant with the Education Global Practice; the Social Protection and Jobs Global Practice; and the Finance, Competitiveness, and Innovation Global Practice. His experience spans projects and programs in Africa, Central Asia, Europe, Latin America, South Asia, and Southeast Asia. Herat is experienced in designing, managing, and evaluating World Bank–funded projects across multiple sectors, including industry, the private sector, finance and banking, innovation and technology development, small and medium enterprise financing, privatization of public enterprises, and public finance and taxation. He holds a graduate degree in business administration in international finance from the George Washington University.

Seo Yeon Hong is an economist focusing on the analytics and science for food and nutrition at the World Food Programme. She previously was a consultant economist in the South Asia Region of the World Bank Education Global Practice for more than 10 years. Her specialization is in development economics. Hong has studied and engaged in human development sector (health, education, and social protection) policies in many developing countries around the world. She holds a doctoral degree in public analysis from the Pardee RAND Graduate School and an MBA from the KDI School of Public Policy and Management.

Shobhana Sosale is a senior education specialist in the South Asia Region of the World Bank Education Practice in Washington, DC. She was global co-lead for the Education and Gender thematic area and the climate change and education focal point for South Asia from 2019–23. Sosale has more than 25 years of experience in education and skills development and has published on education and related fields, analyzing topics linking political economy and cross-sectoral issues in education, technology, climate change, skills development and jobs, entrepreneurship, public-private partnerships, and finance. She has led the preparation and implementation of education and skill development projects and programs and led the World Bank's education engagement in more than 14 countries in East Asia, Europe and Central Asia, the Middle East and North Africa, South Asia, and Sub-Saharan Africa. Sosale also has academic teaching experience at the graduate and undergraduate levels. She holds graduate degrees in political economy and macroeconomics.

Shalika Subasinghe is a consultant with the World Bank Education Global Practice and the Social Protection and Jobs Global Practice in the South Asia Region. Her most recent work focuses on projects and analytical work relating to early childhood development, skills development, jobs, demographic transition, public expenditure reviews, and social safety nets in Sri Lanka and pension and social protection in Maldives. Previously, she has published in the fields of marketing, consumer behavior, and education. Prior to joining the World Bank, she worked for the Distance Learning Center Ltd. (the Sri Lankan node of the World Bank's Global Development Learning Network) as the learning and development manager and in universities in Australia and Sri Lanka lecturing at the undergraduate and postgraduate levels. Subasinghe is a Fulbright scholar and holds an MBA from the University of New Hampshire, a graduate certificate in university teaching and learning from Charles Sturt University, and a bachelor of commerce from the University of Colombo.

Executive Summary
KEY FINDINGS AND RECOMMENDATIONS TO INFORM POLICY DIALOGUE AND BRIEFS

Sri Lanka is at a crossroads. The country's longstanding structural weaknesses plunged the country into a severe economic crisis in 2022 (World Bank 2023). Acute anxieties have emerged due to rising inflation because of the "triple crisis" (fuel, food, fiscal); shifting leadership; and wide protests in 2022. And although Sri Lankans are eager to move forward, their destination is not entirely clear, underscoring the importance of including all members of the country's society—particularly women and marginalized groups—in charting the future. People of all ages and backgrounds stand to benefit from better training, stronger skills, good jobs, and the improved life that follows from them. A skilled and productive workforce will form the bedrock for mobilizing tax revenue for a brighter future, help increase Sri Lanka's competitiveness, and attract investment.

Strengthening skills and improving education will be crucial to Sri Lanka's recovery. Modern economies place a growing premium on higher-order cognitive skills such as complex problem solving, sociobehavioral skills, reasoning, and self-efficacy. Building these skills requires a strong, effective education and training system. Demand is declining for less skilled workers—such as those with only a basic high school certification—and rising for more skilled ones.

Sri Lanka has fewer entrants into occupations requiring mid-level skills because fewer such jobs are being created, partly because jobs requiring mid-level skills can be replaced by labor-saving technology such as automation. Jobs requiring nonroutine low- or high-level skills, however, can thrive despite labor-saving technology.

Like many developed countries, Sri Lanka seems to be experiencing labor polarization. The occupational skills composition by economic sector in Sri Lanka over the period 2013–18 shows that across the three sectors—agriculture, industry, and services—low- and middle-level skills were predominant in the agriculture sector; low-, middle-, and marginally high-level skills were prevalent in industry; and middle- and high-level skills composition was greatest in the services sector. Consistently across the three sectors, occupational skills in Sri Lanka are clustered around low- and mid-level skills. However, the services sector has a growing concentration of high-level skills. The COVID-19 pandemic was an inflection point. In 2021, during the COVID-19 pandemic period, low-level skills seemed to be growing a little across agriculture, industry, and the services sectors, while mid-level skills remained consistently high in agriculture and industry but also grew in services.

Sri Lankan industries with relatively large production growth saw their skills composition change between 2013 and 2018, and specifically between 2018 and 2021. In finance the share of highly skilled workers rose by 9 percent; in information and communication technology (ICT), by 8 percent; and in electricity (power sector), by 6 percent. Technology is likely to have improved efficiency in those sectors. However, there were substantial increases in low-skilled workers occurred in water supply and waste management (20 percent) and real estate (10 percent). These trends may explain why job growth was not commensurate with production growth in finance, ICT, and electricity (power sector), which had growing numbers of highly skilled, highly productive workers between 2013 and 2018. There were changes between 2018 and 2021: The percentage of highly skilled workers fell in finance (−2.4 percent) and in ICT (−3.1 percent), whereas in the power sector there was a slight increase of highly skilled workers (0.4 percent). During both periods 2013–18 and 2018–21, workers in the health and social sector registered slight growth among high- and low-skilled workers (from 0 percent to 0.6 percent), declining among the mid-level skilled workforce (from 2 percent to −0.5 percent). The effects during the 2018–21 period were due to the exogenous shock of the COVID-19 pandemic to the economy.

SRI LANKA'S SKILLS STATUS

Sri Lanka is transitioning from a rural-based to a modern, urbanized economy, with better jobs being created, especially in services. The country's economic development depends on social stability, and education plays a crucial role in developing the human capital and promoting the social stability required for development, especially given the country's history of ethnic-based secessionist conflict and its current social strife. Still, too many poor-quality, labor-intensive, low-productivity jobs remain, mostly in the informal sector. And despite their growing aspirations, many educated youth and women are underemployed.

Employers cannot find enough skilled workers. A recent survey found that nearly 500,000 vacancies—in a country with a population of 21.7 million—exist in the private sector, with most of the unmet labor demand occurring in industry, services, and trade. This skills shortage will likely worsen as Sri Lanka aspires to full-fledged upper-income country status.

Few workers enter the job market with appropriate skills training. Of the 450,000 students who complete grade 11 in a typical academic year, only 20 percent move on to higher education, and only about a third of the rest enroll in technical and vocational education and training (TVET). The result is that nearly half of students leave secondary school with no opportunity for further education or training. In addition, female workforce participation is just 35 percent, further limiting the supply of trained labor. Almost half of employers think the TVET system does not provide graduates with adequate practical skills and timely knowledge, including in English communications and computer and digital literacy. Employers also feel that workers' cognitive skills (reading, writing, and numeracy) are insufficient for highly skilled occupations.

Skills development is crucial to Sri Lanka's economic transformation and global competitiveness. To become globally competitive, Sri Lanka's workforce must gain the technical competencies and higher-order cognitive skills needed in domestic and foreign labor markets. Those skills include working knowledge of English, digital skills, and soft or transferable skills. Structural changes in the country's workforce—proportionally fewer younger workers and more older ones—require stronger skills for new and existing workers to support Sri Lanka's economic transformation. To bolster livelihoods, upgrading, reskilling, and upskilling are needed across the board.[1]

Sri Lankans who have TVET are more likely to work (controlling for education level) than those who do not. The relationship between education and working is not necessarily linear, however. For example, people with O-level diplomas are not more likely to work than those with lower-secondary education or less. Those with A-level qualifications or university degrees are more likely to work. Although there have been annual fluctuations, no significant observable changes to these patterns have occurred in recent years. If they are unemployed, it is likely due to voluntary decision, mismatch in expectations due to high reservation wage expectations, and/or search time to find jobs.

COVID-19 has disrupted lives and livelihoods, and widespread losses in education, skills, jobs, and incomes have occurred. Although there has been a gradual shift to online education, learning losses remain quite high. TVET enrollments have dropped by nearly 50 percent and completions, by 57 percent. This situation is demanding skills development among people searching for employment in the new economic environment. The challenges precipitated by COVID-19 are demanding the sudden, intensive use of digital technologies and applications for delivering services such as education, health care, social protection, e-government, and financial services and banking.

Advancing human capital will be central to regaining pre-COVID-19 growth and to modernizing agriculture, deepening industrial development, and expanding services. At the same time, rapid technological progress lends urgency to developing a skills delivery system that keeps pace with the changing nature of work. Addressing the flow of new graduates, the stock of existing graduates, and the return of migrant workers will require a renewed policy and strategy for action. To become globally competitive, young Sri Lankans require better working knowledge of English, digital skills, and soft or transferable skills. Moreover, job opportunities must be open to all, including women, marginalized groups, and workers of all ages.

INTERVENTIONS AND OPPORTUNITIES

The Skills Sector Development Program (SSDP)—supported by many development partners including the World Bank and the Asian Development Bank—was implemented between 2014 and 2020 to build an efficient skills development system for Sri Lanka. Although the program increased access to TVET, it failed to make training institutes more efficient. The number of public and private TVET students rose by an average of 20 percent annually during the SSDP implementation period, but there was no improvement in completion rates across the TVET sector—they rose at private institutes but fell at public ones, resulting in no net change. The increase in enrollments was likely due to the government's new policy of making TVET free of charge.

Although there appear to be few obstacles for Sri Lankan employers seeking to hire new workers, rigid employment regulations prevent them from dismissing redundant workers. Such regulation constrains employers from hiring permanent staff and shapes firms' incentives to enter and exit an economy, with implications for job creation and economic growth.

Between 2013 and 2018, growth in employment and production was highest in real estate, construction, electricity, ICT, finance, and water supply and waste management. In 2018, agriculture contracted by 10 percent and mining, by 32 percent. Although manufacturing, wholesale and retail services, and transportation are the largest industries in terms of output, in recent years their contribution to job creation has been marginal. In the meantime, the high growth and relatively low employment elasticity (fewer jobs created per unit of output growth) in finance and ICT means a mismatch between supply and demand. However, between 2018 and 2021, employment and production fell in all sectors except finance and ICT. With growing unemployment and underemployment, labor supply in these sectors has not been meeting available demand, likely due to a dearth of appropriately skilled, reskilled, and upskilled labor. Consequently, the available jobs are going unfilled. Thus, investment is needed to develop workers' skills in these industries. Further research on and analysis of subsector and occupation-specific skills are needed to understand the links between labor intensity, automation processes, and skills mismatch over time and why growth in certain industries has not led to employment creation.

Green recovery can create opportunities for growth in incomes and jobs. Green industries are important for generating environmentally sustainable economic growth and are expected to create more jobs than conventional industries do. Moreover, greening projects can be labor intensive. Most such initiatives focus on transforming traditional economies into green ones, with the aim of boosting economic efficiency gains over the long term (OECD 2020).

OBSTACLES AND IDEAS

Sri Lanka's workforce suffers from low female participation. In 2021, only 32 percent of women were economically active, meaning that the gender gap in labor force participation was 39 percentage points. Further, in 2021 nearly 3.3 percent of working women were underemployed compared with 2.1 percent of working men. There have been no significant changes in the gender gap over time. The labor market outcome is favorable for women in high-skilled jobs: 24 percent in 2021 compared with 16 percent for working men. In some industries gender divisions are more pronounced. In 2018, industries with high shares of female workers included education (70 percent), health (62 percent), manufacturing (47 percent), and finance (42 percent).

Sri Lanka needs to promote women's participation in fields where their presence is already strong. It also needs to increase female participation in science, technology, education, and mathematics (STEM) fields by lowering barriers and by coordinating and facilitating opportunities. Social and systemic barriers to participation in STEM need to be broken, starting with training to transitioning into work, to retention in the sectors involved.

TVET has an important role to play in education's digital transformation. TVET is responsible for supplying skilled technicians to expand network connections, building energy and ICT infrastructure in schools, developing software for digital content, and upgrading teacher skills for digital learning environments.

Five systemic issues contribute to Sri Lanka's skills constraints:

- The country's TVET system is complex and fragmented, involving multiple providers and variety of instructional approaches to skills training. Public provision of skills training involves several ministries and 30 statutory bodies that account for approximately 70 percent of TVET enrollment. The remaining 30 percent of TVET is provided by private institutions and nongovernmental organizations (NGOs). Weak coordination is likely to create inefficiencies and complicates overall implementation of a skills development plan.

- There is a disconnect between the curricula pursued in TVET institutions and the demands of the job market. Some of the difference between the demand for and supply of skills is due to weak links with employers and industry, especially in curriculum design, development of training programs, instructors' and teachers' professional development, apprenticeships, and industry visits.

- The alignment of training standards and competencies to labor market needs, as defined in the National Qualifications Framework, is progressing slowly. This continued misalignment further weakens the TVET system's link with employers' needs.

- TVET suffers from serious shortages of qualified instructors and teachers, especially those with industrial experience. Teacher career development and performance incentive structures undermine teacher motivation and make it difficult to attract quality instructors and teachers. Moreover, the lack of modern equipment and facilities makes the teaching-learning environment challenging. A career progression policy for TVET instructors, teachers, and trainers is absent.

- The quality assurance system for TVET is at a nascent stage, and many private providers and courses are still not registered or accredited. Regular tracking of TVET graduate outcomes and feedback mechanisms are largely absent.

RECOMMENDATIONS

Skills development is crucial to Sri Lanka's economic transformation and global competitiveness. The country's workforce must gain the technical competencies and higher-order cognitive skills needed to meet the demands of local and foreign labor markets. Demographic changes also have important implications for skills training and workforce development. The share of young people entering the workforce is declining, and the share of older workers is rising. These structural changes in the workforce call for efforts to upgrade skills for new and existing workers to support Sri Lanka's economic transformation in the medium and long term. Crucial to boosting the supply of workers is the upgrading, reskilling, and upskilling of youth, women, and men to meet the challenges imposed by COVID-19 and to bolster employment and livelihoods in informal and formal labor markets.

Government policies and strategies signal strong support for the skills development agenda. Sri Lanka aims to drive economic transformation with targets to increase export income, address skills development, and create job opportunities. Developing skills and competencies to match the demands of a new economy remains one of the core strategies for supporting the new government's vision. To that end, the following efforts are needed:

- Increase access to TVET to enhance employability, especially for women and marginalized groups.
- Improve the quality of TVET programs.
- Foster digital skills acquisition.
- Reorient and introduce new programs to enhance options for employability.
- Strengthen governance and accountability.
- Deepen private sector involvement.
- Foster entrepreneurship.
- Broaden skills development by harnessing chambers of commerce and employment councils.
- Improve social perceptions of TVET.

Not all sectors carry equal weight. The government will need to identify and prioritize sectors that truly need skilling, reskilling, and upskilling. A hybrid mode of teaching and learning is required, one that is based on learning management or e-learning platforms that facilitate anywhere, anytime learning.

With skills development being a government priority and gender being a binding constraint, skills development needs to be adjusted. Support should facilitate equal opportunity for high-quality, relevant skills. Targeted populations need to include marginalized, vulnerable, and disabled populations as well as girls and women.

TVET needs modular programs to help with lifelong learning and skills development. Specifically, employees and employers should be given options for stacking skills, building theoretical and practical expertise over time. Facilitating the acquisition of microcredentials (short, focused credentials for skills in demand) and of stackable microcredentials to provide pathways for students to acquire certificates or to pursue full degree programs will enhance opportunities for lifelong learning. Making TVET skills more flexible, credible, and stackable is essential to bridge gaps in livelihoods and skills.

Quality enhancements should be made using existing infrastructure:

- *Instructor and teacher training.* Review and upgrade teacher training standards in priority areas for the economy. Put in place a dynamic system to help instructors and teachers to reskill and upskill themselves. Review and assess the stock and flow of qualified instructors and teachers. Make use of visiting industry experts as teaching faculty outside of office hours and on weekends. Consider global knowledge exchange seminars to enhance local knowledge and expand beyond local perspectives.
- *Instructor and teacher recruitment.* Establish a performance-based system of pay for instructors and teachers through a new cadre of contractual instructors and teachers. Natural attrition is occurring among existing instructors and teachers, who currently have permanent jobs and draw a monthly salary without any performance appraisal or promotion system,

reskilling, or upskilling. Consider hiring instructors who can grasp digital trends and apply new digital options for skilling, reskilling, and upskilling.

- *Large centers with enhanced facilities.* At present, there are 600 public sector institutions and 700–800 private sector institutions. Rationalize institutions by introducing a revamped accreditation system for private sector institutions; providing incentives for consolidating small private sector institutions; consolidating public sector institutions to close small, inefficient ones; introducing centers of excellence; consolidating programs by closing unsubscribed programs and adding new 21st-century skills programs (such as stackable microcredentials in areas such as collaboration, creative problem solving, critical thinking, empathy, initiative, oral and written communication, intercultural awareness and fluency, and resilience) in public sector institutions to improve market relevance and quality; assessing the overall governance of the system; and introducing new financing modalities and conducting a public expenditure review of the public skills development system. Centers of excellence in some provinces would help improve the image of TVET.

- *Green infrastructure solutions.* Rehabilitating existing TVET infrastructure should include the use of renewable energy solutions (such as solar and wind) and climate-resilient building materials.

- *Improving coverage and access.* Adopting hybrid or blended teaching and learning modes and, where applicable and necessary, building face-to-face service delivery modes would help double the capacity of the TVET system to respond to growing demand.

- *Digitalization.* Digitalization of systems, including the introduction of e-teaching and e-learning materials and assessments, is necessary. Address the digital divide from four dimensions: geographic/spatial, connectivity, affordability, and as it relates to marginalized and vulnerable populations.

- *Digital skills.* Develop programs for building the digital skills of instructors and teachers, trainers, tutors, assessors, and administrators and managers.

- *Building skills bridges and ladders* and *skills identification.* Adopting the approach of linking to O-level and A-level high school certification, career interest tests for students to assess areas of interest would be important. Career paths for grade 9 students, the option and possibility for students to acquire National Vocational Qualification (NVQ)-level credentials, career and success standards, and career counseling and guidance deserve attention. Further, giving credence to the Government of Sri Lanka's Skills Passport is important. The Skills Passport includes details of NVQ certificates and the trade, number of years of work experience, and other employment information. Because it is more like a driver's license, workers can carry it with them. The Skills Passport is valid for five years. After five years, the Skills Passport holder can apply to extend the validity period. Reskilling requirements have not yet been articulated and communicated but are an important area to address.

- *Curriculum and standards development.* Review the number of occupations for which NVQ-based standards have not yet been developed. Enhance capacity for curriculum assessment and change (which currently takes three years per occupation). Put in place new approaches to curriculum assessment and standards setting. Modularize TVET to permit the stacking of credentials and adopt a qualifications-based approach to skilling. Also of importance to preparing an internationally competitive workforce is the inclusion of soft skills (teamwork, effective communication, self-presentation, problem solving, and so on) in the curriculum and English-language skills. Making English-language curricula a mandatory requirement for all skills development courses would be a driving factor (Amarasekera 2019).

- *Fostering fungible skills.* Curricular reform should result in transformation of skills. Create opportunities for developing fungible skills rather than specialized skills.

- *Districtwide assessment centers for awarding NVQs.* Assess the feasibility and establish, where possible, assessment centers in each district for the purpose of conducting competency-based assessments for the Tertiary and Vocational Education Commission (TVEC) to award NVQ certificates through collaboration with the public, private, and NGO TVET institutes. The proposed centers would be set up within the premises of existing public sector institutions operating under the Ministry of Skills Development. This measure is expected to expedite and facilitate the assessment process of the two pathways of obtaining NVQs.

- *Recognition of prior learning (RPL).* An RPL system can be used to promote a more inclusive and sustainable skills development system that benefits everyone. Building trust around the assessments offered via Sri Lanka's RPL system is important to support the RPL system. Further, Sri Lanka would benefit from assessing the outcome and impact of its RPL system to determine the effectiveness of the knowledge and skills certification provided under the system.

- *Reskilling for returning migrants to help them to take up new jobs.* Introduce new certification options for returning migrants and upload the credentials on the Skills Passport. This practice would foster the portability of knowledge and skills more readily.

- *Entrepreneurship skills.* Promoting self-employment is a priority for the government. Entrepreneurship skills will need to be included in the curriculum to expand the opportunities for individuals to become entrepreneurs. This training is especially needed for women who can enter the labor market through home-based work. Combining entrepreneurship with digital skills will help to facilitate their entry into the workforce on their time and terms. With more women entering the labor market, they could productively contribute to the economy. This will likely also create additional job opportunities in the areas of child care and health care. The availability of child care would facilitate women's participation in the labor market as employees or entrepreneurs in both traditional (for example, child care and elder care) and nontraditional sectors.

- *Communications for sensitization and mindset change about TVET.* This report finds that more young graduates are entering the labor market. This finding is corroborated by the number of young people graduating from secondary school. The number who passed all three subjects in the General Certificate of Education Advanced Level rose from 126,971 (61 percent) in 2014 to 154,905 (66 percent) in 2019. Most parents, students, and communities prefer academic qualifications to professional qualifications. Conditional on working, education and earnings have a positive relationship. That is, the more educated a person is, the greater their earnings. In Sri Lanka in 2018, people with A-level diplomas earned 31 percent more than those with only O-level diplomas. TVET graduates earn 11–18 percent more than secondary school graduates with only O- or A-level credentials. Returns from education are highest for university graduates. The research described in this volume further has found that although academic qualifications are important to acquire a university education, only a fraction of A-level graduates meet university entrance requirements.

- *Government research*. Identify Sri Lanka's competitive and comparative advantages relative to the national and global markets. The Sri Lanka Department of Census and Statistics' Labour Force Survey is an annual survey of the national labor market and labor demand. In addition to this source, consider using sources of global demand for skilled workers. This would help Sri Lanka match the skilling, reskilling, and upskilling requirements of its workforce to the needs of the global marketplace. This is a vital space for investments not least because Sri Lanka has an aging population but because there is globally a need for health care and child care providers. In addition, TVEC and other institutions can be encouraged to conduct more research in the TVET sector.
- *Graduate tracer system*. No system is in place to capture the dynamic nature of graduates and employment. Establish a dynamic system that captures qualifications and experience. The Skills Passport is a good option, but it needs to be improved and expanded.
- *Monitoring and evaluation system*. The TVET system lacks a credible management information system to monitor and evaluate the ecosystem, from access to relevant quality of TVET education to links with the labor market. Develop a viable and credible monitoring and evaluation system to facilitate dynamic measurement, assessment, adjustment, and reforms.

Skills development must continue to be high on the government's agenda for Sri Lanka to become a "smart nation" with digitally skilled workers who possess job-ready soft and technical skills.

NOTE

1. "Upskilling" is the acquisition of skills that build on an existing knowledge base and skills to take up new jobs. "Reskilling" involves refreshing skills to reinforce one's existing knowledge base and skills and to maintain a license or certification.

REFERENCES

Amarasekera, C. L. 2019. "Background Review on English Language Curriculum." World Bank Country Office, Colombo.

OECD (Organisation for Economic Co-operation and Development). 2020. "Green Recovery and Job Creation." Paris.

World Bank. 2023. "Sri Lanka Development Update: Mobilizing Tax Revenue for a Brighter Future." World Bank, Washington, DC. https://openknowledge.worldbank.org/handle/10986/40420.

Abbreviations

A/L	Advanced Level
ACVE	Advanced Certificate in Vocational Education
ADB	Asian Development Bank
AI	artificial intelligence
CBT	competency-based training
CGTTI	Ceylon–German Technical Training Institute
COVID-19	coronavirus 2019
DAI	Digital Adoption Index
DCS	Department of Census and Statistics
DTET	Department of Technical Education and Training
ECTS	European Credit Transfer and Accumulation System
EI	Employment Insurance (Republic of Korea)
EIF	Employment Insurance Fund (Republic of Korea)
EU	European Union
GCE	General Certificate of Education
GDP	gross domestic product
GoSL	Government of Sri Lanka
GVA	gross value added
HCI	Human Capital Index
HCP	Human Capital Project
HRD	Human Resources Development Service (Republic of Korea)
ICR	Implementation Completion and Results Report
ICT	information and communication technology
IRR	internal rate of return
ISCO	International Standard Classification of Occupations
ISO	International Organization for Standardization
IT	information technology
LAYS	learning-adjusted years of schooling
LKR	Sri Lanka rupee
MoE	Ministry of Education
MOU	memorandum of understanding
MoWCD	Ministry of Women and Child Development, Preschool and Primary Education, School Infrastructure, and Education Services

NAITA	National Apprentice and Industrial Training Authority
NCS	national competency standard
NEC	National Education Commission
NEET	not in education, employment, or training
NGO	nongovernmental organization
NIE	National Institute of Education
NITAC	National Industrial Training Advisory Committee
NPV	net present value
NVQ	National Vocational Qualification
O/L	Ordinary Level
OECD	Organisation for Economic Co-operation and Development
OU	Ocean University
PDV	present discounted value
PPF	production possibility frontier
QIS	Quality Improvement System
QMS	Quality Management System
RBL	results-based lending
RPL	recognition of prior learning
SAR	special administrative region
SDO	skills development officer
SDP	Skills Development Program
SLBFE	Sri Lanka Bureau of Foreign Employment
SLIOP	Sri Lanka Institute of Printing
SLQF	Sri Lanka Qualifications Framework
SMSDVERI	State Ministry of Skills Development, Vocational Education, Research and Innovations
SSDP	Skills Sector Development Program
STEM	science, technology, education, and mathematics
STEP	Skills Toward Employment and Productivity
TVEC	Tertiary and Vocational Education Commission
TVET	technical and vocational education and training
UGC	University Grants Commission
UNESCO	United Nations Educational, Scientific, and Cultural Organization
UNIVOTEC	University of Vocational Technology
US$	US dollar
VCDP	Vocational and Competency Development Plan (Republic of Korea)
VET	vocational education and training
VTA	Vocational Training Authority

Introduction

BACKGROUND

Sri Lanka recognizes the central importance of education and skills development for economic and human development. The country does well in providing access to primary education, with a net enrollment rate of 99 percent, and secondary education, with a net enrollment rate of 84 percent. However, only about 70 percent of children aged 3 to 4 years have access to early childhood education. Further, access to higher education is low, with an enrollment rate of 21 percent, well below the level for upper-middle-income countries (UMICs), which have an average GER of 44 percent. Findings of World Bank analytical work in the education sector point to the need to improve the quality of education at all levels. The World Bank's 2020 Human Capital Index (HCI) shows that although the average expected duration of schooling is 13 years, when adjusted for learning, it falls to only 8.3 years (Aturupane et al. 2021). Improving the labor market orientation of technical and vocational education and training (TVET) and of promoting the economic relevance of higher education would be key drivers to preparing the workforce of the future.

In 2010 8.9 percent of Sri Lanka's population was below the national poverty line of US$3,025. Sri Lanka has confronted and is grappling with a number of exogenous shocks over the past 40 years, including the devastating 2004 tsunami; the 2008 global recession; the COVID-19 global pandemic; and, more recently, the ongoing "triple crisis" (fuel, food, fiscal) (figure I.1). Despite the challenges, in 2021 Sri Lanka's per capita GDP was estimated to be US$3,815 (World Bank 2022).

In this context, Sri Lanka has the following priorities:

- Establishing a foundation for universal access to quality early childhood education and care.
- Modernizing the primary and secondary education sector, with a key focus on improving learning outcomes of children, especially in rural and plantation sector areas.

FIGURE I.1

GDP per capita in Sri Lanka, 1961–2022

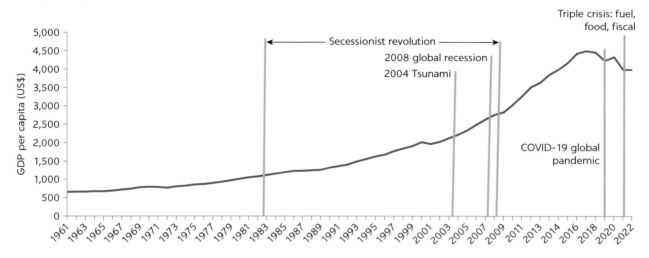

Source: Original figure for this publication.
Note: GDP = gross domestic product.

- Generating the vocational and technical skills needed for the labor market in priority economic sectors, with a special focus on developing private sector TVET institutions.
- Expanding access to higher education in science, engineering, technology, and mathematics (STEM) areas and promoting the economic relevance of university education, research, and innovation.

Skills development is crucial to Sri Lanka's rapid economic transformation and global competitiveness. Sri Lanka is a lower-middle-income country. Its per capita GDP reached US$4,059 in 2018 (UMIC status) but declined toUS$3,815 in 2021, which resulted in the country being downgraded in income status. Meeting the demand for higher-level skills to boost productivity is important to the country's efforts to jumpstart the economy and regain UMIC status in the wake of the 2022 triple crisis (fuel, food, fiscal) and the significant economic, technological, and demographic changes already underway.

Demographic changes also have important implications for skills training and workforce development. Sri Lanka is confronted with a dwindling demographic dividend. The share of youth entering the workforce is declining, and the share of older workers is rising. The structural changes in the workforce call for efforts to upgrade skills for new and existing workers in supporting Sri Lanka's path of economic transformation.

As the country moves forward, human capital will remain critical for modernizing agriculture, deepening industrial development, and expanding services. At the same time, rapid technological progress lends urgency for the development of a skills delivery system that keeps pace with the changing nature of work. The Sri Lankan workforce must gain the relevant technical competencies and higher-order cognitive skills to meet the skills needed in local and foreign labor markets and to remain globally competitive.

Issues in skills development

Confronted with rapidly changing skills demands, Sri Lanka is facing the challenges of skills shortages and mismatch in the labor market. Systemic shortcomings underpin the skills constraint.

Sri Lankan employers are unable to find sufficient numbers of appropriately skilled workers. With the post-2009 growth dividend, the skills shortage has been exacerbated and will likely deepen as the country aspires to reach UMIC status. Approximately 16 percent of Sri Lankan firms surveyed view the lack of well-trained workers as a major barrier to their productivity and growth (World Bank 2017). Almost a third of the surveyed firms considered TVET skills to be more important than general education when recruiting for mid- and high-level technical positions, compared to only 16 percent of firms that prioritized general education. However, the reality is that few workers enter the job market with appropriate skills training. Of a cohort of about 450,000 students who take the General Certificate of Education Ordinary Level exam (Grade 11 completion) during a typical academic year, only 20 percent move on to higher education; of the remainder, only about a third enroll in a TVET program (World Bank 2017). Almost half of students leave secondary schools with a plethora of low-quality skill development options due to a fragmented service delivery system and limited career guidance. The policy of free TVET introduced in 2019 reinforces the poor quality of TVET service delivery. Therefore, many students remain not in education, employment, or training (NEET). In addition, the female workforce participation rate is low, only 35 percent.[1] This low rate of participation further limits the supply of trained labor and prospects for higher returns from training and employment for women. The TVET system has failed to signal the importance of technical education to students and parents, who often undervalue technical skills in favor of general academic skills.

TVET graduates are not meeting employers' skills needs, especially in modern, high-value-added industries. According to the Skills Toward Employment and Productivity (STEP) Employer Survey 2012 (Dundar et al. 2014), more than half of Sri Lankan employers stated that the TVET system was not producing the skills they seek. The survey revealed a disconnect with industry needs: almost half of the survey respondents felt the TVET system did not provide graduates with adequate practical skills and up-to-date knowledge of methods, materials, and technology. Other job-specific skills that employers felt were short in supply include English communication (oral and written) and computer skills. Moreover, employers also expressed that cognitive skills (reading, writing, and numeracy) among workers were insufficient for high-skilled occupations. The issues persist.

Systemic issues contribute to the skills constraints:

- First, the TVET sector in Sri Lanka is complex and fragmented, involving multiple providers and varied skills training media. Public provision of skills training involves 15 ministries and 30 statuary bodies, accounting for around 70 percent of all TVET enrollment. The remaining 30 percent of TVET is provided by private institutions and NGOs. Weak coordination creates inefficiencies and complicates implementation of a skills development plan.
- Second, there is a disconnect between the curricula pursued in technical educational institutions and the demands of the job market. Weak linkages

with employers and industry, especially in curricula design, development of training programs, professional development of teachers and instructors, apprenticeships, and industry visits, explain part of the difference between the demand and supply of skills.

- Third, the alignment of training standards and competencies to labor market needs, as defined in the National Qualifications Framework (NQF), is progressing slowly. This further weakens the TVET system's link with employers' needs.
- Fourth, the TVET sector suffers from serious shortages of qualified teachers, especially those with industrial experience. The career development and performance incentive structures undermine teacher motivation and recruitment of quality teachers. Moreover, the lack of modern equipment and facilities make the education environment challenging.
- Finally, the quality assurance system is at a nascent stage, and a significant number of private providers and courses are not registered or accredited. Regular tracking of TVET graduate outcomes and feedback mechanisms are largely missing.

Goals of this report

This report aspires to

- Inform the government's commitment to support the development of skills among a populace whose jobs and livelihoods have been adversely affected since the 2020 start of the COVID-19 pandemic, which threatened human capital accumulation due to closures of educational institutions, fewer youth transitioning to the labor market, and loss of jobs and livelihoods for the vulnerable. Skills development is also needed to recover from 2022 economic downturn and other exogenous shocks and, ultimately, to build resilience and prepare for future shocks. The COVID-19 pandemic resulted in the lengthy closure of educational institutions. Despite significant efforts in remote learning, available data have revealed that students did not learn during the closures and that, on average, one month of school closure led to one month of lost learning. The observed learning losses are estimated to result in reduced future earnings around the world by US$21 trillion (Schady et al. 2023). Youth in a crucial stage of the life cycle, when they need to decide whether to stay in school, work, or raise a family, experienced dramatic drops in employment and a declining transition into the labor market.
- Inform Sri Lanka's national strategy for skills development for 2024–33 (currently under preparation) by assessing related policies and institutions, ultimately creating efficiencies, economies of scale and scope, and facilitating job creation. The report reviews the many factors other than skills that can limit productivity and job creation, including weak governance, bureaucracy, infrastructure, and taxation policies that directly affect skills development, the business environment, and entrepreneurship.

The report is based on the authors' empirical analyses of growth accumulation effects and the skills ecosystem through the education and training system (skills accumulation effects). Economic growth, employment trends, and gross value addition to the economy are analyzed to assess and lay out the constraints for the demand and supply of skilled and unskilled labor in Sri Lanka. Since labor markets are dynamic, there will always be skills gaps and mismatches; the report reviews the education and training system and its potential to be flexible, to transform the skilling ecosystem to adapt to changing labor market needs, and to build a skilled workforce for both the formal and informal labor markets from an accumulation perspective. Value chain studies for priority sectors in Sri Lanka need to be undertaken to inform the skills needs and guide TVET institutions to produce appropriately trained and informed graduates. It is likely that the findings will be predominantly a study of medium and small enterprises since there are few large firms in Sri Lanka at present. For instance, green jobs are typically labor intensive in nature. Therefore, digitalizing economy recovery in Sri Lanka would not displace workers who might otherwise be unable to participate in the economy. Finally, an evaluation of active labor market programs would also add value.

This report presents a comprehensive diagnostic of skills development policies and institutions in Sri Lanka. It analyzes the economic imperative for attention to skills development; various mechanisms for skilling, reskilling, and upskilling youth and citizens; the need for government and the private sector to collaborate to manage the flow and stock of a skilled workforce to develop a critical mass of skilled workers, and workforce alignment with emerging sector demand. The underlying idea is that the development of a critical mass of skilled labor with strong foundational and higher-order skills can improve competitiveness, meet the labor needs of the transforming economy, and promote growth. The skills ecosystem faces several challenges that require attention, including a fragmented and disparate institutional structure; weak governance; excessive bureaucracy; inadequate infrastructure; a no-taxation policy for TVET that is resulting in inefficiencies; and the absence of a robust system for quality assurance, accreditation, and recognition of prior learning. The deadweight loss[2] to the economy due to the predominance of low- and mid-level skills, underemployment, a relatively small private sector, the absence of good jobs, limited entrepreneurship skills and banking options for youth, and excessive dependence on public sector jobs that offer security such as regular pay and pension have limited Sri Lanka's competitiveness.

The report bridges the analytical work completed by a World Bank team in 2014 (Dundar et al. 2014) to update the body of knowledge about the emerging challenges of skills mismatch in Sri Lanka and projects the financial requirements for the country to transform the skills development system. This introductory chapter defines the context, rationale, and scope of the study on which the report is based; sets out the conceptual framework; describes the questions addressed by the study; explains the methodology; and identifies the data sources.

CONCEPTUAL FRAMEWORK FOR THE STUDY

Rescripting delivery of skills development services in the post-COVID-19 economy requires a people-centered approach for inclusive and resilient recovery in Sri Lanka. It must cover all sectors and include women and vulnerable populations. Skilling, upskilling, reskilling, and lifelong learning will foster adaptability, facilitate resilience, and generate dividends for Sri Lanka.

With an HCI of 60 percent (compared to the South Asian average of 48), Sri Lanka could potentially attract foreign direct investment provided the political economy environment and regulations are conducive. Sri Lanka would benefit from strengthening skills in the STEM fields while continuing to maintain its approach to deepening investment in general education. Higher levels of technical and specialized education, rather than only generalized skills, could facilitate creation of the required workforce for structural transformation; however, it will take time.

Sri Lanka has the potential to capitalize on its growing digital infrastructure. Since 2017, when the government increased its focus on digital infrastructure, Sri Lanka has done well to build a base for its digital development. However, gaps remain and are significant or growing in some areas. In 2022, Sri Lanka ranked 81 of 131 countries in the Network Readiness Index (a measure of broad digital readiness) (Portulans Institute n.d.) and 44 of 78 countries in the Global Services Location Index (a measure of a country's attractiveness as an offshore location for business services) (Kearney n.d.), a drop from 25 in 2019. The latter includes a measure of people's skills and availability. Limited digitalization of economic activities and public services, a factor in a country's desirability as an offshore location, has created major bottlenecks for digitalization, however. For example, in 2021, Sri Lanka had 44 internet users for every 100 inhabitants, far fewer than the OECD average of 87 in 2021 and lower than the OECD average in the early 2000s (World Bank, 2021).[3]

The study adopts the life-cycle approach to skilling for lifelong learning using the Aggregation-Accumulation Framework (Sosale and Majgaard 2016; World Bank 2022). The framework shows that, all else held equal, changes in educational attainment can increase GDP over time. The proposed life-cycle framework for skilling (figure I.2) uses the Accumulation-Aggregation Model, which

FIGURE I.2

A life-cycle approach to skilling for lifelong learning

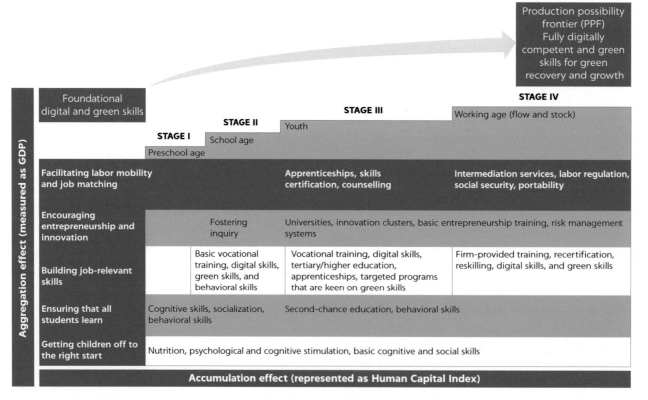

Sources: Original figure for this publication based on Sosale and Majgaard 2016 and World Bank 2010, 2022.
Note: GDP = gross domestic product; PPF = production possibility frontier.

applies the principles of a dynamic calculus that factors four elements: the intertemporal accumulation of skills, the layered nature of skills acquisition, a life-cycle approach to skilling, and moving the production possibility frontier (PPF)[4] over time.

The conceptual framework integrates themes of the demand for skills; the supply of the flow and stock of the skilled, reskilled, and upskilled workforce; and skills for the new age. Therefore, the study incorporated the following considerations:

- The *stock of workers* in the selected sectors and their characteristics—especially skill levels (opportunities and constraints). The analysis examines job-relevant skills, workers' constraints to obtaining job-relevant skills, barriers to finding employment, demand for skills, and socioeconomic constraints to developing a sufficient supply of skills in each sector?.
- The *flow of future workers,* by analyzing the current education and training sector using the life-cycle approach to education and skills development and the potential contribution of the life-cycle approach to economic growth. Skills are disaggregated into developing foundational skills (early childhood development); ensuring that all children learn literacy and numeracy; building job-relevant skills; encouraging entrepreneurship, innovation, and management skills; and fostering skills for labor mobility to permit ease of movement from the formal to the informal sector and vice versa.

MAIN QUESTIONS ADDRESSED BY THE STUDY

The report is structured to respond to six main questions.

1. What has been the trajectory of Sri Lanka's economic growth, and what is the structure of the labor market and which sectors have contributed to growth?
2. Where are the jobs?
3. What types of skills are being used in the sectors where the largest percentages of the population are employed, and are the employed productive?
4. What are the demand and supply barriers to skills development among workers?
5. Which policies, regulations, and institutions are driving the skills development sector, and are they appropriate to address the skills development challenge and sufficient for Sri Lanka to regain its former UMIC status?
6. What needs to be or could be reformed to enhance skills development and productivity in Sri Lanka to contribute to economic growth, competitiveness with a job-ready workforce, facilitate the creation of good jobs, and boost tax revenue for the country to regain its economic footing?

METHODOLOGY AND DATA SOURCES

The study conducts a dynamic analysis, accounting for intertemporal and data constraints. Analytical inputs include the following:

- Based on an intertemporal analysis of the dynamics in the labor market, the study identifies the priority sectors for which job readiness would be required to facilitate structural transformation from an LMIC to a full-fledged MIC.

The intertemporal analysis serves as the basis for understanding the demand for workers by analyzing change over time of sector activity and the stock of workers and their composition, education levels, and value added to the sector; assessing existing skills and competencies; and understanding skills needs, skills gaps, and potential skills upgrading strategies for workforce development over the next 15 years. The key skills considered pertinent here are mid-level and higher-order skills for men and women, new-age digital skills for the 21st century, green skills for fueling green growth, skills for women in the nontraditional sectors, entrepreneurial skills, managerial skills, and socioemotional skills (teamwork, behavioral skills, presentation skills, and so on).

- Analyses of the latest available labor force survey data and government analytical reports, which provide key information on the current state of employment and the gross value addition to the economy along with the current education levels of employees. The key skills considered pertinent here are cognitive, noncognitive, and job-relevant skills.

- A descriptive analysis of the impact of the growing school-age and youth population on educational attainment and its potential effects on the working-age population and labor market outcomes. The quantitative simulation helps to explain how gaps in the skills required by firms could be bridged. Here, foundational skills, higher-order job-relevant skills, and skills for labor mobility are considered important.

- Finally, due to the intertemporal exogenous shocks to the economy, data analysis is based on two distinct time periods—2013 to 2018 and 2018 to 2021 (the latest year for which the most comprehensive data are available).

The analyses for the study were undertaken over a two-year period using primarily secondary data, and through consultations with stakeholders in the government and private sector and with development partners. The analyses include the strengths and weaknesses of the system, especially in transforming a system that is responsive to 21st-century labor markets and serve as the basis for prioritizing interventions and estimating financial forecasting.

NOTES

1. International Labour Organization Statistics (ILOStat) Database, 2019.
2. Deadweight loss primarily arises from an inefficient allocation of resources created by various interventions, such as price ceilings and price floors, monopolies, and taxes. These factors lead to the price of a service or product not being accurately reflected, meaning that services and goods are either overvalued or undervalued. This in turn leads to changes in consumer (students and learners) and producer behavior (service delivery), which usually has a negative impact on the economy. For instance, with a no-fee TVET policy, students can test and reject programs. They move freely across programs without committing to any one program or on-the-job training to accumulate skills. This practice leads to significant investment by the government in programs that do not generate the commensurate skilled workforce. Price differentiation by programs based on the demand for high-, middle-, and low-level skills and the quality of learning (as determined by independent assessors and appropriately evaluated by the market) could usher in more discipline in the demand for skills programs. A base price across all programs, with marginal additions based on market-referenced jobs availability (as determined by value chain studies across market sectors), could turn the tide in favor of TVET.
3. See https://data.worldbank.org/indicator/IT.NET.USER.ZS?locations=LK-OE.

4. The PPF is a graphical representation showing the marginal rate of transformation that a society can make by accumulating human capital, where all possible options for outputs can be produced by harnessing all the other factors of production, given resources are fully and efficiently utilized, per unit of time. The PPF illustrates several economic concepts, such as *allocative efficiency, economies of scale, opportunity cost* (or marginal rate of transformation), *productive efficiency,* and *scarcity* of resources (the *fundamental economic problem* that all societies face). The aspects contribute to output aggregation over time in the economy measured by GDP.

REFERENCES

Aturupane, Harsha, Hideki Higashi, Roshini Ebenezer, Deepika Attygalle, Shobhana Sosale, Sangeeta Day, and Rehana Wijesinghe. 2021. *Sri Lanka Human Capital Development: Realizing the Promise and Potential of Human Capital.* International Development in Focus. Washington, DC: World Bank. doi:10.1596/978-1-4648-1718-2.

Dundar, Halil, Benoît Millot, Yevgeniya Savchenko, Harsha Aturupane, and Tilkaratne A. Piyasiri. 2014. *Building the Skills for Economic Growth and Competitiveness in Sri Lanka.* Directions in Development. Washington, DC: World Bank. doi:10.1596/978-1-4648-0158-7.

Kearney Advisor Network. n.d. "Regenerative Talent Pools: The 2023 Global Services Location Index." A.T. Kearney, Chicago, IL. https://www.kearney.com/service/digital/gsli/2023-full-report.

Portulans Institute. n.d. "Network Readiness Index 2022: Sri Lanka." University of Oxford, Oxford, U.K. https://networkreadinessindex.org/country/sri-lanka/.

Schady, Norbert, Alaka Holla, Shwetlena Sabarwal, Joana Silva, and Andres Yi Chang. 2023. "Collapse and Recovery" How the COVID-19 Pandemic Eroded Human Capital and What to Do about It." Executive Summary. World Bank, Washington, DC.

Sosale, Shobhana, and Kirsten Majgaard. 2016. *Fostering Skills in Cameroon: Inclusive Workforce Development, Competitiveness, and Growth.* Directions in Development. Washington, DC: World Bank. doi:10.1596/978-1-4648-0762-6.

World Bank. 2017. "Sri Lanka Education Sector Assessment: Achievement, Challenges and Policy Options. Directions in Development." World Bank, Washington DC.

World Bank. 2021. *World Development Indicators 2021.* Washington, DC: World Bank. https://databank.worldbank.org/data/download/GNIPC.pdf.

World Bank. 2022. "South Asia's Digital Economy: An Opportunity to Build Back Better, Digitally." Washington, D.C.: World Bank Group. https://documentsinternal.worldbank.org/search/33780484

1 The Economy
TRENDS AND PERSPECTIVES FOR PROGRESS

INTRODUCTION: THE PROBLEM, NEED, OR EXISTING DEFICIENCY

Between 2014 and 2018 in Sri Lanka, large gains in employment and productivity resulted in employment elasticities[1] being greater than 1 in the education, construction, water supply and waste management, and real estate sectors. At 4.9, education had the highest employment elasticity. The finance, real estate, health and social work, electricity (power sector), information and communication technology (ICT), and water supply sectors grew more than average. However, between 2018 and 2021, the landscape changed. There was a decline in the intensity of employment growth. Employment elasticity was highest in agriculture (>1), followed by public administration. All other occupations registered no employment growth, and some even had negative employment elasticity (for instance, transportation was <1).

Although manufacturing, wholesale and retail services, and transportation are the largest industries in terms of output (measured in gross value added [GVA]), in recent years their growth has been struggling with low employment elasticity (<1). Hence, their contribution to job creation has been marginal. In the meantime, the high growth and relatively low employment elasticity (fewer jobs created per unit of output growth) in finance and ICT means a mismatch between supply and demand. With growing unemployment and underemployment, labor supply in these sectors has not been meeting available demand, likely due to a dearth of appropriately skilled, reskilled, and upskilled labor. Consequently, the available jobs are going unfilled. Investment is needed to develop workers' skills in these industries. Further research on and analysis of subsector and occupation-specific skills are needed to understand the links among labor intensity, automation processes, and skills mismatch over time and why growth in certain industries has not led to employment creation.

Modern economies place a rising premium on higher-order cognitive skills such as complex problem solving, sociobehavioral skills, reasoning, and self-efficacy. Building such skills requires a strong, effective education and training system. Demand is declining for less skilled workers—such as those with only a basic high school certification—while it is rising for more skilled workers.

From education and demographic features perspectives, most technical and vocational education and training (TVET) trainees and graduates have an O-level secondary education or higher.

In recent years, Sri Lanka has experienced changes in occupational skills. Like many developed countries, labor polarization seems to be occurring, with growing shares of occupations requiring low- or high-level skills and fewer requiring mid-level skills. Labor polarization was most pronounced in services, where the share of occupations requiring high-level skills rose from 35 to 41 percent between 2013 and 2018, and the share requiring mid-level skills fell from 52 to 43 percent. By contrast, the share of occupations requiring mid-level skills in agriculture stayed essentially the same—possibly because technology cannot yet replace many agricultural tasks. The industries with relatively large production growth saw their skills composition change between 2013 and 2018. The COVID-19 pandemic (declared in early 2020) and the 2022 political and economic downturn resulting in the triple crisis (fuel, food, and fiscal) ushered in new trends in the job market. For instance, in 2021, the services sector registered an increase in mid-level skills to 56 percent, up from 43 percent in 2018. Low-level skills in the economy grew from 16 percent in 2018 to 25 percent in 2021. This increase is likely due to higher skilled people undertaking lower level jobs to make a living but working fewer hours, resulting in greater underemployment.

This trend is observed in many developed countries, where there are fewer entrants into occupations requiring mid-level skills because fewer such jobs are created (World Bank 2019c). A potential explanation is that occupations requiring mid-level skills are easily replaceable by labor-saving technological advancements such as automation. Occupations requiring non-routine low- or high-level skills can thrive despite labor-saving technologies (World Bank 2019c). Still, more research is required to study country and industry conditions. In some industries digital technology threatens not only mid-level skilled workers but also low-skilled workers. Automation in factories and commerce can displace occupations requiring low-level skills such as factory workers in manufacturing, sales clerks in stores, and waiters in restaurants as well as occupations requiring mid-level skills in logistics, processing, data digitization, and clerical support.

The Skills Sector Development Program

The Skills Sector Development Program (SSDP), a seven-year plan, was implemented between 2014 and June 2023. The program's goal was to build an efficient skills development system to meet both domestic and foreign labor market demands by improving the quality, access, and relevance of skills to labor markets and skills training systems. The SSDP was technically and financially supported by various development partners including the World Bank and the Asian Development Bank (annex 1A). The estimated cost of the SSDP amounted to 42 percent of the US$648 million spent on skills development over its implementation. The program was partly successful in that it increased access to technical and vocational training, but it failed to make training institutes more efficient. In 2020, external financing for skills development dropped to 13 percent of the total.

The number of TVET graduates increased by an average of 20 percent annually during the SSDP implementation period, although outcomes were better in some previous years. The increase in TVET admissions reflected the rising number of students enrolled in both public and private TVET institutes. Yet there was no improvement in completion rates across the entire TVET sector— completion rates rose at private institutes but fell at public ones, resulting in no net change. The increase in enrollments was likely due to the government's new policy of making TVET free of charge.

Confronted with changing skills demands,[2] Sri Lanka is facing the challenges of skills shortages and mismatch in the labor market. Systemic shortcomings underpin the skills constraint. Sri Lankan employers are unable to find sufficient numbers of appropriately skilled workers. The GoSL DCS conducted the Labour Demand Survey for the first time in 2017 and found nearly half a million vacancies in the private sector, with most of the labor demand stemming from the industry, services, and trade sectors (DCS 2017a). The challenge of skills shortages will likely increase as the country aspires to move toward full-fledged upper-income country status. Approximately 16 percent of surveyed Sri Lankan firms viewed the lack of well-trained workers as a major barrier to their productivity and growth (World Bank 2017). Almost a third of the surveyed firms considered TVET skills to be more important, compared to only about 16 percent for general education, when recruiting for mid- and high-level technical positions. However, the reality is that few workers enter the job market with appropriate skills training. Of a cohort of about 450,000 students who take the General Certificate of Education Ordinary Level (grade 11 completion) during a typical academic year, only 20 percent move on to higher education, and only about a third of the rest enroll in a TVET program (World Bank 2017). Put another way, almost half of students leave secondary school with no opportunity for further education or training. They are not in education, employment, or training (NEET). In addition, the female workforce participation rate was low, at approximately 35 percent. This further limits the supply of trained labor and the prospects for higher returns from training and employment for women.[3] Finally, the TVET system has failed to signal the importance of technical education to students and parents, who often undervalue technical skills in favor of general academic skills.

Findings of the World Bank 2020 jobs diagnostic (Ruppert Bulmer 2020) indicate that Sri Lanka has undergone structural transformation over the past two decades and better-quality jobs are being created. However, there are too many poor-quality, labor-intensive, and low-productivity jobs, mostly in the informal sector. In addition, despite their rising aspirations, educated youth and women are increasingly underemployed; most firms are micro in nature, and they face constraints to grow and compete; and economic distortions restrain the creation of better jobs. Recommendations of the jobs diagnostic report are as follows: enhance the capacity of youth and women to obtain better jobs; improve the matching of job seekers and employers; increase the productivity of self-employed workers; reduce barriers for firm growth and productivity; and revise labor market, government employment, and competition policies.

TVET graduates are not acquiring the skills employers need, especially in modern, high-value-added industries. According to the 2012 Skills Toward Employment and Productivity (STEP) Employer Survey (World Bank 2012), more than half of Sri Lankan employers stated that the TVET system was not producing the skills they seek. The survey revealed a delink with industry needs: almost half of the employers surveyed felt the TVET system did not provide graduates with adequate practical skills and up-to-date knowledge of methods, materials, and technology. Other job-specific skills that employers felt were in short supply included English communication (oral and written) and computer and digital literacy. Only 20 percent of Sri Lankan workers were found to be fluent in English, and only 15 percent had computer skills—far below the expected demands of employers. Moreover, employers also expressed that cognitive skills (reading, writing, and numeracy) among workers were insufficient for high-skill occupations.

The challenges persist in 2023. There is a need for TVET to respond through the introduction of modular skill development programs to assist with lifelong learning. Specifically, employees and employers need to be provided with options for stacking skills[4] credentials to build theoretical and practical expertise over time. The COVID-19 pandemic revealed the importance of introducing flexibility, credibility, and stackability of TVET credentials.

Systemic issues contribute to the skills constraints discussed in preceding sections:

- The TVET sector in Sri Lanka is complex and fragmented, involving multiple providers and varied media for skills training. Public provision of skills training involves several ministries and 30 statutory bodies, accounting for approximately 70 percent of all TVET enrollment. The remaining 30 percent of TVET is provided by private institutions and nongovernmental organizations. Weak coordination is likely to create inefficiencies and complicates overall implementation of a skills development plan.
- There is a disconnect between the curricula pursued in technical educational institutions and the demands of the job market. Weak links with employers and industry, especially in curricula design, development of training programs, instructors' and teachers' professional development, apprenticeships, and industry visits explain part of the discrepancy between the demand and supply of skills.
- The alignment of training standards and competencies to labor market needs, as defined in the National Vocational Qualifications Framework (TVEC 2016b, 2021b), is progressing slowly. This further weakens the TVET system's link with employers' needs.
- The TVET sector suffers from serious shortages of qualified instructors and teachers, especially those with industrial experience. The teacher career development and performance incentive structures undermine teacher motivation and the ability to attract quality instructors and teachers for the job. Moreover, the lack of modern equipment and facilities makes the teaching and learning environment challenging.
- Finally, the quality assurance system is at a nascent stage, and a significant number of private providers and courses are not registered or accredited. Regular tracking of TVET graduate outcomes and feedback mechanisms is largely missing.

This report serves to update the findings from the 2014 World Bank report *Building the Skills for Economic Growth and Competitiveness in Sri Lanka* (Dundar and others 2014). It analyzes the rapidly changing trajectory of skills needs in the country, while noting that the skills sector is making progress in some areas but is largely stagnant in others. Policies need review and adaptation to create a dynamic 21st-century skills strategy and to respond to the setbacks arising from the COVID-19 pandemic and the ongoing economic crisis that began in 2022.

The rest of chapter 1 provides analytical insights into the economy, the trends, and the outlook for progress in Sri Lanka. Chapter 2 focuses on the labor market and skills, trends, and outlook for progress in Sri Lanka.

Chapter 3 lays out the education, training, and skills ecosystem in the country. Chapter 4 addresses the governance, quality assurance, and relevance of TVET. Chapter 5 focuses on the financing of TVET. The report concludes with overarching recommendations in chapter 6.

FILLING THE EXISTING GAP IN THE SECTOR

Sri Lanka is transitioning from a predominantly rural-based economy toward a modern, urbanized, and digital economy. The modern economy places an increasing premium on higher-order cognitive skills, such as complex problem solving, sociobehavioral skills, reasoning, and self-efficacy. Building these skills requires a strong and effective education system. Sri Lanka's economic development also depends on its social stability, and education has a vital role to play in promoting good citizenship. Education is especially important given the history of ethnic-based secessionist conflict that Sri Lanka experienced for nearly three decades as well as the social instability in the country resulting from the COVID-19 pandemic. Education has a critical role in developing the country's human capital and promoting the social stability required for the success of its development agenda.

The COVID-19 pandemic and its effects

The COVID-19 pandemic has disrupted lives and livelihoods, but the demand for higher-level skills continues to grow. The pandemic has resulted in widespread impacts on education, skills, jobs, and income. Further, many expatriate Sri Lankans working overseas have returned to the country. Their upskilling and reskilling[5] will be critical for integrating them into the job market. Strategies are needed to prepare students and workers in the post-COVID-19 era for recovery and to promote resilience.

Sri Lanka's human development indicators are threatening to go below lower-middle-income country levels. For the country to regain the pre-COVID-19 growth rate and move forward, human capital will be central and critical for modernizing agriculture, deepening industrial development, and expanding services. At the same time, rapid technological progress lends urgency for a skills delivery system that will keep pace with the changing nature of work. Addressing the flow of new graduates, the stock of existing graduates, and the return of migrant workers will require a renewed policy and strategy for action.

Sri Lanka's 2019 national policy framework, *Vistas of Prosperity and Splendour* (GoSL 2019), articulates the GoSL's recognition of, and commitment to, improving general education in Sri Lanka. It also recognizes the importance of skills, jobs, and empowerment:

> The other important task will be to create a progressive national economy and a pluralistic society; we have to create an environment that provides our youth and local entrepreneurs with new opportunities, gives everyone new hope and a sense of pride, where people can use their skills, talents and business acumen to be the world leaders in any field of their choice. It is only by empowering our people that we can strengthen and expand the national economy (GoSL 2019, i).

The GoSL's agenda for growth includes the expansion of compulsory education and the reorienting of the education and skills development systems to the needs of the labor market. Government policies seek to promote a globally competitive, export-led economy that generates inclusive, sustained growth. Accordingly, accelerating human capital and skills development is of central importance for Sri Lanka's successful return to upper-middle-income country status and eventually high-income status.

Government policies and strategies signal strong support for an agenda focused on developing skills. *Vistas of Prosperity and Splendour* recognizes that the dynamism of Sri Lanka's economy depends on its labor force and that the country's development depends on its productivity. Thus, the goal is to encourage and develop a trained, energetic workforce with a culture of working for the country's accelerated development (GoSL 2019, 19).

Skills development is crucial to Sri Lanka's rapid economic transformation and global competitiveness. The Sri Lankan workforce must gain the relevant technical competencies and higher-order cognitive skills to meet the skills needs in local and foreign labor markets and remain globally competitive. Demographic changes also have important implications for skills training and workforce development. Sri Lanka is confronted with a dwindling demographic dividend. The share of youth entering the workforce is declining, while the older workforce is increasing. The structural changes in the workforce call for efforts to upgrade skills for new and existing workers to support Sri Lanka's path of economic transformation in the medium term and long term. Crucial to this goal is the upskilling and reskilling of youth, women, and men to meet the challenges imposed by the COVID-19 pandemic and bolster employment and livelihoods in the informal and formal labor markets.

Economic and demographic trends

Sri Lanka is a lower-middle-income country with a gross domestic product (GDP) per capita of US$3,815 in 2021. In 2018, the country's GDP per capita was US$4,059, so the decline seen in the 2019 data resulted in the country's downgrade from upper-middle-income status (World Bank 2022). This shift resulted from the onset of the COVID-19 pandemic, which hit the country hard. In 2022, the economic crisis pushed the country into a recession, spiraling inflation, and a steep decline in the value of the Sri Lankan rupee (from US$1 = LKR 136 in 2015 to approximately US$1 = LKR 314 in 2022).

Sri Lanka's population is 21.7 million. After the 26-year secessionist conflict ended in 2009, the country's economy registered rapid growth, averaging 5.3 percent annually between 2010 and 2019. The economy is transitioning from predominantly rural to modern, urbanized, and digital. Between 1977 and 2019 the share of agriculture, forestry, and fisheries in GDP fell from about 31 percent to 7 percent. The share of industry declined slightly, from about 29 percent to 26 percent, while services jumped from about 41 percent to 58 percent (Central Bank of Sri Lanka 2019). This change reflects determined policies for reconstruction and growth. The COVID-19 pandemic and the 2022 economic crisis have severely affected the gains made by the country in the last decade (2010–20).

Although unemployment fell from 9 percent to 4 percent between 2000 and 2012—and rose slightly to nearly 5 percent in 2019—20 percent of 15- to 24-year-olds were still unemployed in 2019. Since then, that proportion has swelled. The number of young people with a basic high school certification is growing, so the stock and flow of postsecondary education graduates are increasing as well. Despite the growing number of educated young workers, the skills of new labor market entrants are not commensurate with demand. Accordingly, Sri Lanka's labor market has high youth unemployment and high overall underemployment, with most of the labor force being employed informally. Underemployment and informal employment are major concerns for the government.

By 2013, Sri Lanka's workforce was the most educated in South Asia. In 2016, learning-adjusted years of schooling (LAYS) were estimated at 8.5, compared with the South Asian average of 6.5 (Azevedo and others 2020; Filmer and others 2018; World Bank 2019b). Importantly, there was gender parity in school completion. Modern economies place a rising premium on higher-order cognitive skills such as complex problem solving, sociobehavioral skills, reasoning, and self-efficacy. Building such skills requires a strong, effective education and training system. Demand is declining for less skilled workers—such as those with only a basic high school certification—while it is rising for more skilled workers.

Sri Lanka also has an increasingly aging population, especially relative to its peers. This trend will affect the composition of households, provision of education and health services, and structure of employment and has long-term implications. Moreover, the large gap in labor force participation rates between men and women has hardly changed. To buffer the effects of a reduced number of workers, it will be important to narrow the gender gap in labor force participation, implement policies to foster women's entry into labor markets, boost education attainment to raise productivity and the participation of youth, reallocate workers toward emerging sectors to support productivity gains, and increase economic growth.

Government policies and strategies signal strong support for an agenda focused on developing skills. *Vistas of Prosperity and Splendour* recognizes that the dynamism of the country's economy depends on its labor force, and the country's development depends on its productivity. Thus, the goal is to encourage and develop a trained, energetic workforce with a culture of working for the country's accelerated development (GoSL 2019, 19).

Compared with other countries, Sri Lanka's performance on the World Bank's Human Capital Index (HCI) has been modest (figure 1.1).[6] A study by the World Bank's Human Capital Project in 2016–17 found that the country had an HCI of 58 percent and a ranking of 74 of 157 countries included in the HCI (World Bank 2019a). Children born in Sri Lanka in 2018 were estimated to be only 58 percent as productive in adulthood relative to their full potential. This was far lower than in Southeast Asian economies such as Hong Kong SAR, China, Japan, the Republic of Korea, and Singapore but higher than in Bangladesh, India, Nepal, and Pakistan (see figure 1.1).[7] Indeed, Sri Lanka has the highest HCI in South Asia. In 2020, Sri Lanka showed improvement in HCI, reaching 60 percent compared to the South Asian average of 48 percent, and the lower middle-income countries' average (also 48 percent). Therefore, with the highest HCI, Sri Lanka continues to lead South Asia (Aturupane et al. 2021). Yet, Sri Lanka has some way to go to catch up with other Southeast Asian economies.

The country appears to be doing better on some components of the HCI than others. The probability of a child surviving to age 5 is 99 percent, and the expected number of years of schooling averages 13.2 years—both are on par with high-income countries. Further, the probability of a child surviving to adulthood, at 90 percent, is just above the 86 percent for upper-middle-income countries. These achievements offer promise and potential for Sri Lanka.

The country does less well on learning outcomes and stunting[8] rates. On learning outcomes, with a score of 400, Sri Lanka is only a little above the

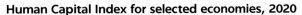

FIGURE 1.1

Human Capital Index for selected economies, 2020

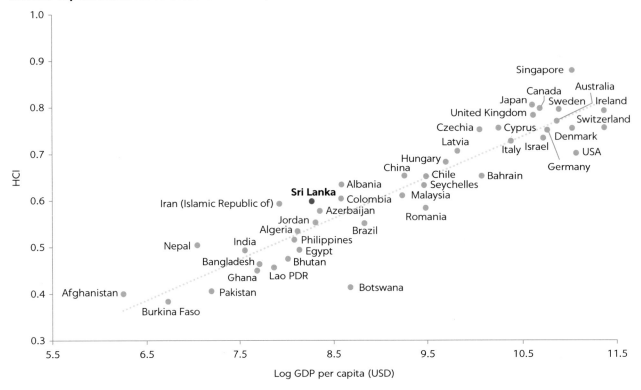

Source: Original calculations based on data from World Bank 2020b.
Note: HCI = Human Capital Index; PPP = purchasing power parity.

FIGURE 1.2

LAYS in Sri Lanka and in selected regions and country income groups, 2018

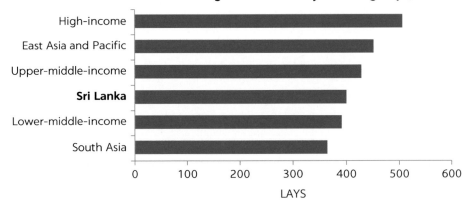

Source: World Bank 2019a.
Note: LAYS = learning-adjusted years of schooling.

average of 391 for lower-middle-income countries, and less than the 428 for upper-middle-income countries; it is well below the mean score of 451 for East Asia and Pacific (figure 1.2). On stunting, at 83 percent, Sri Lanka is above the average for lower-middle-income countries, at 73 percent, but below the 87 percent average for upper-middle-income countries.

Government policies seek to promote a globally competitive, export-led economy that generates inclusive, sustained growth. Accordingly, accelerating human capital and skills development is of central importance for Sri Lanka's successful return to upper-middle-income country status and, eventually, to high-income status.

Labor market features

Research in Brazil shows that enforcement of labor regulation affects firms' use of informal workers and firm performance. Where enforcement is stricter, firms employ fewer informal workers. Reducing firms' access to unregulated workers lowers average wages, productivity, and investment; enforcement of labor regulation constrains firm size and leads to higher unemployment; enforcement of labor regulation in the formal sector may push workers into the informal sector because it increases the costs of formal labor; and lower-paying formal jobs become attractive to some informal workers, making them want to move to the formal sector (Almeida and Carneiro 2005, 2009, 2012). These findings resonate with Sri Lanka's formal and informal labor markets.

Sri Lanka's labor force is made up of formal public sector workers, formal private sector workers, and informal workers. The features that distinguish them are shown in table 1.1.

In 2017, the Department of Census and Statistics (DCS)—part of the Ministry of National Policies and Economic Affairs—conducted the first countrywide survey on labor demand (DCS 2017a).[9] The International Standard Classification of Occupations 2008 (ILO 2008) served as the basis for classifying jobs for data analysis. The survey revealed the quality and quantity of private sector workers and the labor demand for skills by job categories.

TABLE 1.1 **Characteristics of Sri Lanka's workforce**

CHARACTERISTIC	FORMAL PUBLIC SECTOR WORKERS	FORMAL PRIVATE SECTOR WORKERS	INFORMAL WORKERS
Remuneration	High–low, but benefits (including pension, hours of work, job security, and so on) are attractive	A range; closer to informal	Low
Wage gap	Low	Varies	Persistent
Working conditions	Stable	Stable to precarious	Precarious
Redundancy costs	Very high (second highest globally)	Varies	Ad hoc
Capital costs	Lower	Varies	Higher
Labor productivity	Higher	Varies	Lower
Mandated taxes and benefits	Cannot be avoided	Cannot be avoided	Can be avoided
Business registration procedures	n.a.	High	Varies
Access to credit	Requires collateral	Requires collateral	Requires collateral
Work hours	Shorter	Longer	Not fixed
Holidays	Many	Some	Varies
Leave	Paid with benefits	Some	Varies
Job security	High	A range; closer to informal	Limited
Social security	Yes	Yes	None

Source: Original table for this publication based on World Bank 2020a.
Note: n.a. = not applicable.

The results captured the skills being demanded and the skills gaps among education system outputs, that is, graduates. This approach was taken to facilitate understanding of how appropriately trained graduates could become eligible for higher-quality, more relevant jobs. The survey found huge disparities between the outputs of the education system and the demands of the labor market. It appears that the education and training system is preparing students to aspire to permanent employment. However, the labor market demands skills that are fungible and directly relevant to production chain jobs. The fast-changing technology in the markets today requires a different skill set than what the education and training system is providing students. The system continues to impart knowledge and skills that are more suitable for permanent jobs that provide security and assured income, but the labor market is increasingly less able to ensure permanent employment. Therefore, graduates can no longer hold out for permanent jobs.

Labor market outcomes

The DCS survey found that the preparedness of first-time job seekers varied significantly by academic background. The range of preparedness was as follows:

- Fifty percent of young people had only a secondary school education. This group had the most promising results.
- Forty percent had secondary school and technical or vocational qualifications.
- Thirty-eight percent had technical and vocational qualifications.
- Thirty-six percent had qualifications from a university or some other institution of higher education.
- Twenty-six percent had qualifications from a university or other institution of higher education and with technical or vocational qualifications, making this the group with the least promising results.

The survey also revealed that private employers believed that young people were unwilling to take the vacancies that did exist. Even for vacancies that had been filled, young people were inadequately prepared by the school system, despite Sri Lanka's high literacy level (92 percent) and digital literacy (46 percent). Reasons cited for poor preparedness were that secondary school graduate new hires lacked job-specific, required competencies such as technical, information technology (IT), problem-solving, and teamwork skills; that among graduates of secondary school and TVET, there was a lack of work and life experience or maturity (including general knowledge and common sense); that technical and vocational school graduates exhibited limited basic education (literacy and numeracy); and that first-time job seekers coming from a university or other higher education institution had bad attitudes or lacked motivation (for example, on work ethic, punctuality, appearance, and manners). Private employers also did not think remedial programs were available for socioemotional, higher-order problem-solving, and critical thinking skills.

In addition, the DCS survey found the following rank order of labor demand and employment by sector and subsector: services, industry, trade, tourism, construction, and agriculture. Labor demand by occupation was highest for sewing machine operators, security guards, manufacturing laborers, and commercial and sales representatives, but these areas were least attractive to all potential workers. The highest demand for workers in services was in the Western Province. For professional jobs, mechanical engineering technicians, assistant accounting professionals, and nurses were in high demand. In tourism, waiters were in greatest demand, and in the plantation sector, it was tea pluckers and building construction laborers. Such routine jobs require semiskilled labor.

Finally, the survey identified the main reasons for hard-to-fill vacancies. On the demand side, 21.3 percent of employers surveyed said there was significant competition to attract available, interested workers, and 13.5 percent said the salaries demanded by graduates were too high. On the supply side, the pool of interested applicants was relatively small to start with: 25.4 percent of job seekers surveyed had insufficient interest in pursuing jobs in high demand, and 9.5 percent considered the terms and conditions (such as pay) to be unattractive for such jobs.

In 2018, the World Bank offered policy recommendations for boosting labor demand:

- Introduce reforms to move to a trade-led growth model, because changes in trade policies and openness to foreign direct investment could lead to more productive, higher-paying jobs.
- Improve opportunities for innovation and entrepreneurship through early-stage financing and incubation facilities.
- Focus on sectors likely to generate a lot of jobs (especially for women), improving the investment climate for small and medium-size enterprises, and providing incentives for large, informal firms to formalize.
- Provide protections for both formal and informal workers.
- Improve the quality of and access to education to mitigate the skills mismatch. Such efforts are directly related to improving TVET and ensuring that graduate training better prepares students for private sector jobs (World Bank 2018).

Several related issues arise when analyzing the above in conjunction with the finding that low- and middle-income countries tend to regulate employment more than do high-income countries (World Bank 2020a). Although there appear to be few obstacles for employers seeking to hire new staff, rigid employment regulation prevents them from dismissing redundant workers. Such regulation constrains employers from hiring permanent staff.

Employers are often unsure whether employees can perform the tasks associated with permanent work at their firms. Strict employment protection regulation shapes firms' incentives to enter and exit an economy, which has implications for job creation and economic growth. It also tends to foster larger informal sectors (World Bank 2020a). In other words, economies with flexible employment regulation tend to have smaller informal sectors. That is not the case in Sri Lanka, which has a large informal sector. The share of wage earners in the informal sector, by industry group, stayed more or less constant between 2012 and 2021. However, the percentage of informal workers engaged in agriculture, forestry, and fishing increased slightly from 2012 to 2021, whereas the percentage of informal workers in the education sector decreased (figure 1.3).

Since 2000, from a labor demand perspective, better wage than nonwage jobs have been created in Sri Lanka. However, 70 percent of jobs continue to be of low quality and informal (Ruppert Bulmer 2020). The labor supply has the following characteristics:

- More young graduates are entering the labor market. This finding is corroborated by the number of young people graduating from secondary school. The

FIGURE 1.3

Distribution of informal workers in Sri Lanka, by industry group, 2012 and 2018–21

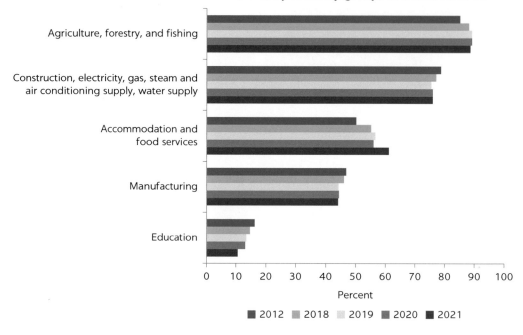

Sources: DCS 2012, 2018, 2019, 2020b, 2021.

number who passed all three subjects in the General Certificate of Education Advanced Level (GCE A/L) rose from 126,971 (61 percent) in 2014 to 154,905 (66 percent) in 2019.

- The skills of new graduates are underused despite graduates' rising aspirations.
- Urban and rural youth alike see social connections as the way to obtain the best jobs.
- Female youth have narrower occupational options because of social norms, which leads them to prefer government jobs. Those who cannot get a public sector position tend to drop out of the labor market because other occupational options are not available.
- Male youth also see public sector jobs as preferable because of the significant wage premium (for example, pension, hours of work, and job security) compared to the private sector.
- Entrepreneurship is not considered a viable career option.
- There are only a few large private firms in some sectors, including export manufacturing, that dominate the market. There are few job opportunities in these firms compared to the supply of graduates.
- There are no vibrant private small and medium-size firms to drive competitiveness and raise productivity.
- The wage premium and job security in the public sector are crowding out the private sector.
- Labor laws that protect workers constrain demand for workers.

Combined with traditional norms and social biases, the formal labor market favors men (Ruppert Bulmer 2020).

Ruppert Bulmer (2020) provides five recommendations to mitigate these shortcomings: reduce barriers to firms' growth and productivity; revise labor market, government employment, and competition policies; enhance women's and young people's capacity to obtain better jobs; raise productivity among the self-employed; and improve job matching (demand and supply). Private sector job-matching e-platforms exist, as does a formal civil service hiring process. Thus, there is no reason for the government to invest in setting up private platforms or even a public sector one.

Employment growth and trends

Between 2014 and 2018, Sri Lanka saw annual economic growth of 3.3 percent in value-added terms (table 1.2), and a further increase to about 4 percent during the 2018–21 period. Between 2014 and 2018, Sri Lanka saw annual economic growth of 3.3 percent in value-added terms (table 1.2). Most of that growth was due to services, which grew by 3.8 percent on average between 2014–18 and to 4.4 percent between 2018 and 2021; agriculture grew by just 1.3 percent between 2014 and 2018 but decreased to an average of only about 0.5 percent between 2018 and 2021. Overall employment was not commensurate with economic growth, however, increasing by just 0.8 percent on average between 2014 and 2018, and a little higher to 1.2 percent between 2018 and 2021. This disparity resulted in an employment elasticity of 0.3 overall between 2014 and 2018 but registering 1.0 percent between 2018 and 2021. Still, that was a slight improvement during the 2014–18 period over the previous two periods (2002–10 and 2011–14), but a decline during 2018–21 attributable to the exogenous and endogenous shocks to the economy. Employment elasticity in agriculture registered a significant increase on average by 16.9 percent during the period 2018–21.

Among the three economic sectors, agriculture has been creating the most jobs, with an employment elasticity of 16.9 between 2018 and 2021. That is, agriculture led to larger growth in informal employment relative to services

TABLE 1.2 **Annual economic and employment growth in Sri Lanka, by sector, 1996–2021**

SECTOR	1996–2002	2002–10	2011–14	2014–18	2018–21	TREND
Agriculture						
Value-added economic growth (%)	1.9	5	4.2	1.3	0.5	
Employment growth (%)	2.3	0.8	−3.7	−1.2	8.3	
Employment elasticity	1.2	0.2	−0.9	−0.9	16.9	
Industry						
Value-added economic growth (%)	4.5	8.0	6.5	2.7	-4.0	
Employment growth (%)	2.3	3.2	4.3	2.3	−5.8	
Employment elasticity	0.5	0.4	0.7	0.9	1.5	
Services						
Value-added economic growth (%)	5.4	8.0	7.3	3.8	4.4	
Employment growth (%)	5.0	1.0	2.7	1.1	1.6	
Employment elasticity	0.9	0.1	0.4	0.3	0.4	
All sectors						
Value-added economic growth (%)	4.3	8.0	6.5	3.3	1.3	
Employment growth (%)	5.0	1.0	1.0	0.8	1.2	
Employment elasticity	1.2	0.2	0.2	0.3	1.0	

Sources: Original table for this publication based on ADB and ILO 2017; CBSL 2022; and Department of Census and Statistics data.
Note: Data for 2014–18 is in constant 2010 prices; data for 2018–21 is in constant 2015 prices.

and industry. However, its employment generation rate has not been consistent across all years, registering declines between 2011 and 2018. Employment elasticity in industry registered some increase during the period, but its contribution to growth and productivity declined sharply between 2018 and 2021. Employment elasticity in the services sector registered small increases during 2011–18 but a significant increase from 2018 to 2021, with its value addition to growth showing an increase to 4.4 percent, up from 3.8 percent during 2014–18, indicating positive labor productivity. The increasing use of digital infrastructure during the 2018–21 period is likely to have contributed to this growth in employment elasticity, as has growth in other essential basic services (education, health and social services, transportation, finance, and real estate).

Job growth sectors

Across subsectors, between 2013 and 2018 the highest growth in both employment and production occurred in real estate, construction, electricity, ICT, finance, and water supply and waste management (figure 1.4a). The largest job expansion was in water supply and waste management, where the number of workers skyrocketed 165 percent in 2018. That same year, agriculture contracted by 10 percent and mining by 32 percent. Real estate and construction, electricity, and ICT—with job growth of 102 percent, 70 percent, and 25 percent, respectively—also created more employment than other industries. In terms of production, the largest increases were in finance (75 percent growth), water supply and waste management (68 percent), and ICT (64 percent) in GVA.

There were significant changes between 2018 and 2021 across subsectors (figure 1.4b). Changes in employment and GVA in most sectors stagnated. Albeit positive, there were minimal increases in both working-age population and production in agriculture, public administration, health and social services, and education. Finance, health and social work, education, real estate, professional activities, public administration, electricity (power sector), and wholesale/retail registered positive GVA to the economy. However, in terms of working population, there were mixed results. Only public administration, education, health and social work and agriculture registered increasing working population, ranging from 0.3 percent to 15.6 percent. The working-age population in agriculture grew by 15.6 percent (likely through informal employment) and contributed a little and positively to growth (0.5 percent). However, while the ICT sector registered a small decline in working age population (-0.1 percent), its contribution to value-added growth was significant (54.1 percent). Overall, the combined effect of changes in working-age population (1.2 percent) and value addition (5.5 percent) from all the sectors was low, but positive.

Between 2013 and 2018, large gains in employment and output growth occurred in education, real estate, construction, and water supply and waste management, all of which achieved employment elasticities above 1 (figure 1.5a). At 4.9, education had the highest employment elasticity. Finance, real estate, health and social work, electricity, ICT, and water supply grew more than average, although employment did not expand as much as growth in production, except in real estate and water supply and waste management.

Between 2013 and 2018, although manufacturing, wholesale and retail services, and transportation were the largest industries in terms of output (in terms of GVA), in recent years their growth has been struggling with low employment elasticity (<1), and their contribution to job creation has therefore

FIGURE 1.4

Economic and job growth in Sri Lanka, by industry, 2018 and 2021

a. 2013–18

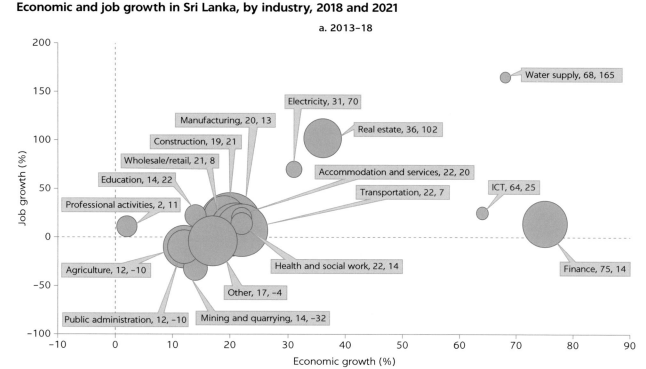

b. 2018–21

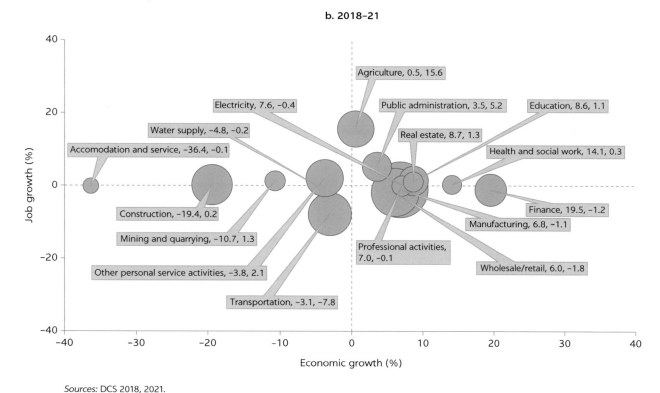

Sources: DCS 2018, 2021.
Note: The x axis indicates GVA economic growth from 2013–18 by industry. The y axis indicates job growth (employment) between 2013 and 2018 in each industry. The percentages listed after each sector correspond to the value on the x and y axes, respectively. The size of each circle indicates the size of industry measured in GVA. GVA = gross value added; ICT = information and communication technology.

FIGURE 1.5

Employment elasticity and annual output growth in Sri Lanka, by economic size of sector, 2013–21

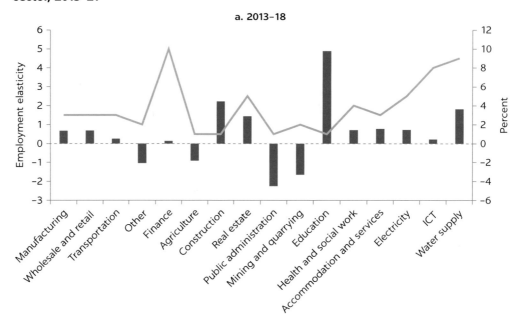

a. 2013–18

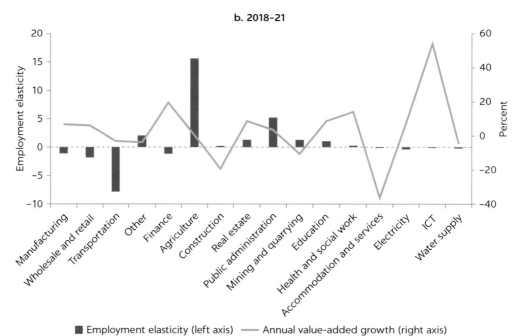

b. 2018–21

■ Employment elasticity (left axis) — Annual value-added growth (right axis)

Sources: Original calculations for this publication based on CBSL 2022 and DCS 2013, 2018, 2021.
Note: Data for 2014–18 is in constant 2010 prices; data for 2018–21 is in constant 2015 prices. ICT = information and communication technology.

been marginal (figure 1.5a). Meanwhile, finance, real estate, health and social work, ICT, and water supply were the sectors contributing maximum in terms of output (measured by GVA) signaling higher labor productivity compared to the other sectors. However, those sectors also registered low employment elasticity (<1) as did public administration. Further, the supply of skilled workforce in the finance and ICT sectors is lagging growing demand. The education sector alone registered high employment elasticity (>1), implying employment opportunities. However, its GVA was very low.

Between 2018 and 2021, two noteworthy changes took place: First, employment elasticity was near zero in all sectors except in agriculture (16 percent) and public administration (5 percent), and second, transportation registered a decline (–8 percent). The average annual employment during the period grew by only about 0.2 percent (figure 1.5b). This is likely due to the start of the COVID-19 health emergency in early 2020 and the intermittent lockdowns. The increasing use of digital infrastructure during the 2018–21 period is also likely to have contributed to growth. However, employment elasticity in the ICT sector was low. Other sectors had low but positive contribution to growth, specifically, essential basic services—health and social services, education, finance, and real estate). Investment is needed to develop workers' skills in these industries. Further analysis of subsector and occupation-specific skills is needed to understand why growth in certain industries has not led to increased employment. Value chain analysis of small, medium, and large enterprises would help to inform employment levels and skills needs.

Skills composition

Skills polarization is prevalent in Sri Lanka across sectors. This polarization is most pronounced in services, where the share of occupations requiring high-level skills rose from 35 to 41 percent between 2013 and 2018, and the share requiring mid-level skills fell from 52 to 43 percent (figure 1.6a). By contrast, the share of occupations requiring mid-level skills in agriculture stayed essentially the same. The occupational skills composition by economic sector in Sri Lanka over the period 2013–18 shows that across the three sectors—agriculture, industry, and services—low- and mid-level skills were predominant in the agriculture sector, low- middle- and marginally high-level skills were prevalent in industry, and middle- and high-level skills composition was greatest in the services sector. Consistently across the three sectors, occupational skills in Sri Lanka are clustered around low- and mid-level skills. However, the services sector has a growing concentration of high-level skills. The COVID-19 pandemic was an inflection point. In 2021, during the COVID-19 pandemic period, low-level skills seemed to be growing a little across agriculture, industry, and the services sectors, while mid-level skills remained consistently high in agriculture and industry but also grew in services (figure 1.6b).

The industries with relatively large production growth saw their skills composition change between 2013 and 2018. In finance the share of highly skilled workers rose by 9 percentage points, in ICT by 8 points, and in electricity by 6 points (figure 1.7). Substantial increases in low-skilled workers occurred in water supply and waste management (20 percentage points) and real estate (10 points). These trends may explain why job growth was not commensurate with production growth in finance, electricity (power sector), and ICT, which have growing numbers of highly skilled, highly productive workers. At the height of the COVID-19 pandemic, while the availability of midlevel skilled workers increased in water supply and waste management, finance, and real estate, it declined for health and social work, electricity (power sector), and ICT (figure 1.7b).

FIGURE 1.6

Occupational skills composition in Sri Lanka, by economic sector, 2013, 2018, and 2021

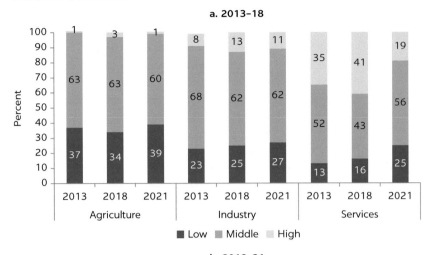

a. 2013–18

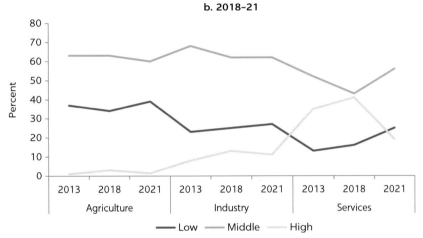

b. 2018–21

Sources: DCS 2013, 2018, 2021.

Note: High-skill occupations are managers, professionals, technicians, and associate professionals. Middle-skill occupations are clerical support workers; sales and services workers; craft and related trades workers; skilled agricultural, forestry, and fishery workers; and plant and machine operators and assemblers. Low-skill occupations are elementary occupations such as cleaners and helpers; laborers in agriculture, forestry, and fisheries; laborers in mining, construction, manufacturing, and transport; food preparation assistants; and street and related sales and services workers.

Labor market returns to technical and vocational education and training

In Sri Lanka people who have TVET qualifications are more likely to work, controlling for education level, than those who have no TVET qualifications (figure 1.8). But the relationship between education and working is not necessarily linear. For example, people with O-level diplomas do not have a higher probability of working than do those with lower-secondary education or lower. Those with an A-level qualification or a university degree are more likely to work. Although there have been annual fluctuations, no significant observable changes to these patterns have occurred in recent years.

FIGURE 1.7
Changes in skills composition in growing industries in Sri Lanka, 2013–21

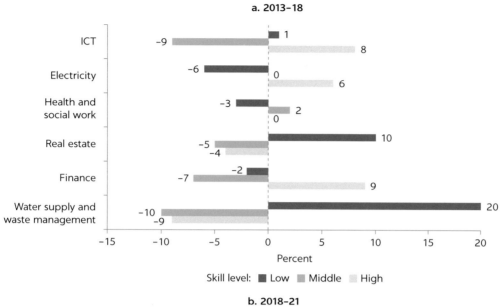

a. 2013–18

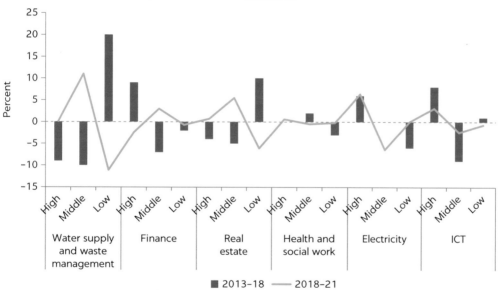

b. 2018–21

Sources: DCS 2013, 2018.
Note: ICT = information and communication technology.

Conditional on working, education and earnings have a positive relationship. That is, the more educated a person is, the greater their earnings. In Sri Lanka in 2018, people with A-level diplomas earned 31 percent more than those with only O-level diplomas (figure 1.9). TVET graduates earn 11–18 percent more than secondary school graduates with only O- or A-level credentials. Returns to education are highest for university graduates.

The varying returns to TVET across education levels are measured by the higher probability of people with TVET working (figure 1.10, panel a) and the earnings ratios of those with TVET to those without it (figure 1.10, panel b).

FIGURE 1.8

Returns to education in Sri Lanka: Probability of working, 2013–18

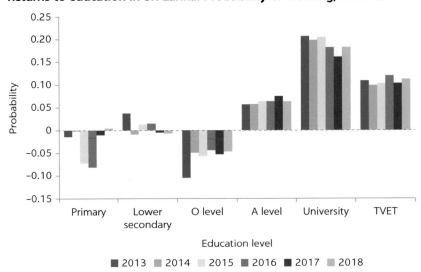

Sources: Original calculations for this publication based on DCS 2013, 2014, 2015, 2016b, 2017b, 2018.
Note: The figure shows the probability of working for each education level relative to the level that is one step below it (for example, university degree compared with A level). For primary, the returns are relative to workers with no or incomplete primary education. For TVET, the returns are relative to workers with no TVET. The authors calculated the data by regressing the probability of working (*y* = 1 if employed) on education level, gender, age, and age squared using Department of Census and Statistics *Labour Force Surveys* from 2013 through 2018. TVET = technical and vocational education and training.

FIGURE 1.9

Returns to education in Sri Lanka: Changes in earnings, 2013–18

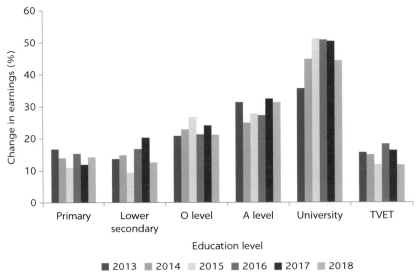

Sources: Original calculations for this publication based on DCS 2013, 2014, 2015, 2016b, 2017b, 2018.
Note: The figure shows the returns to each education level relative to the level that is one step below it (for example, university degree compared with A level). For primary, the returns are relative to workers with no or incomplete primary education. For TVET, the returns are relative to workers with no TVET. The authors calculated the data by regressing the log of yearly earnings on education level (dummies), TVET, gender, and polynomial function of age using Department of Census and Statistics *Labour Force Surveys* from 2013 through 2018. TVET = technical and vocational education and training.

FIGURE 1.10

Differences in returns to TVET in Sri Lanka, by education level, 2013–18

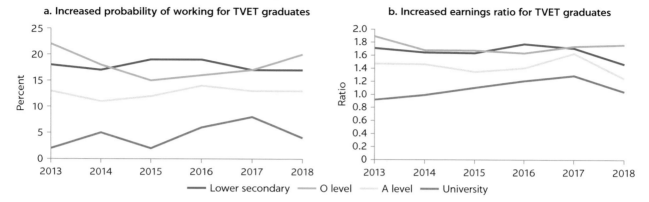

Sources: Original calculations for this publication based on DCS 2013, 2014, 2015, 2016b, 2017b, 2018.
Note: The earnings ratio is earnings of TVET graduates / earnings of non-TVET graduates. TVET = technical and vocational education and training.

For both measures, during 2013–18, people with lower-secondary education or O levels had the highest returns to TVET, while those with university degrees had the lowest.

Education and demographic features of TVET graduates and trainees

Most recent TVET graduates have an O-level secondary education or higher. During 2013–18, graduates with A-level education accounted for 40–45 percent of this group (figure 1.11, panel a). Compared with current workers, TVET graduates tended to be younger, with an average age of 36, and female, accounting for 51–54 percent. Current workers were, on average, 43 years old, and women accounted for 35 percent.

Demographic characteristics of TVET trainees differed slightly from those of TVET graduates. First, the share of female TVET trainees averaged 43 percent over the 2013–21 period. Second, the share of TVET trainees with A-level education has been increasing from 47 percent in 2013 to 54 percent in 2018 and 52 percent in 2021. The share of trainees with lower-secondary or O-level education has been decreasing (figure 1.11, panel b). This shift reflects labor market outcomes showing that TVET graduates with A-level education have the highest relative returns to employment.

Efficiency of recent public investment in TVET

The Skills Sector Development Program (SSDP), a seven-year plan, was implemented between 2014 and June 2023. The program's goal was to build an efficient skills development system to meet both domestic and foreign labor market demands in Sri Lanka by improving the quality, access, and relevance of skills to labor markets and skills training systems. The SSDP was technically and financially supported by various development partners including the World Bank and the Asian Development Bank (see annex 1A). The estimated cost of the SSDP amounted to 42 percent of the US$648 million spent on skills development over its implementation period.[10] The program was partly successful in that it increased access to technical and vocational training. However, it failed to make training institutes more efficient. In 2020, external financing for skills development dropped to 13 percent of the total.

FIGURE 1.11

Educational characteristics of TVET graduates and trainees in Sri Lanka, 2013–21

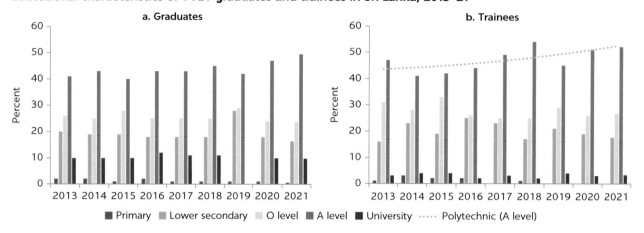

Sources: Original calculations for this publication based on DCS 2013, 2014, 2015, 2016b, 2017b, 2018, 2019, 2020, 2021.
Note: TVET = technical and vocational education and training.

FIGURE 1.12

Number of TVET graduates, enrollees, and completion rates in Sri Lanka, 2012–18

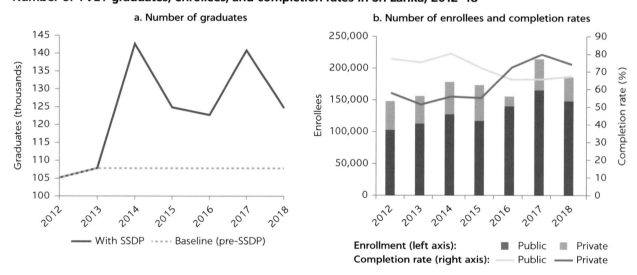

Sources: TVEC 2012, 2013, 2014, 2015, 2016a, 2017, 2018.
Note: SSDP = Skills Sector Development Program; TVET = technical and vocational education and training.

The number of TVET graduates increased by an average of 20 percent annually during the SSDP implementation period (figure 1.12, panel a), although outcomes were better in some previous years. The increase in TVET admissions reflected the rising number of students enrolled in both public and private TVET institutes (figure 1.12, panel b). Yet there was no improvement in completion rates across the entire TVET sector—completion rates rose at private institutes but fell at public ones, resulting in no net change. The increase in enrollments was likely due to the government's new policy of making TVET free of charge.

Analysis of the SSDP's efficiency focuses on the increased number of TVET graduates during the program period and the program's cost.[11] Cost-benefit

TABLE 1.3 **Total benefit, cost, net present value, and internal rate of return of the Skills Sector Development Program under two scenarios**

INDICATOR	US$, MILLIONS	
	BASE SCENARIO	HIGH-IMPACT SCENARIO
Total benefit (present value)	$271.3	$380.1
Total cost (present value)	$126.3	$126.3
Net present value	$145.0	$253.9
Internal rate of return (%)	6	9

Source: Original calculations for this publication.
Note: Amounts are in constant 2014 US dollars.

analysis was conducted using the program's estimated impact—that is, the increase in TVET gradates—their estimated labor market outcomes using the DCS *Labour Force Survey* (2013–18), and the increased public spending on skills development during this period. The economic benefit is estimated as the higher lifetime earnings of the increased number of TVET graduates. Lifetime earnings are estimated using the present discounted value (PDV) method, and the net present value (NPV) and internal rate of return are estimated using the project cost of the World Bank–financed Skills Development Project (2014–19)—that is, the World Bank's contribution to the SSDP. The sensitivity analysis is conducted using various assumptions on earnings projections and their impact (table 1.3).

The cost-benefit analysis largely relies on project beneficiary projections, beneficiary earnings profiles, and the project years covered. To check the sensitivity to assumptions, additional cost-benefit analysis is conducted with estimated benefits based on cohort-based, age-specific earnings profiles[12] and the five project years from 2014 to 2019. The base scenario assumes no lasting impact of the SSDP on TVET graduate trends after it ended. The high-impact scenario assumes that the SSDP's impact lasts five years; in other words, the last-year impact of the SSDP on increased TVET graduates would last five years after the end of the SSDP in 2020. Under the base scenario, the SSDP generated NPV in the amount of US$145 million (in 2014 dollars) and had an internal rate of return of 6 percent during the project years (2014–20). Under the high-impact scenario, the SSDP investment NPV rises to US$253.9 million, and the internal rate of return increases to 9 percent.

Impacts of COVID-19

Like all countries, Sri Lanka is facing the socioeconomic challenges of the COVID-19 pandemic. The first wave of infections occurred between March and July 2020, and the second wave commenced in October 2020 and lasted until mid-February 2021 (figure 1.13). In May 2021, the country began experiencing a third wave that started in mid-April. Infections—potential or actual—and deaths have led to contractions in the economic and social sectors. Even before the pandemic, in the first quarter of 2020 Sri Lanka was experiencing an economic slowdown, especially in construction, textiles, mining, and tea. Pandemic-driven periodic national lockdowns and border closures, along with weaker global demand, have exacerbated the economic contraction, lowering garment exports, tourism, and remittances.

FIGURE 1.13

Daily new confirmed COVID-19 cases in Sri Lanka, March 2020–May 2021

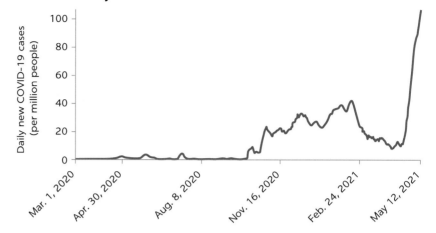

Source: Johns Hopkins University, Center for Systems Science and Engineering COVID-19 database, https://systems.jhu.edu/tracking-covid-19/.
Note: The data shown are rolling seven-day averages. The number of confirmed cases is lower than the actual number, mainly due to limited testing.

As a result, the Sri Lankan economy contracted by 3.6 percent in 2020, with tourism, manufacturing, construction, and transportation suffering the largest economic declines. Specifically, industrial activities such as construction and textile manufacturing experienced a 6.9 percent contraction due to weak export demand. This triggered an increase in the poverty rate from 9.2 percent in 2019 to 11.7 percent in 2020. In the medium term, while the economy is expected to recover gradually, recovery is expected to be slow because of lower export demand, tourism, and remittances as well as the challenging macroeconomic situation (World Bank 2021). The April–May 2022 economic crisis compounded the problems, making recovery a medium-term macroeconomic challenge to be surmounted.

Impacts on business and employment

The pandemic reversed the poverty reduction path that had occurred through labor reallocation and employment in recent years. Industrial activities, such as construction and manufacturing, and services, such as transportation and accommodations, were the main drivers of job growth before the pandemic and were hit the hardest by it. Employment fell by 1.1 percent in industry and by 0.8 percent in services (World Bank 2021).

According to a survey of businesses conducted in April–May 2020, only 3 percent were operating at full capacity, 44 percent were operating under capacity, and 53 percent had closed (DCS 2020b). Prolonged effects of COVID-19 will exacerbate economic disruptions, likely forcing the failure of many small and medium-size enterprises (World Bank 2020b).

The pandemic has had the greatest adverse effect on education, with nation-wide school closures reaching 76 percent (figure 1.14). Although many reports indicate that businesses intend to reopen when the pandemic ends, the damage of the longer-than-expected outbreak is likely to have lingering effects over the long term. Lingering effects would have substantial implications for

FIGURE 1.14

Status of business operations during the COVID-19 lockdown in Sri Lanka, April–May 2020

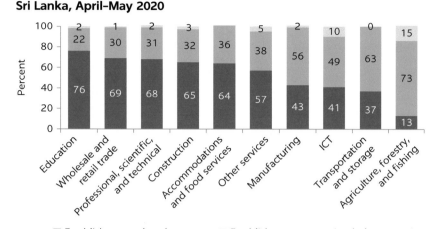

Source: Original analysis for this publication based on GoSL 2020.
Note: Covers only private formal enterprises. ICT = information and communication technology.

employment—especially for female workers—because education has the highest share of female workers and the highest employment elasticity.

Wholesale and retail trade, professional services, construction, and accommodations have also been hit hard by the pandemic, with business closures above 60 percent. And although agriculture has been the least affected sector, 73 percent of agribusinesses have been operating under capacity. Business closures and operations under capacity are inversely correlated with firm size: nearly 70 percent of small businesses (fewer than 15 employees) closed fully, but only about 15 percent of large businesses (more than 50 employees) have done so (Department of Labor 2020).

Private employment plummeted 36 percent in May 2020 (GoSL 2020). The damage has been worse in industries where remote work is not generally possible. As of April 2020, the pandemic's effects on employment were most severe in real estate (91 percent reduction), construction (88 percent), and accommodations and food services (81 percent) (figure 1.15). The effects were less severe in agriculture (13 percent reduction), ICT (20 percent), and education (45 percent). Some of the reduction in employment could be temporary, a result of travel restrictions. However, some workers will remain unemployed for extended periods and will have to upgrade their skills to be able to access better jobs or employment opportunities when the economy recovers after COVID-19 and prevailing restrictions are lifted.

Impacts on learning and earnings

In response to COVID-19, the Sri Lankan government closed public schools twice in 2020. The first closure lasted from mid-March to mid-June. Schools were reopened between mid-June and end-September, then had to close again in October. As of end-December 2020, they had remained closed, but they have since reopened. To ensure continuity in education, the Ministry of Education provided alternative learning for children during the school closures through

FIGURE 1.15

Reductions in employment in Sri Lanka, by industry, March–April 2020 relative to 2019

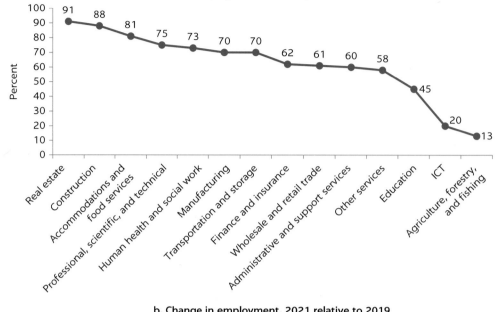

a. Reductions in employment, March–April 2020 relative to 2019

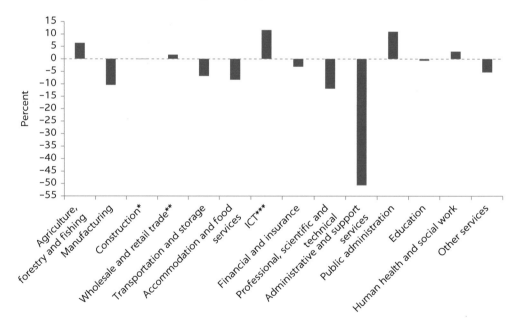

b. Change in employment, 2021 relative to 2019

Source: Original analysis for this publication based on GoSL 2020 and DCS 2021.
Note: Construction includes electricity, gas, steam and air conditioning supply, water supply, sewage, and waste. Wholesale and retail trade includes repair of motor vehicles and motorcycles. ICT = information and communication technology.

multiple distance-learning formats: an online platform combined with WhatsApp and Viber messaging from instructors and teachers and more traditional methods such as radio and television.

In 2016, only about 7 percent of households lacked access to a radio, television, DVD or CD player, or computer (DCS 2016a). Alternative learning modes were rolled out despite just 34 percent of Sri Lankans having internet access (World Bank 2019b). How effective are alternative learning modes, especially for students in poor households? To estimate the average effect of school closures on learning loss in Sri Lanka, the authors used simulation tools developed by the World Bank (Azevedo and others 2020) that take into account the duration of school closures and the mitigation strategies that have been used, such as access to and effectiveness of distance learning across income groups.[13] The simulation shows results for three scenarios: optimistic, intermediate, and pessimistic. It assumes that the duration of school closures in a school year ranges from 60 percent (optimistic) to 80 percent (pessimistic), that access to distance learning ranges from 14 percent (for the poorest quintile) to 100 percent (for the richest), and that the average effectiveness of distance education ranges between 10 percent (pessimistic) and 40 percent (optimistic).

Before the pandemic, Sri Lankan students had an estimated 8.5 learning-adjusted years of schooling (LAYS). This measure combines the 13.2 expected years of schooling with the quality of learning, indexed by Sri Lanka's score of 400 on Harmonized Test Scores (in a range from 300 to 625; Filmer and others 2018; World Bank 2020b). Relative to other countries in South Asia, where the average is 6.5 LAYS, Sri Lanka is faring well. This is testimony to the country's strong school system in terms of both quantity (access) and quality of teaching.

But with aspirations for regaining upper-middle-income country status and reaching high-income country status, Sri Lanka needs to continue investing in education and skills to reach the levels of the benchmark countries in Asia: the Republic of Korea and Malaysia (figure 1.16). The simulation results for Sri Lanka due to COVID-19 show that learning drops to 7.3 LAYS in the pessimistic scenario and 7.7 LAYS in the optimistic one (figure 1.17, panel a). As estimated, the learning loss will be approximately 1.2 LAYS because of intermittent school closures (as mentioned above) in 2020 and 2021—implying that learning loss is tending toward the pessimistic scenario.

FIGURE 1.16

LAYS, various countries, 2020

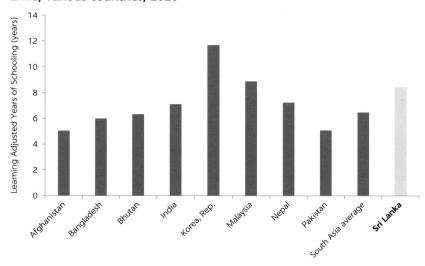

Source: World Bank 2020b.
Note: LAYS = learning-adjusted years of schooling.

If this learning loss is projected into the future, earnings losses could be expected to range between the intermediate and pessimistic scenarios. Per capita annual earnings are estimated to fall by US$550 (2017 purchasing power parity, adjusted dollars)—about 8 percent of average earnings (figure 1.17, panel b).

Impacts on overseas workers

Remittances from Sri Lankans working overseas were the country's largest source of foreign exchange, accounting for 8 percent of GDP in 2018 (table 1.4). But in recent years the reliance on remittances has been steadily falling due to declining overseas employment. The average number of migrant workers who left for foreign employment fell from 824 per day in 2014 to 579 per day

FIGURE 1.17

Simulated learning losses and earnings losses in Sri Lanka due to COVID-19, various scenarios

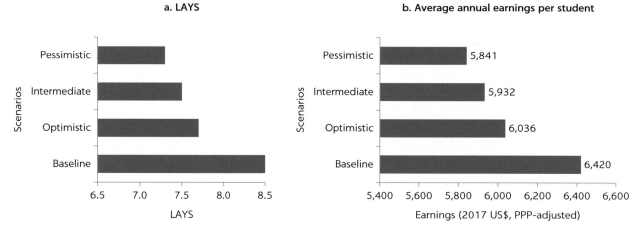

Source: Original data using the simulation tools developed by Azevedo and others 2020.
Note: LAYS = learning-adjusted years of schooling; PPP = purchasing power parity.

TABLE 1.4 **Remittances and overseas employment among migrant workers from Sri Lanka, 2014–20**

	2014	2015	2016	2017	2018	2019	2020	TREND
Remittances as % of GDP	8.9	8.7	8.8	8.2	8.0	8.0	8.8	
Remittances as % of export earnings	63	66	70	63	59	56	71	
Total number of migrant workers	300,703	263,443	242,816	211,992	211,211	203,087	53,875	
Average migrants for employment per day	824	722	665	581	579	556	148	
Female share (%)	37	34	34	34	39	40	40	
Employment by source								
Through government-registered sources (%)	59	44	36	32	32	34	34	
Through direct sources (%)	41	56	64	68	68	66	66	
Destinations for employment								
Middle Eastern countries (%)	86	84	80	55	79	86	83	
Non-Middle Eastern countries (%)	14	16	20	45	21	14	17	

Sources: De and Ratha 2012; SLBFE 2014, 2015, 2016, 2017, 2018, 2019, 2020.

in 2018, and to a very low level of 148 per day in 2020 due to the onset of the COVID-19 pandemic. Consequently, remittances also decreased from 8.87 percent of GDP in 2014 to 7.97 percent in 2018, but picked up slightly to 8.8 percent in 2020. This is likely due to the inflows from foreign remittances to assist family and communities during the COVID-19 pandemic and the ensuing intermittent lockdowns.

Meanwhile, more recruitments have occurred directly rather than through government-registered channels. The share of recruitment through direct sources—such as company portals, private recruitment sites, individual contacts, and the like—jumped from 41 to 68 percent between 2014 and 2018 and decreasing to 66 percent in 2020 as the pandemic set in (see table 1.4). The share of women engaged in overseas employment increased slightly, from 37 percent in 2014 to 39 percent in 2018, although for the three years in between, the average share dropped to 34 percent. It picked up to 40 percent in 2019 but remained at that level in 2020. Most overseas female workers are housemaids in Middle Eastern countries.

Occupations requiring skilled workers comprise the largest percentage of foreign employment, followed by housemaids and unskilled categories (figure 1.18, panel a). The share of skilled workers in foreign employment decreased significantly from 21 percent in 2014 to 14 percent in 2017, and further declined to 5 percent in 2020 due to the pandemic. It picked up in 2022, rising to 10 percent. (figure 1.18, panel b). This is likely a result of national foreign employment policies over the past decade, which have increasingly focused on foreign employment for skilled workers and require female domestic workers to have at least National Vocational Qualification (NVQ) level 3 skills (SLBFE 2014, 2015, 2016, 2017, 2018, 2019, 2020, 2021, 2022). Semiskilled workers were the least required in foreign employment.

There are some indications of a growing mismatch between recruitment (supply) and job vacancies (demand) in foreign employment, with increasing supply shortages—especially for skilled jobs.[14] Job vacancies for foreign employment have been stable. Yet supply has been falling faster than demand. Government-registered sources show this mismatch, with supply having more than halved between 2014 and 2018, falling steadily until 2019, and plummeting to an all time low of 7 percent in 2021; it picked up in 2022 to register 13 percent (figure 1.19, panel a). In recent years the supply and demand gap has widened, with only 34 percent of job vacancies through government-registered sources filled in 2020, far below the 2014 level of 59 percent, and more vacancies being filled through direct sources at up to 66 percent in 2020 compared to about 41 percent in 2014 (table 1.4). The mismatch exists across all skill levels and has been growing evenly over the years, but it is much higher for skilled workers, for whom only 10 percent of job vacancies (demand) were filled in 2022, up from 5 percent in 2020 and 2021 due to the pandemic (figure 1.19, panel b). Housemaids were in greater supply, with approximately 17 percent of vacancies filled in 2022 compared to 18 percent in 2020 and 11 percent in 2021. This shows some signs of recovery.

To minimize uncertainties originating from foreign labor markets and economies, the government has tried to gradually reduce dependence on remittances, especially from unskilled workers. For example, high youth employment in Middle Eastern countries lowers demand for unskilled workers from overseas. The national foreign employment policy focuses on investing in a skilled

FIGURE 1.18

Trends in skills composition of overseas workers from Sri Lanka, 2014–22

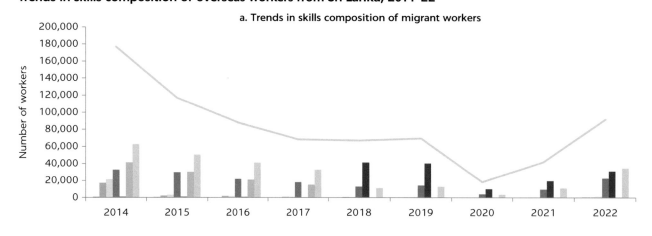

a. Trends in skills composition of migrant workers

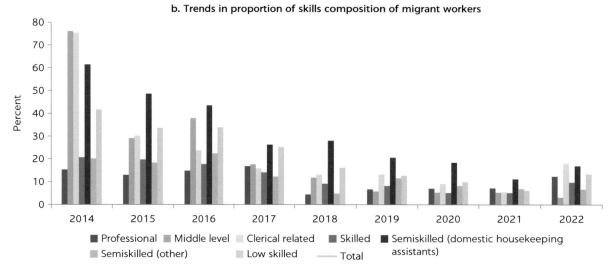

b. Trends in proportion of skills composition of migrant workers

Professional ■ Middle level ■ Clerical related ■ Skilled ■ Semiskilled (domestic housekeeping assistants)
■ Semiskilled (other) ■ Low skilled —— Total

Sources: SLBFE 2014, 2015, 2016, 2017, 2018, 2019, 2020, 2021, 2022.

workforce through vocational and professional training. The Foreign Employment Bureau advises all workers to receive NVQ through the recognition of prior learning route or by attending training courses at a training institute. This approach is intended to ensure that workers have qualifications of internationally verifiable standards for their employment in both domestic and high-income countries. This also helps to reduce the number of unskilled and mid-level workers for domestic industries that have been facing labor supply shortages in these categories (GoSL 2020).

The policy focus on skilled workers with verifiable international standards may be economically beneficial in the short run, guaranteeing a stable source of foreign exchange. But in the long run, the country could consider measuring the potential economic costs of brain drain caused by the emigration of skilled workers and the economic benefits of remittances. Accommodating the return of experienced migrants could help revitalize the economy.

Brain drain is a well-known international phenomenon. For example, in the 1980s and 1990s, India lost an estimated US$2 billion annually due to the

FIGURE 1.19
Foreign employment and skills mismatch in Sri Lanka, 2014–22

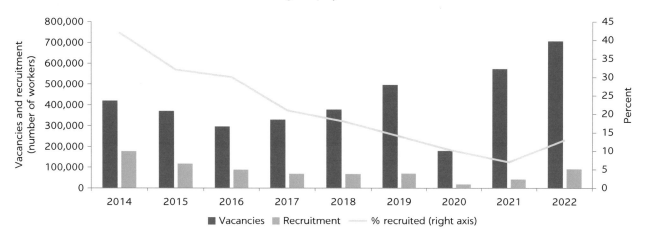

a. Foreign employment mismatch

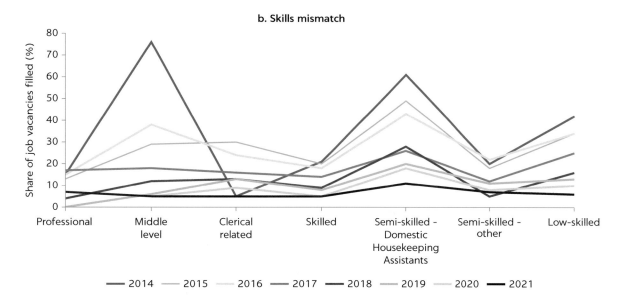

b. Skills mismatch

Sources: SLBFE 2014, 2015, 2016, 2017, 2018, 2019, 2020, 2021, 2022.
Note: Vacancies and recruitment are through government-registered sources only.

emigration of IT experts to the United States, after having borne the costs of their education (UNDP 2001, 92). Yet there is also brain circulation, with high-skilled emigrants contributing to the economic development of their home countries by bringing new technologies, entrepreneurial skills, and experience (Saxenian 2005). Brain circulation is mainly observed and studied in China and India. Creating incentives to attract skilled, experienced workers back to their home countries and vitalizing economies with their entrepreneurship could be key to redesigning policies on foreign employment to minimize the cost of brain drain. Sri Lanka has the advantage of an educated population capable of acquiring 21st-century IT skills to energize its economy and build a solid foundation for driving its economy with a skilled labor force.

Impacts on return migrants

COVID-19 has affected migrant workers globally. In 2020, nearly 28 percent of the stock of migrant workers emigrated from the 20 countries with the highest COVID-19 infection rates, and in 2019 they transferred 37 percent of all remittances to their countries of origin (IOM 2020). Migrants in those countries are likely to be essential workers and more affected by the pandemic. For example, 13 percent of key workers in the European Union are immigrants (Fasani and Mazza 2020), and 69 percent of migrants in the United States work in critical infrastructure sectors—where lockdowns, travel restrictions, and border closures have affected and will continue to affect migrants working in these sectors (Kerwin and Warren 2020).

Globally, some of the deleterious effects of the pandemic have been staggering job losses and displacement for migrants and decreasing remittances. These trends will have long-term economic consequences. In South Asia alone, they will hurt 122 million migrant workers from India, 36 million from Bangladesh, 19 million from Pakistan, and 2 million from Nepal (ILO 2020). A recent study suggests an unmet need for occupation-specific skills training for Nepalese migrants who have returned from India due to the pandemic (Sharma, Sherpa, and Goyal 2021). A similar situation could occur in Sri Lanka.

Like all regions, the Middle East was hit hard by the pandemic, and that is where nearly 80 percent of Sri Lankan foreign workers were registered in 2018 (see table 1.4). Most Middle Eastern countries closed borders, halted international travel, and imposed lockdowns at various stages. Nearly half of all migrant workers in the Middle East are in sectors—such as transportation, accommodations and food, real estate, business administration, manufacturing, and wholesale and retail services—with medium to high risk of being stricken by COVID-19. In addition, migrant workers are engaged in subsectors of essential services such as health care, child care, food production, and cleaning, which are also disproportionately affected by COVID-19. Consequently, many migrant workers have seen their work contracts terminated and have been deported to their home countries. Some are stranded (ILO 2020). Sri Lanka is experiencing the effects of returning migrants.

At the end of 2020, 361,000 COVID-19 infections were reported in Saudi Arabia, the top destination for foreign workers from Sri Lanka (WHO 2020). In May 2020, 75 percent of confirmed new cases were among migrants, and an estimated 1.2 million foreign workers—approximately 9 percent of all employees—were expected to leave the Saudi labor market that year (Nereim 2020). A recent study on low-skilled Indian migrant workers in Saudi Arabia estimated that they were likely to lose up to 36 percent of their expected earnings (Abella and Sasikumar 2020).

COVID-19 vaccines offered hope, but their rollout and administration were delayed. Meanwhile, given that the pandemic and associated travel restrictions and border closures continued in 2021, new foreign employment was far lower than the pre-pandemic levels. Existing migrant workers—especially unskilled or semiskilled ones in affected industries such as construction, sales, and accommodations and hospitality—continued to return to their home countries. Sri Lanka's government prepared a policy framework for the return and reintegration of migrant workers (SMFEPMD 2020).

The National Action Plan on Return and Reintegration is being implemented by the Sri Lanka Bureau of Foreign Employment (SLBFE). This subpolicy framework covers the social and economic reintegration of migrant returnees, physical and psychological well-being of returnees and their family members, civil and political empowerment of returnees, and management and dissemination of information in the migration cycle. The plan's strategies include standardizing the quality and certifying the skills of migrant workers before their departure and upon return, promoting a savings and financial management culture among migrant workers, promoting entrepreneurship among migrant returnees and family members, and securing domestic jobs for returnees through public-private partnerships. It also emphasizes the role of district and divisional resource centers and collaboration with civil society organizations (ILO 2015; SMFEPMD 2020).

Returning migrants are valuable to the workforce. They can transfer skills across borders, provide social capital from foreign environments, and stimulate investment in new enterprises (Cassarino 2014). But it is likely that, due to the pandemic, current migrants returning to Sri Lanka are less prepared to perform these functions since their migration cycles have been abruptly interrupted, even halted. Further evaluation is needed of the current flow of returning migrants and those who have already returned. To support their social, economic, and psychosocial reintegration, Sri Lanka needs to adopt evidence-based return and reintegration planning and services generated through a registration system that provides survey information on returnees by gender, skills, occupations practiced abroad, legal status, reasons for return, preparedness for return, and geographic distribution (Wickramasekara 2019). Such a system would help identify skills gaps and design needed training programs to upgrade skills or reskill returning migrants to meet both domestic labor markets immediately and potentially new labor markets overseas in the future.

An interim review of existing profiles of foreign workers and an assessment of how the pandemic has affected them indicates that a large portion of returning migrants will be low-skilled male workers engaged in the most affected sectors (such as construction, wholesale and retail sale services, accommodations, and food services) and female workers engaged in domestic household work. Upgrading their skills and/or reskilling them would help cater to immediate and future labor demands in the post-COVID-19 era in Sri Lanka. Returning female migrants could be seamlessly absorbed in health care, child care, and elder care services with skills acquired informally in foreign countries and systematic upgrading of specific skills suitable for Sri Lankan industries.

ANNEX 1A: SUPPORT FOR THE SKILLS SECTOR DEVELOPMENT PROGRAM FROM DEVELOPMENT PARTNERS

TABLE 1A.1 **Development partners and skill development programs in Sri Lanka**

DEVELOPMENT PARTNER AND PROJECT	FUNDING AND DURATION	IMPLEMENTING AGENCY	ACTIVITIES
Asian Development Bank SSEP	US$100 million Period: 2014–17	SMSDVERI	**Sectorwide intervention** Supporting activities under the SSDP (2014–20) using the RBL approach covering programs in the SSDP. The focus is on systemwide improvements, and it is an islandwide project.
	Additional financing US$100 million Period: 2018–21 Loan	SMSDVERI	**Sectorwide intervention** Supporting activities under the SSDP (2014–20) using the RBL approach covering programs in the SSDP. The focus is on systemwide improvements, and it is an islandwide project.
	US$3 million Grant. Japan Fund for Poverty Reduction	SMSDVERI	**Focused intervention** To complement the existing assistance to strengthen private sector engagement and women's participation in TVET and employment.
GIZ Vocational training in the north and east of Sri Lanka	€8 million €4 million grant + €4 million loan Period: 2011–18	SMSDVERI	**Focused intervention** KfW Development Bank financed the construction of Sri Lanka-German Training Institute, teacher training, equipment, curriculum development, and so on. GIZ is assisting 15 satellite centers in the north and east of Sri Lanka in improving their training courses. Entrepreneurial skills training, on-the-job training, career guidance, curriculum development, teacher training, and so on. English and information technology skills are built into the courses.
Government of Australia, Department of Foreign Affairs and Trade Skills for Inclusive Growth Project	$A15 million Grant Period: 2016–20	SMSDVERI	**Focused intervention** The project piloted a flexible, market-oriented TVET program in Sri Lanka's poorest provinces, focusing on the poor (especially women and people with a disability) in the informal sector. It seeks to improve the ability of the poor to gain jobs in the expanding tourism sector. Support the full value chain of the tourism sector—for example, food suppliers, hospitality trainers, artisans, surf instructors, spa owners, accommodation providers, and taxi drivers—as well as district planners, park rangers, industry regulators, and business chambers in four districts in Sri Lanka: Trincomalee, Ampara, Batticaloa (Eastern Province), and Polonnaruwa (North Central Province).
Government of Austria Institute of Engineering Technology	€9.5 million Loan Period: 2017–20	SMSDVERI	**Focused intervention** Upgrading of Institute of Engineering Technology, Katunayake
Government of India	LKR 199 million Period: 2017–19	SMSDVERI	**Focused intervention** Thondaman Vocational Training Centre, Hatton
Government of the Netherlands National Vocational Training Institute	€42 million (US$33 million) Loan + grant Period: 2016–20	SMSDVERI	**Focused intervention** Establishment of National Vocational Training Institute, Polonnaruwa. Construction, training, equipment, and model hostel

continued

TABLE 1A.1, *continued*

DEVELOPMENT PARTNER AND PROJECT	FUNDING AND DURATION	IMPLEMENTING AGENCY	ACTIVITIES
International Labour Organization Skills to support local economic development European Union support to reconstruction and development in selected districts in Sri Lanka	€2 million Period: July 1, 2012–March 31, 2018	UNICEF, UNDP, UNOPS, FAO, IFC, SMSDVERI, and other partners	**Focused intervention** Activities: (a) implement modified/new demand-oriented training programs with selected partner institutions; (b) implement capacity-building programs for selected training institutions; (c) strengthen the District Enterprise and TVET providers Networks Project Outcomes; and (d) strengthen the delivery of the district-level employment services. Upgrading of technical colleges in Batticaloa and Ampara in the Eastern Province and Vavuniya and Mannar in the Northern Province. Providing equipment to upgrade 10 courses in those technical colleges. Providing career guidance and soft skills training of instructors and teachers and supporting selected VTA and NYSC centers in the four selected districts. Partners: UNICEF, UNDP, UNOPS, FAO, IFC, Ministry of Labor and Trade Union Relations, MYASD, registered vocational providers, district administrations, worker organizations, employers' organizations, and district chambers.
Korea International Cooperation Agency	US$3 million Period: 2010–21	DTET, SMSDVERI	**Focused intervention** Modernization and Upgrading of Technical Colleges and Colleges of Technology Project in Sri Lanka. It provided equipment and teacher training in the automobile sections of Maradana College of Technology, Kandy College of Technology, Kegalle Technical College, Sammanthurai Technical College, and Bandarawela Technical College. Signing memoranda of understanding with KIA Motors (Lanka) Ltd and MICRO Holdings to develop industry and training institute links and provide on-the-job training opportunities for students
Korea International Cooperation Agency *(continued)*	US$2.5 million Period: 2017–21	Ocean University, SMSDVERI	**Focused intervention** Establishment of the Master Plan and Capacity Building of the Ocean University (previously the National Institute of Fisheries and Nautical Engineering)
Republic of Korea EXIM Bank	US$26 million Period: 2016–19 Loan	SMSDVERI	**Focused intervention** • Construction of Korea-Sri Lanka National Vocational Training Institute in Orugodawatte • Upgrading of Gampaha Technical College • Supply of training equipment and installation • Overseas training in the Republic of Korea for teachers • Dispatch of Korean experts • Textbook development (for 10 trades)—mechatronics, welding, robotics, computer numerical control, pneumatics and hydraulics, refrigeration and air conditioning, automotive, electrical, electronics, and telecommunication

continued

TABLE 1A.1, *continued*

DEVELOPMENT PARTNER AND PROJECT	FUNDING AND DURATION	IMPLEMENTING AGENCY	ACTIVITIES
United States Agency for International Development Youth Employment and Business Startup Project (YouLead Project)	US$12 million Period: 4 years US$1.8 million partner support Period: 2017–21 Grant	Administered by Volunteers for Economic Growth Alliance and implemented by IESC and other partners	**Focused intervention** YouLead creates a more skilled and flexible workforce through activities that support and strengthen students, teachers, and institutions. It fosters increased opportunities for self-employment by improving the skills of young entrepreneurs and working with financial institutions to encourage more lending to youth-led start-ups in the Sabaragamuwa, Central, Southern, and Northern Provinces; improve career guidance and counseling; provide foundational skills critical to finding and maintaining a job; introduce new demand-driven courses, conduct training of trainers; and so on. Volunteers for Economic Growth Alliance administers the program, and IESC implements it. IESC has partnered with the Ceylon Chamber of Commerce, the American Chamber of Commerce, Arizona State University, Global Communities, Skills for Life, and Verité Research.
World Bank Skills Development Program	US$101.5 million (US$47.8 million disbursed) Period: 2014–19	SMSDVERI	**Sectorwide intervention** Supporting activities under the SSDP (2014–20) using the RBL approach covering programs in the SSDP. The focus is on systemwide improvements, and it is an islandwide project.
World University Services of Canada ASSET Project	Amount: Can$14 million Period: 2015–19	SMSDVERI	**Focused intervention** Four thousand scholarships given to students from 11 districts to pursue vocational training programs in the public sector and private sector vocational training institutes. This covers all districts in the north and east, as well as Puttalam, Matara, and Hambantota. Work with the private sector to identify demand for courses and ensure that scholarships are provided to students to pursue courses.

Source: Original table for this publication.
Note: Originally approved amounts of funding are presented; actual disbursement figures are not included in most cases. DTET = Department of Technical Education and Training; FAO = Food and Agriculture Organization; GIZ = German Agency for International Cooperation (Deutsche Gesellschaft fur Internationale Zusammenarbeit); IESC = International Executive Service Corps; IFC = International Finance Corporation; KfW = Kreditanstalt für Wiederaufbau; MYASD = Ministry of Youth Affairs and Skills Development; NYSC = National Youth Services Council; RBL = results-based lending; SMSDVERI = State Ministry of Skills Development, Vocational Education, Research and Innovations; SSDP = Skills Sector Development Program; SSEP = Skills Sector Enhancement Plan; TVET = technical and vocational education and training; UNDP = United Nations Development Programme; UNICEF = United Nations Children's Fund; UNOPS = United Nations Office for Project Services; VTA = Vocational Training Authority.

NOTES

1. An employment elasticity of 1 implies that with every 1 percentage point growth in GDP, employment increases by 1 percent.
2. The Department of Census and Statistics *Labour Demand Survey* 2017 evaluates employers' skills demands over the next few years and discusses the rapidly changing nature of skills demand: "Most of the new jobs created over the next few years will be higher skilled. There are thousands of lower skilled jobs and these can be rewarding careers or pathways to other jobs. Employers' needs can change quickly. Workers who are willing to learn, gain experience and build their skills will be well placed to find and keep a job" (DCS 2017a, 44).
3. International Labour Organization Statistics (ILOStat) Database, 2019.
4. "Stacking skills" refers to organizing skills in layers, from foundational to expert, skilled professional.
5. "Upskilling" is the acquisition of skills that build on an existing knowledge base and skills to take up new jobs. "Reskilling" involves refreshing skills to reinforce one's existing knowledge base and skills and to maintain a license or certification.

6. "Given the vital importance of human capital for economic growth, the World Bank has launched the Human Capital Project (HCP), which includes the Human Capital Index (HCI). The HCI is different from the [United Nations Development Programme's] Human Development Index, which is a composite measure of three key dimensions of human development: adult life expectancy, education, and per capita income. As such, it differs from the HCI, which is designed to capture the main dimensions of human capital development. The objective of the HCP is to accelerate human capital development around the world. The HCI is a cross-country metric designed to measure and forecast a country's human capital. The index follows the trajectory, from birth to adulthood, of a child born today. It measures the amount of human capital that a child can expect to attain by the end of secondary school, given the risks of poor health and low education that exist in the country at the time of birth. The HCI has three components: (a) a measure of whether children survive from birth to school age (age 5); (b) a measure of expected years of quality-adjusted school, which combines information on the quantity and quality of education; and (c) two broad measures of nutrition and health, stunting rates, and adult survival rates" (World Bank 2019a, 8).

7. Sri Lanka also lags behind East Asian countries such as China, Malaysia, Mongolia, Thailand, and Vietnam (World Bank 2019c).

8. The World Health Organization (WHO n.d.) defines "stunting" as low height for a child's age. It results from chronic or recurrent undernutrition (a form of malnutrition) and is usually associated with poverty, poor maternal health, frequent illness, or inappropriate care early in life. Stunting can lead to physical and cognitive deficits. For more information, see the WHO website at https://who.int/health-topics/malnutrition#tab=tab_1.

9. There were many reasons for the survey. The most important was to identify the influence of new technological developments on the labor market. Employers' demand for skills had changed over time. To better understand the characteristics of the new labor market, the Department of Census and Statistics conducted a survey of private enterprises with assistance from the International Labour Organization. In all, 3,500 enterprises engaged in industry, trade, and services (including tourism) were selected. (Public enterprises were not included because information on them could be drawn from administrative data.) Because demand was high in the plantation sector, all plantation companies were surveyed. The distribution of employment was surveyed based on current employment by occupation type, age group, gender, and average salary by occupational group. The occupational groups were managers, professionals, technicians, and associate professionals; clerical support workers; service and sales workers; skilled agricultural, forestry, and fisheries workers; craft and related trades workers; plant and machine operators and assemblers; and elementary occupations.

10. Actual spending on the Skills Sector Development Program (SSDP) was not possible to identify based on the government's spending category. The amount was estimated based on increased government spending on skills development relative to the pre-SSDP period (that is, 2013).

11. Because data on technical and vocational education and training graduates for 2019 and 2020 were not available as of November 2020, the last available data (World Bank 2018) are used to project the impacts in 2019 and 2020.

12. Because earnings increase as workers age, the average earnings difference between technical and vocational education and training (TVET) and non-TVET workers of all age groups is used, as workers at the beginning of their careers will distort the discounted value of the benefit at present.

13. Other parameters include learning-adjusted years of schooling, monthly earnings of employees in 2017 dollars adjusted for purchasing power parity, and income disparities across quintiles.

14. Actual demand may be lower than the total number of job vacancies because there is redundancy in job vacancies across multiple sites.

REFERENCES

Abella, Manolo I., and S. K. Sasikumar. 2020. "Estimating Earnings Losses of Migrant Workers Due to COVID-19." *Indian Journal of Labour Economics* 63: 921–39. https://doi.org/10.1007/s41027-020-00281-y.

ADB (Asian Development Bank) and ILO (International Labour Organization). 2017. "Sri Lanka: Fostering Workforce Skills through Education: Employment Diagnostic Study." Manila and Geneva.

Almeida, Rita, and Pedro Carneiro. 2012. "Enforcement of Labor Regulation and Informality." *American Economic Journal: Applied Economics* 4 (3): 64–89. https://doi.org/10.1257/app.4.3.64.

Almeida, Rita, and Pedro Manuel Carneiro. 2005. "Enforcement of Labor Regulation, Informal Labor, and Firm Performance." Policy Research Working Paper 3756, World Bank, Washington, DC.

Almeida, Rita, and Pedro Manuel Carneiro. 2009. "Enforcement of Labor Regulation and Firm Size." *Journal of Comparative Economics* 37 (1): 28–46.

Aturupane, Harsha, Hideki Higashi, Roshini Ebenezer, Deepika Attygalle, Shobhana Sosale, Sangeeta Day, and Rehana Wijesinghe. 2021. *Sri Lanka Human Capital Development: Realizing the Promise and Potential of Human Capital.* International Development in Focus. Washington, DC: World Bank. doi:10.1596/978-1-4648-1718-2.

Azevedo, Joao Pedro, Koen Geven, Diana Goldemberg, Amer Hasan, and Syedah Aroob Iqbal. 2020. "Country Tool for Simulating the Potential Impacts of COVID-19 School Closures on Schooling and Learning Outcomes, Version 6." World Bank, Washington, DC.

Cassarino, Jean-Pierre, ed. 2014. *Reintegration and Development.* San Domenico di Fiesole, Italy: European University Institute. http://hdl.handle.net/1814/30401.

Central Bank of Sri Lanka. 2019. *Annual Report.* Colombo.

CBSL (Central Bank of Sri Lanka). 2022. *Annual Report.* Colombo.

DCS (Department of Census and Statistics). 2012. *Sri Lanka Labour Force Survey Annual Report—2012.* Colombo.

DCS (Department of Census and Statistics). 2013. *Sri Lanka Labour Force Survey Annual Report—2013.* Colombo.

DCS (Department of Census and Statistics). 2014. *Sri Lanka Labour Force Survey Annual Report—2014.* Colombo.

DCS (Department of Census and Statistics). 2015. *Sri Lanka Labour Force Survey Annual Report—2015.* Colombo.

DCS (Department of Census and Statistics). 2016a. *Sri Lanka—Household Income and Expenditure Survey 2016.* Battaramulla: Sri Lanka.

DCS (Department of Census and Statistics). 2016b. *Sri Lanka Labour Force Survey Annual Report—2016.* Battaramulla: Sri Lanka.

DCS (Department of Census and Statistics). 2017a. *Sri Lanka Labour Demand Survey.* Colombo.

DCS (Department of Census and Statistics). 2017b. *Sri Lanka Labour Force Survey Annual Report—2017.* Colombo.

DCS (Department of Census and Statistics). 2018. *Sri Lanka Labour Force Survey Annual Report—2018.* Colombo.

DCS (Department of Census and Statistics). 2019. *Sri Lanka Labour Force Survey Annual Report—2019.* Colombo.

DCS (Department of Census and Statistics). 2020a. *Sri Lanka Labour Demand Survey.* Colombo.

DCS (Department of Census and Statistics). 2020b. *Sri Lanka Labour Force Survey Annual Report—2020.* Colombo.

DCS (Department of Census and Statistics). 2021. *Sri Lanka Labour Force Survey Annual Report—2021.* Colombo.

De, Prabal Kumar, and Dilip K. Ratha. 2012, October 25. "Impact of Remittances on Household Income, Asset, and Human Capital: Evidence from Sri Lanka." *Migration and Development* 1 (1): 1–43. https://doi.org/10.1080/21632324.2012.719348.

Dundar, Halil, Benoît Millot, Yevgeniya Savchenko, Harsha Aturupane, and Tilkaratne A. Piyasiri. 2014. *Building the Skills for Economic Growth and Competitiveness in Sri Lanka.* Directions in Development. Washington, DC: World Bank. doi:10.1596/978-1-4648-0158-7.

Fasani, F., and J. Mazza. 2020. "A Vulnerable Workforce: Migrant Workers in the COVID-19 Pandemic." Technical Report. European Commission, Joint Research Centre, Brussels.

Filmer, Deon, Halsey Rogers, Noam Angrist, and Shwetlana Sabarwal. 2018. "Learning-Adjusted Years of Schooling: Defining a New Macro Measure of Education." Policy Research Working Paper 8591, World Bank, Washington, DC.

GoSL (Government of Sri Lanka). 2019. *Vistas of Prosperity and Splendour*. Colombo: Ministry of Finance, Treasury of Sri Lanka.

GoSL (Government of Sri Lanka). 2020. "COVID-19 and Beyond—The Impact on the Labor Market of Sri Lanka." GoSL Department of Labor, Colombo.

ILO (International Labour Organization). 2008. "International Standard Classification of Occupations (ISCO:08)." https://www.ilo.org/public/english/bureau/stat/isco/isco08/.

ILO (International Labour Organization). 2015. "Return and Reintegration in Sri Lanka: Creating an Empowerment Landscape for Returnee Migrant Workers." Policy Brief. ILO, Geneva.

ILO (International Labour Organization). 2020. "COVID-19: Labor Market Impact and Policy Responses in Arab States." Briefing Note. ILO, Geneva.

IOM (International Organization for Migration). 2020. *UN Migration*. IOM Sri Lanka. https://srilanka.iom.int/.

Kerwin, Donald, and Robert Warren. 2020. "US Foreign-Born Workers in the Global Pandemic: Essential and Marginalized." *Journal on Migration and Human Security* 8 (3): 282–300.

Nereim, Vivian. 2020. "Expat Departures to Benefit Saudi Arabia's Unemployed." *Bloomberg*. https://www.bloomberg.com/news/articles/2020-06-15/expat-exodus-to-curb-unemployment-among-saudis-at-time-of-crisis.

Ruppert Bulmer, Elizabeth. 2020. "Sri Lanka Jobs Diagnostic." Report Number P168904, World Bank, Washington, DC. https://openknowledge.worldbank.org/entities/publication/b48f653d-1b2a-561b-b503-38559ac26b4a.

Saxenian, Anna Lee. 2005. "From Brain Drain to Brain Circulation: Transnational Communities and Regional Upgrading in India and China." *Studies in Comparative International Development* 40: 35–61.

Sharma, Uttam, Maya Sherpa, and Sangeeta Goyal. 2021. *Understanding the Skills Needs of Migrant Workers from Nepal*. Washington, DC: World Bank Group. http://documents.worldbank.org/curated/en/103831611117571692/Understanding-the-Skills-Needs-of-Migrant-Workers-from-Nepal.

SLBFE (Sri Lanka Bureau of Foreign Employment). 2013. *Annual Statistical Report of Foreign Employment 2013*. Colombo: SLBFE.

SLBFE (Sri Lanka Bureau of Foreign Employment). 2014. *Annual Statistical Report of Foreign Employment 2014*. Colombo: SLBFE.

SLBFE (Sri Lanka Bureau of Foreign Employment). 2015. *Annual Statistical Report of Foreign Employment 2015*. Colombo: SLBFE.

SLBFE (Sri Lanka Bureau of Foreign Employment). 2016. *Annual Statistical Report of Foreign Employment 2016*. Colombo: SLBFE.

SLBFE (Sri Lanka Bureau of Foreign Employment). 2017. *Annual Statistical Report of Foreign Employment 2017*. Colombo: SLBFE.

SLBFE (Sri Lanka Bureau of Foreign Employment). 2018. *Annual Statistical Report of Foreign Employment 2018*. Battaramulla. SLBFE.

SLBFE (Sri Lanka Bureau of Foreign Employment). 2019. *Annual Statistics of Foreign Employment 2019*. Battaramulla. SLBFE.

SLBFE (Sri Lanka Bureau of Foreign Employment). 2020. *Annual Statistics of Foreign Employment 2020*. Colombo: SLBFE.

SLBFE (Sri Lanka Bureau of Foreign Employment). 2021. *Annual Statistics of Foreign Employment 2021*. Colombo: SLBFE.

SLBFE (Sri Lanka Bureau of Foreign Employment). 2022. *Annual Statistics of Foreign Employment 2022*. Colombo: SLBFE.

SMFEPMD (State Ministry of Foreign Employment Promotion and Market Diversification). 2020. "National Policy on Migration for Employment for Sri Lanka and National Action Plan (2020–2023)." Draft. Colombo.

TVEC (Tertiary and Vocational Education Commission). 2012. *Labour Market Information Bulletin*. Colombo.

TVEC (Tertiary and Vocational Education Commission). 2013. *Labour Market Information Bulletin*. Colombo.

TVEC (Tertiary and Vocational Education Commission). 2014. *Labour Market Information Bulletin*. Colombo.

TVEC (Tertiary and Vocational Education Commission). 2015. *Labour Market Information Bulletin*. Colombo.

TVEC (Tertiary and Vocational Education Commission). 2016a. *Labour Market Information Bulletin*. Colombo.

TVEC (Tertiary and Vocational Education Commission). 2016b. *NVQ Operations Manual 2016 Update*. Colombo.

TVEC (Tertiary and Vocational Education Commission). 2017. *Labour Market Information Bulletin*. Colombo.

TVEC (Tertiary and Vocational Education Commission). 2018. *Labour Market Information Bulletin*. Colombo.

TVEC (Tertiary and Vocational Education Commission). 2019. *Labour Market Information Bulletin*. Colombo.

TVEC (Tertiary and Vocational Education Commission). 2020. *Labour Market Information Bulletin*. Colombo.

TVEC (Tertiary and Vocational Education Commission). 2021a. *Labour Market Information Bulletin*. Colombo.

TVEC (Tertiary and Vocational Education Commission). 2021b. *National Vocational Qualifications Framework of Sri Lanka: Operations Manual*. Colombo.

UNDP (United Nations Development Programme). 2001. *Human Development Report 2001*. New York: UNDP.

WHO (World Health Organization). n.d. "Malnutrition." https://who.int/health-topics/malnutrition#tab=tab_1.

WHO (World Health Organization). 2020. *Epidemiology Unit*. Sri Lanka Situation Reports. https://www.epid.gov.lk/web/index.php?option=com_content&view=article&id=225&lang=en&Itemid=0.

Wickramasekara, Piyasiri. 2019. "Effective Return and Reintegration of Migrant Workers with Special Focus on ASEAN Member States." International Labour Organization, Geneva.

World Bank. 2012. Skills Toward Employment and Productivity (STEP) Employer Survey 2012. World Bank, Washington, DC.

World Bank. 2017. *Sri Lanka Education Sector Assessment: Achievement, Challenges, and Policy Options*. Directions in Development. Washington, DC: World Bank.

World Bank. 2018. "Sri Lanka Development Update: More and Better Jobs for an Upper-Middle-Income Country." World Bank, Colombo.

World Bank. 2019a. "Sri Lanka Human Capital Development: Realizing the Promise and Potential of Human Capital." Report AUS0000819. World Bank, Washington, DC.

World Bank. 2019b. *World Development Indicators 2019*. Washington, DC: World Bank.

World Bank. 2019c. *World Development Report 2019: The Changing Nature of Work*. Washington, DC.

World Bank. 2020a. "Informality, Job Quality, and Welfare in Sri Lanka." World Bank, Washington, DC. https://elibrary.worldbank.org/doi/abs/10.1596/34399.

World Bank. 2020b. "Human Capital Project, Sri Lanka Brief." World Bank, Washington, DC.

World Bank. 2021. "Sri Lanka Development Update: Economic and Poverty Impact of COVID-19." World Bank, Washington, DC.

2 Labor Market and Skills
TRENDS IN STOCK AND FLOW OF WORKFORCE FOR PROGRESS

GENDER DISPARITIES IN LABOR FORCE PARTICIPATION

Sri Lanka's labor market is marked by low labor force participation of women. In 2021, only 34 percent of women were economically active (table 2.1). For women, the gender gap in labor force participation was 39 percentage points below that for men. Further, in 2021, nearly 32 percent of working women were underemployed compared with 21 percent of working men. There have been no significant changes in the gender gap over time. The labor market outcome is favorable for women in high-skilled jobs: 25 percent in 2021 compared with 18 percent for working men. As noted, the share of high-skilled workers has been increasing for both genders over time.

The gender gap partly reflects women's lower education levels, employment, earnings, and working hours. Compared with men having the same education level, age, and location, women were 37 percent less likely to work, earned 60 percent less, and were 12 percent more likely to be underemployed over the 2013–18 period. However, there is no gender gap with women's skills or their probability of working in high-skilled occupations once differences in education level, age, and location are taken into account (table 2.2).

Having technical and vocational education and training (TVET) certification reduces gender gaps in labor market outcomes, especially the probability of underemployment. TVET increases the probability of women being employed by 9 percent, of having higher earnings by 5 percent, and of working in high-skilled jobs by 4 percent; it lowers women's probability of underemployment by 3 percent (table 2.2). Nevertheless, the effects of TVET on labor market outcomes are better for men, except for underemployment.

In certain industries gender divisions are more pronounced. In 2021, industries with high shares of female workers included education (70 percent), health (64 percent), manufacturing (43 percent), public administration (41 percent), and finance (40 percent). Industries with low female representation included real estate, electricity, mining and quarrying, transportation, and construction. Although overall the gender compositions are stable within industries, the share of women working in the real estate sector is increasing, and women's share is decreasing in the financial services sector (figure 2.2).

TABLE 2.1 **Labor force trends for men and women in Sri Lanka, 2013–21**

Percent

INDICATOR		2013	2015	2018	2021	TREND
Labor force participation	Men	75	54	73	71	
	Women	35	27	34	32	
Working	Men	73	53	71	68	
	Women	33	25	31	29	
Underemployment	Men	16	15	12	21	
	Women	26	26	27	32	

Sources: DCS 2013, 2015, 2018, 2019, 2020, 2021.

FIGURE 2.1

Skills composition among female and male workers in Sri Lanka, 2013–21

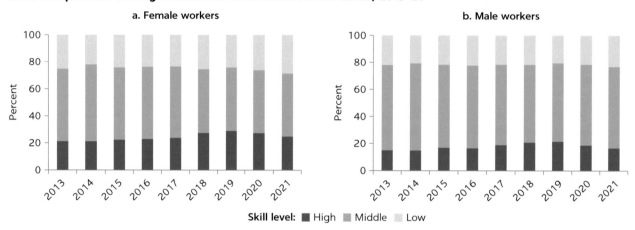

a. Female workers

b. Male workers

Skill level: ■ High ■ Middle ■ Low

Sources: Original calculations for this publication based on DCS 2013, 2014, 2015, 2016, 2017, 2018, 2019, 2020, 2021.
Note: Skills classification is based on ISCO-08 occupational categories. High-skill occupations are managers, professionals, technicians, and associate professionals. Middle-skill occupations are clerical support workers; sales and services workers; craft and related trades workers; skilled agricultural, forestry, and fishery workers; and plant and machine operators and assemblers. Low-skill occupations are elementary occupations such as cleaners and helpers; laborers in agriculture, forestry, and fisheries; laborers in mining, construction, manufacturing, and transport; food preparation assistants; and street and related sales and services workers. Armed forces occupations and unidentified occupations are excluded. ISCO = International Standard Classification of Occupations.

TABLE 2.2 **Differences in returns to TVET in Sri Lanka, 2013–18**

INDICATOR	TVET GRADUATES AND NON-TVET GRADUATES	WOMEN AND MEN	WOMEN WITH TVET AND WOMEN WITHOUT
Probability of being employed	0.11	−0.37	0.09
Log of earnings (% of earnings)	0.12	−0.60	0.05
Probability of being in a high-skilled occupation	0.08	0.00	0.04
Probability of underemployment	0.02	0.12	−0.03
Probability of working in small business	−0.07	−0.05	0.17

Sources: Original calculations for this publication based on DCS 2013, 2014, 2015, 2016, 2017, 2018.
Note: The table shows coefficients from regressions controlling for education, age and age squared, rural or urban, and year fixed effect. Standard errors are clustered in sampling unit. All coefficients shown are significant at the 1 percent level. All regressions except the probability of being employed are conditional on working. TVET = technical and vocational education and training.

FIGURE 2.2

Share of female workers in Sri Lanka, by industry, 2013–21

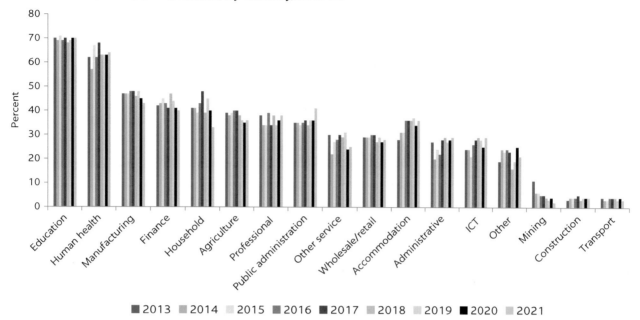

Sources: DCS 2013, 2014, 2015, 2016, 2017, 2018, 2019, 2020, 2021.
Note: These industry groups are based on International Standard Industrial Classification of All Economic Activities (ISIC), Rev. 4. Accommodation = accommodation and food service activities; administrative = administrative and support service activities; agriculture = agriculture, forestry and fishing; construction = construction, electricity, gas, steam and air conditioning supply, water supply, sewerage, waste; education = education services, institutions, managers, authorities, programs, facilities at all levels of education; household = activities of households as employers, undifferentiated goods- and services-producing activities of households for own use; human health = human health and social work activities; other service = other service activities; ICT = information and communication technologies; finance = financial and insurance activities; manufacturing = companies, managers, operations, production supervisors, and so on; mining = mining and quarrying; other = real estate, arts, entertainment, and recreation, activities of extraterritorial organizations and bodies; professional = professional, scientific, and technical activities; public administration = public administration and defense, compulsory social security; wholesale/retail = wholesale and retail trade, repair of motor vehicles and motorcycles; transport = transportation and storage.

Potential explanations for gender gaps in labor market outcomes

Women's sociophysical constraints and unequal responsibilities in households

Reducing barriers to women's labor force participation requires an understanding of gender differences in factors contributing to labor participation decisions and careers among young people. World Bank (2018) posits that women's unequal household roles and responsibilities and sociophysical constraints on their mobility are major factors explaining their low labor force participation. This hypothesis is supported by a large-scale qualitative study on factors influencing working decisions among young people. Girls first consider factors oriented to responsibilities of taking care of family and meeting parents' expectations, whereas boys assess their quality of education, employability, families' economic background, and parental financial support (exhibit 2.1). Moreover, girls report seeking job opportunities closer to home and public subsidies as important contributing factors for their labor force participation (Dissanayake 2020).

EXHIBIT 2.1 Factors contributing to employment among young people in Sri Lanka, by gender

WOMEN	MEN	BOTH GENDERS
Jobs close to home	Strong education background	Inspiring people
Jobs to support family and take care of parents	Work experience	Meeting family's expectations
Government subsidies	Family economic background	Support from instructors and teachers/school and employers
Children's life aspirations	Parental financial support for business	Subsistence living

Source: Dissanayake 2020.

Gender discrimination in job search, hiring, and promotion

Another potential barrier for women seeking to participate in the labor market is gender discrimination in job search, hiring, and promotion. Job advertisements in Sri Lanka are heavily targeted toward male job seekers, with 37 percent of job advertisements in 2021 mentioning men as a preferred criterion and only 13 percent specifically targeting women. Gender-neutral job advertising is proportionate for technical, professional, and managerial occupations (figure 2.3). For less-skilled jobs, such as craft and related trades and plant machine operators, more than 60 percent of employers specify men as preferred candidates. This gender-targeted hiring is reflected in the gender compositions of the occupation categories shown in figure 2.2.

From 2016 to 2019, gender discrimination in hiring intensified. Gender-specific advertisements increased for both genders but more for men: from 33 to 45 percent. For women, gender-specific job ads rose from 12 to 18 percent. However, gender-specific advertisements declined in 2020. The decline was more drastic for male-specific advertisements, with the reduction from 45 to 23 percent between 2019 and 2020, and registering an increase from 23 to 34 percent between 2020 and 2021, whereas female-specific advertisements declined from 18 to 14 percent from 2020 to 2021 (figure 2.4).

FIGURE 2.3

Job advertisements in Sri Lanka, by occupational category and gender targeted, 2021

Source: TVEC 2021.
Note: Covers only high-demand jobs.

FIGURE 2.4

Gender-specific job advertisements in Sri Lanka, 2016–21

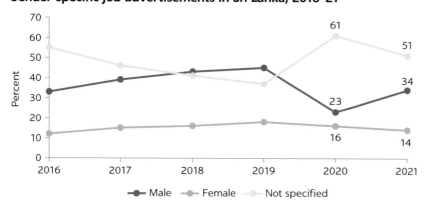

Sources: TVEC 2016, 2017, 2018, 2019, 2020, 2021.

Job advertisements in Sri Lanka show bias in favor of male-specific or female-specific advertisements (figure 2.5). The articulation of job vacancies and the required background, skills, and experience for positions appear to be favoring males. This is evident in the job advertisements for high- and middle-skilled workers in the following areas: plant and machine operators and assemblers, craft and related workers, skilled agricultural and fishery workers, service workers and shop and market workers, and technicians and associated professionals. Female-specific job advertisements are more polarized and prevalent in the high- and lower-skilled categories: elementary occupations, clerks, professionals, and technicians and associate professionals to some extent. There are variations over time (2017-21). Women are least represented as agricultural and fisheries workers, craft and related workers, plant and machine operators and assemblers, and service workers and shop and market workers.

FIGURE 2.5

Male- and female-specific job advertisements in Sri Lanka, by occupational category, 2016–21

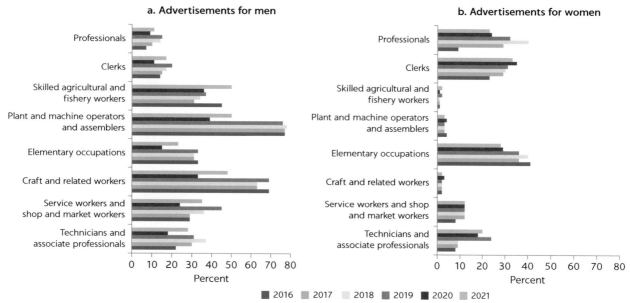

Sources: TVEC 2016, 2017, 2018, 2019, 2020, 2021.

Recommendations for increasing women's labor force participation

The *World Development Report 2012* on gender equality and development highlighted some core elements of women's labor force participation (World Bank 2012b). There are three possible hypotheses to explain gender gaps in labor market outcomes: household roles and responsibilities, which fall disproportionately on women, and the associated sociophysical constraints on women's mobility; a human capital mismatch, whereby women are not acquiring the proper skills demanded by job markets; and gender discrimination in job search, hiring, and promotion processes. More specifically, barriers to women's participation in paid work include lack of child care services and sociophysical constraints on women's mobility, which undermine their ability to travel to work.

Approaches to address the problems are as follows:

- Strengthen girls' early orientation to career development and to acquiring the types of education and skills—such as programs and courses in science, technology, engineering, and mathematics (STEM)—that prepare them for the labor market.
- Improve the job focus of education providers and expand the provision of job-matching services and TVET that respond to employers' needs.
- Ensure gender equity in labor legislation and nondiscriminatory workplace environments, which includes zero tolerance for sexual harassment in—and when traveling to and from—the workplace.
- Provide safe transportation for women.
- Introduce affirmative action and ethics initiatives to help expand women's share of employment and firm ownership.

Gender gaps in STEM careers

In most of the world, STEM disciplines and sectors have been male-dominated areas of study, and many women disproportionately transition out of STEM fields during their studies and careers. For example, in 2020, women's enrollment in engineering, manufacturing, and construction courses was only 8 percent; 5 percent in natural sciences, mathematics and statistics; and 3 percent in information and communication technologies (ICT) (Sosale et al. 2023). Gender disparities in STEM areas have been widely researched, and global evidence shows that individual, societal, institutional, and labor market factors are at play and tend to lower female participation in STEM-related TVET.[1] Gender stereotypes, peer and parental beliefs and attitudes, cultural forces, gender-biased learning materials, lack of female role models, employer preferences, and male-dominated workplaces all deter greater female participation (Sosale et al. 2023). STEM-related TVET plays a significant role in sustainable, inclusive economic growth when STEM skills and competencies for innovation are fostered across sectors.

Gender disparities in STEM professions also exist in Sri Lanka, with some variations across fields. Women's participation is lowest in engineering, yet women dominate health care, bioscience, and biotechnology. Female students accounted for only 12 percent of the engineering stream in grade 12; this underrepresentation continued to the tertiary level, where 22 percent of tertiary graduates in engineering were women in 2015 (figure 2.6). However, in health care and biotechnology, girls have high enrollments in grade 12 (70 percent and 54 percent, respectively), and 58 percent of tertiary graduates in health and welfare are women (Abayasekara 2020; Subasinghe et al. 2023; UNESCO 2015).

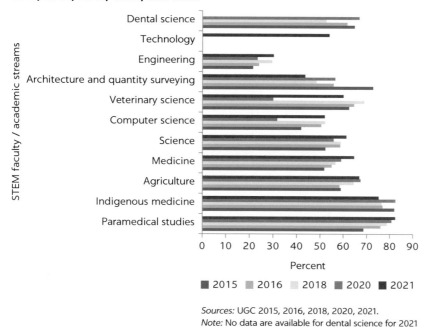

FIGURE 2.6

Female tertiary graduates' participation in STEM fields in Sri Lanka, 2015, 2016, 2018, 2020, and 2021

Sources: UGC 2015, 2016, 2018, 2020, 2021.
Note: No data are available for dental science for 2021 or for technology for 2015, 2016, 2018, or 2020. STEM = science, technology, engineering, and mathematics.

The architecture and quantity survey courses had the largest decrease in female student output during the period 2015 to 2021, from 73 percent down to 44 percent. However, the percentage of female engineering graduates increased from 22 percent in 2015 to 30 percent in 2021. Paramedical studies registered the largest increase, by 14 percentage points, from 69 percent in 2015 to 82 percent in 2021 (figure 2.6).

Overall, women workers tend to be more educated than men in Sri Lanka, and so are engaged in high-skilled occupations as professionals. But whereas women's share of high-skilled professional employment was 69 percent in non-STEM fields, in STEM it was just 52 percent in 2021 (figure 2.7). By contrast, women's share in low- and middle-skilled occupations in STEM is higher than in non-STEM fields. For example, 42 percent of plant and machine operators and assemblers were women in STEM fields, but only 2 percent were women in non-STEM fields in 2021.

Many countries have initiated policies to promote gender equity in STEM fields in education and labor markets. UNESCO-UNEVOC (2020a) recommend systemic responses to gender inequality in labor markets, education, and training (table 2.3). For example, Australia outlines a vision and role for government in redressing gender disparities in the labor market and education in STEM in its *National Women in STEM Strategy* (Government of Australia 2020) and its *Women in STEM Decadal Plan* (Australian Academy of Science 2019). In education, initiatives to close gender gaps in TVET and tertiary education include providing scholarships for women in STEM, expanding professional development for gender-sensitive teaching, providing mentoring and support groups to guide and inspire girls to engage in STEM, and initiating international monitoring efforts on gender gaps in STEM. Sri Lanka needs to promote women's participation in fields where their presence is already strong (such as education and health care). In addition, it needs to increase female

FIGURE 2.7

Female participation in STEM and non-STEM fields in Sri Lanka, 2021

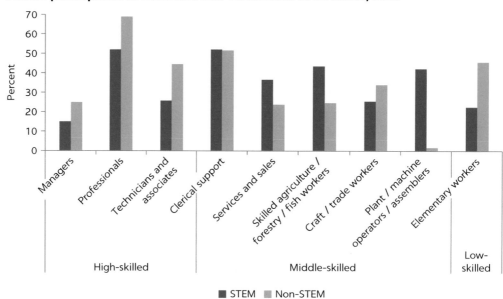

Source: Original calculations for this publication based on DCS 2021.
Note: STEM = science, technology, engineering, and mathematics.

TABLE 2.3 **Country policies addressing gender disparities in STEM in training and labor markets**

INITIATIVE	COUNTRY	DESCRIPTION
TVET and tertiary education		
Scholarships	Chile	Scholarship program aimed at women seeking a scientific-technological vocation.
	Philippines	The Universal Access to Quality Tertiary Education Act, Special Training Program for Employees, Training for Work Scholarship Program, and Private Education Student Financial Assistance actively promote female participation in STEM-related TVET.
Teacher professional development	Various countries	Provides gender-sensitive teaching skills to TVET staff to raise participation and attainment of girls and women in STEM.
Mentoring schemes	Chile	Organizes STEM women's day, pairing school-age girls with female students in STEM in TVET or universities.
Female support group	Costa Rica	The National Training Institute organizes meetings and support groups for women in "nontraditional areas" with the goal of encouraging female students to continue their studies.
UNESCO gender advancement system	Various countries	Systematizes indicators at the country level to identify gender gaps in STEM by collecting high-quality data.
Labor markets		
Gender-specific organizations for STEM	Ghana, Netherlands	Provide modern curricula, gender-inclusive career guidance, female role models, and teacher training for gender-sensitive behaviors and develop a "gender scan" that provides TVET institutes with tips for analyzing the influx and outflow of female students.
Mentoring schemes	Ghana	Internship program for female students in the power sector.
	Netherlands	Improve the flow of female students to technical fields by focusing on talent development, career guidance, and technical subjects in early education.
ICT programs	Australia	Radio team sets a target of 50 percent female guests on-air and actively seeks women's voices using resources such as the Women's Leadership Institute Australia.
	Germany	Provide women with a better understanding of STEM occupations.
Awareness-raising among male leaders	Australia	Provides guidance for male STEM leaders.
Improving labor market opportunities and conditions	Germany	Making career entry easier and more attractive for women through flexible working times, remote working, and family-friendly working environments.

Source: UNESCO-UNEVOC 2020a.
Note: For other examples of labor markets, see Annex 2A. ICT = information and communication technology; STEM = science, technology, engineering, and mathematics; TVET = technical and vocational education and training; UNESCO = United Nations Educational, Scientific, and Cultural Organization.

participation in STEM by lowering barriers, as well as by coordinating and facilitating opportunities. Social and systemic barriers to participation in STEM need to be broken, starting with training to transitioning into work, to retention in the sectors involved.

AGING ECONOMY

Sri Lanka has been experiencing a gradual demographic transition to an aging population and has reached an advanced stage relative to its peers (figure 2.8, panel a) and is projected to increase further from 2025 onward. The share of the population ages 65 and above reached 10.8 percent in 2020 (figure 2.8, panel b)—higher than the average for upper-middle-income countries, which was around 10 percent in 2019. The aging population is increasing rapidly. These trends are like those in upper-middle-income countries, with a dramatic reduction in the fertility rate until the early 1990s (figure 2.9, panel a) and a consistent rise in life expectancy (figure 2.9, panel b).

The age dependency ratio (as a percentage of the working population) reached its lowest level in 2007 at 49.4 percent due to a consistently shrinking young population (figure 2.10). Then it reversed, rising to 52 percent in 2022. Much of the increase in the age dependency ratio for the older population happened between 2011 and 2022, when it spiked by 5 percentage points, up from 1.5 percentage points between 2000 and 2010. Given this rapid demographic shift, Sri Lanka may not be fully prepared to support the aging population (World Bank 2012a). Significant growth in public spending on the health care sector will be needed, yet the health care industry has remained stagnant over the past decade (see the health care section later in this chapter). Further, the COVID-19 pandemic in 2020 and the economic downturn leading to the triple crisis (fuel, food, fiscal) of 2022 have created significant challenges in the labor market and a cascading effect on tax revenues and investments in skills development.

There were minor changes between 2014 and 2018. The proportion of the working population ages 31–40 fell slightly, and it increased slightly among workers ages 51 and over (figure 2.11, panel a). However, with the start of the

FIGURE 2.8

Dependency ratio and population by age group in Sri Lanka, 1950–2095 (projected)

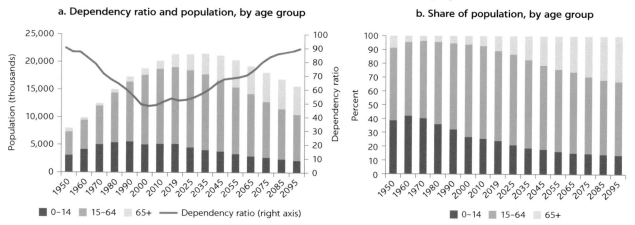

Sources: Original calculations for this publication and World Bank 2019.

FIGURE 2.9

Fertility rate and life expectancy at birth, Sri Lanka and upper-middle-income countries, 1971–2021

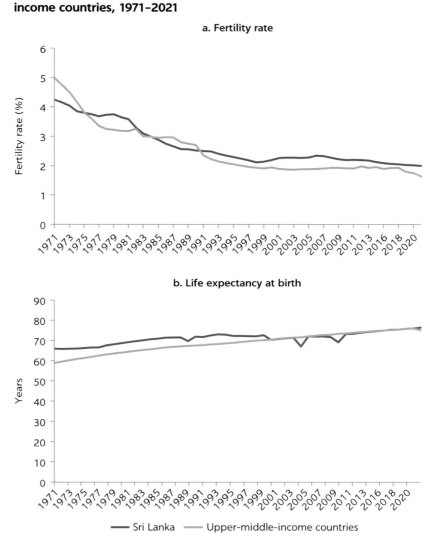

Source: World Bank 2021b.

COVID-19 global health emergency in early 2020, there was steady decline in working-age population across all the age groups between 31 years and 65+ years. As noted, the proportion of middle-skilled workers is increasing and that of low-skilled workers is decreasing. Middle-skilled workers tend to work well into their 60s; high-skilled workers tend not to do so. High-skilled workers tend to seek better opportunities; with a little upskilling and reskilling, they could be fungible and work in any industry. This tendency calls for upskilling and reskilling of high-skilled workers to foster productive work lives for people over 51 into their 60s. Between 2014 and 2021 underemployment among the older population decreased 5–6 percentage points (figure 2.11, panel b). This is attributable to the necessity for older people to remain working due to the effects of the poly crisis.

Between 1992 and 2006, the labor force participation of the older population, especially women, significantly increased from 25.8 percent to 42.1 percent

FIGURE 2.10

Age dependency ratio in Sri Lanka, 1971–2021

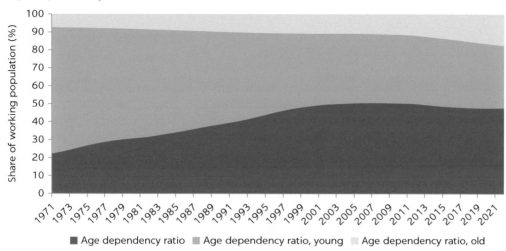

■ Age dependency ratio   ■ Age dependency ratio, young   ■ Age dependency ratio, old

Source: World Bank 2021b.
Note: The age dependency ratio is a measure of the number of dependents ages zero to 14 and over the age of 65, compared with the total population ages 15 to 64. It is a demographic measure of the ratio of the number of people of non–working age compared with the number of those of working age. A high age dependency ratio means those of working age and the overall economy face a greater burden in supporting the aging population.

FIGURE 2.11

Working population and underemployment in Sri Lanka, by age group, 2014, 2018, and 2021

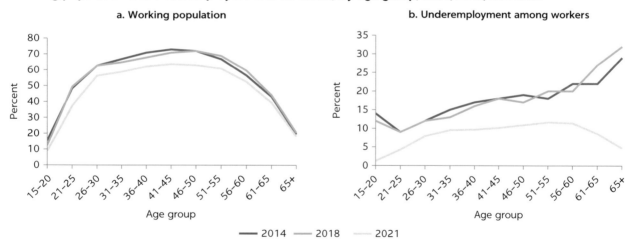

━━ 2014   ━━ 2018   ━━ 2021

Sources: Original calculations for this publication based on DCS 2014, 2018.

(among 50- to 59-year-olds) and from 8.4 percent to 13.0 percent (among workers 60+ years old). Between 2016 and 2019, it remained relatively steady, decreasing only slightly from 33.7 percent to 33.5 percent among 55- to 64-year-olds. Labor force participation among workers 65+ years old increased from 9.9 percent in 2015 to 11.7 percent in 2019, then declined to 9.4 percent in 2021 due to the COVID-19 pandemic (figure 2.12). Since then the labor force participation of the elderly has grown at a low rate for both genders. Although a small fraction of the elderly work more in recent years, they tend to work fewer hours.

Most of the working elderly are engaged in middle-skilled occupations and fewer in high-skilled occupations relative to younger workers (figure 2.13).

FIGURE 2.12

Labor force participation of older population in Sri Lanka, by gender, 2018–2021

Percent

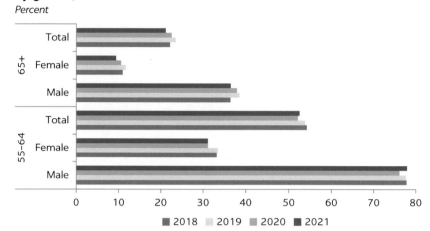

Sources: ADB and ILO (2017) and original calculations using Department of Census and Statistics Labour Force Survey 2021 microdata.

FIGURE 2.13

Skills composition in Sri Lanka, by age group, 2021

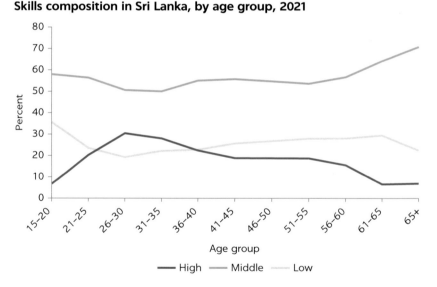

Source: Original calculations for this publication based on DCS 2021.

The reasons for this are difficult to pinpoint because various socioeconomic indicators—such as education, income, and occupation—are correlated with both working and longevity. The high-skilled elderly likely do not need to work, perhaps due to a strong social safety net. The middle- and low-skilled elderly may need to work longer for a living, or employment opportunities for the elderly could largely be limited to middle-skill occupations. Regardless, with its rapidly aging population, the importance of lifelong learning for a longer productive life is becoming more relevant for Sri Lanka. Further, more workers are needed in health care, child care, elder care, and education. COVID-19 has necessitated a social safety net for child care. In addition, the triple crisis (fuel, food, fiscal) due to the economic downturn in 2022 have heightened awareness about social insurance programs to protect vulnerable populations (such as women, children, and people with disabilities) and those who have lost their livelihoods. For recovery and building resilience, social insurance will be a critical complement to skills development.

GLOBAL TRENDS AMID A CHANGING ECONOMIC FRAMEWORK

This section discusses the status and potential of digitalization generally and in education, as well as in green industries and health care.

Digitalization

In many developed countries economic growth through digital diffusion is the top economic policy priority, with a focus on innovative emerging digital technologies such as artificial intelligence (AI), blockchain, and fifth generation (5G) infrastructure, the latter of which is critical to support enhanced mobile broadband, Internet of Things devices, and AI applications. However, gaps in computer skills and digital literacy persist across countries, demographic groups, and firms and are expected to widen the digital divide in societies. More educated, high-income groups use internet and online activities better, enabling them to access knowledge, job opportunities, and health and education services. The gender gap in computer and digital literacy is widespread, and other skills in high demand from digital-intensive industries are more often held by men (OECD 2020a).

Since the early 2000s, digitalization has been transforming business processes in major industries such as ICT, commerce, health, finance, professional services, and manufacturing. The advent of the use and application of technology is defined as the "convergence revolution,"[2] which has implications for future jobs and skills and for the innovation system and requirements for advanced human capital (World Bank 2022c). The COVID-19 pandemic has accelerated digitalization, pressuring countries to adopt high-speed network connections and use digital business solutions more quickly. Skilling, reskilling, and upskilling are going to be key drivers of economic growth in the future in all countries, and especially to enable Sri Lanka to rise from the 2022 economic crisis. Intertemporal accumulation of skills, the layering of skills acquisition, and adopting a life-cycle approach to skilling will be critical drivers for the country to move the production possibility frontier[3] over time (World Bank 2022c).

During the COVID-19 pandemic, Sri Lanka's digital divide emerged as a threat to long-term equality by diverging incomes between workers with and without digital access as well as by widening education gaps between students with and without digital access (World Bank 2021a). Digital adoption in Sri Lanka approximates the global average but is far less than in leading Asian economies such as Malaysia, the Republic of Korea, and Singapore.

Sri Lanka ranked 106th of 183 countries in the overall Digital Adoption Index (DAI), which is a set of normalized indicators measuring the digital adoption rate for people, business, and government (World Bank 2016). Its DAI was higher than the global average in government, for people and businesses (figure 2.14).[4] Since 2017, Sri Lanka has done well to build a base for its digital development. However, gaps remain and are significant or growing in some areas. In 2022, Sri Lanka ranked 81 out of 131 countries in the Network Readiness Index (measures broad

FIGURE 2.14
Digital Adoption Index and subindexes in various countries and globally, 2016

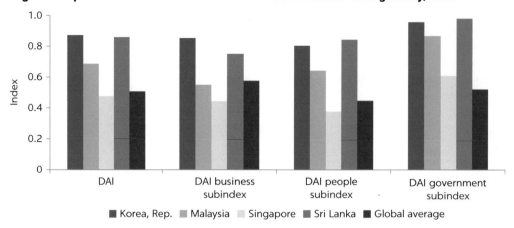

Source: World Bank 2016.
Note: DAI = Digital Adoption Index.

digital readiness) (Portulans Institute n.d.) and 44 out of 78 countries in 2022 in the Global Services Location Index (measures a country's attractiveness as an off-shore location for business services) (Kearney Advisor Network n.d.). The latter includes a measure of people's skills and availability. In this regard, Sri Lanka's rank has dropped from 25 in 2019 to 44 in 2022. The country's affordable entry level internet services are a strength for digitalization (International Telecommunications Union n.d.). However, higher quality services are expensive. Such services are critical for video-based and interactive online education. For example, 20 Mbps+ speeds are unaffordable for most. Such a connection could cost over 8 percent of GNI per capita. Limited digitization of economic activities and public services has created major bottlenecks for digitalization. For example, in 2021, Sri Lanka had 44 internet users for every 100 inhabitants, far fewer than OECD average of 87 in 2021 and lower than the OECD average in the early 2000s (World Bank, 2021a).

In the medium to long term, policies that universalize digital infrastructure and digital literacy are key to making the economy more resilient to shocks (such as the COVID-19 pandemic) and to creating jobs (World Bank 2021a). In 2018, the Government of Sri Lanka articulated its digital economy vision for 2025, creating flagship programs in three industries: manufacturing, agriculture, and tourism. Annex 2B shows select employment and labor market decisions during the COVID-19 pandemic.

Globally—especially in developed countries—shares of low- and high-skilled employment are growing, while the share of middle-skilled occupations is falling because of their susceptibility to digital technology and automation. Sri Lanka seems to be undergoing similar labor market polarizations (see figures 1.6 and figure 1.7 in chapter 1 on skills composition). Because polarizations and labor-saving digital technologies are inevitable, the country should prepare to upgrade the skills of existing and new workers through better TVET and options for lifelong learning. Equipping workers with nonroutine, higher-order cognitive skills; technical skills, including in ICT; and nonroutine interpersonal and socioemotional skills will help reduce job displacement from digital technologies (exhibit 2.2).

EXHIBIT 2.2 Skills needed in a modern economy

Nonroutine, higher-order cognitive skills
Ability to understand complex ideas; deal with complex information processing; adapt to work environments; learn from experience; engage in various forms of reasoning; and overcome obstacles with critical thought, such as unstructured problem solving and critical thinking, learning, and reasoning
Technical skills, including ICT skills
Ability to perform specific occupations, such as skills to repair a water leak (for a plumber), knowledge of how to operate a machine (for a factory worker), knowledge of how to work with software (for a bank employee), and effective application of ICT systems and devices—ranging from ICT specialists who can develop, operate, and maintain ICT systems to basic ICT users who are competent with mainstream tools needed in their working lives (email, Word, Excel, PowerPoint)
Nonroutine interpersonal and socioemotional skills
A broad range of malleable skills, behaviors, attitudes, and personality traits that enable individuals to effectively navigate interpersonal and social situations—such as perseverance to finish a job or achieve a long-term goal, working in teams, punctuality, organization, commitment, creativity, and honesty

Source: World Bank 2016.
Note: ICT = information and communication technology.

To pave the way for an inclusive digital future, seven building blocks need to be considered: access, use, innovation, trust, jobs, society, and market openness (OECD 2019). The policy pillars to build skills needed in a modern economy are summarized in table 2.4. This approach could inform Sri Lanka's efforts to design and redesign training that would help respond to the needs of a digital future and economic growth. The "Use" pillar emphasizes the role of government to ensure that all workers are equipped with the skills needed for a digital economy. People with good literacy, numeracy, and problem-solving skills in a technology-rich environment use digital tools more efficiently, conduct more sophisticated activities online, and adapt better to digital transformations. In addition, skills transferable across jobs and occupations—that is, higher-order cognitive, socioemotional, and technical skills—are essential.

Digitalization and digital transformation in education, digital skills, and literacy

During the COVID-19 pandemic and the postpandemic era, education will need to embrace a new approach to teaching and learning as well as prepare students with the requisite skills to cope in the digitized workplace and in life. The pandemic has accelerated digital transformation in every aspect of life. Governments have taken emergency measures and adapted education to online learning in a very short period. During the pandemic, about 65 percent of lower-middle-income countries and nearly 25 percent of low-income countries initiated remote learning platforms. Still, internet and broadband connectivity are major bottlenecks to the global transformation to digital education: globally, only about 36 percent of lower-middle-income countries had access to the internet (Vegas 2020). Sri Lanka is one of them.

Improving digital school connectivity is the top priority for providing future workers with the right skills. A holistic approach should be taken, including reviewing telecommunications regulation; upgrading school and telecom infrastructure, technology, and devices; developing financial mechanisms to extend access to underconnected areas; developing safe, relevant content and delivering it through secure platforms; and empowering learners, instructors,

TABLE 2.4 **Going digital: Integrated policies for various required skills**

PILLAR	GOVERNMENT'S POLICY GOAL	RELEVANT SKILLS
Access	Providing access to broadband, upgrading networks to the next stage of fixed and wireless broadband, and improving access to data	Technical skills related to specific occupations to build ICT infrastructure
Use	Ensuring all workers are equipped with skills needed for a digital economy	Well-rounded cognitive skills including literacy, numeracy, and higher-order cognitive skills; technical skills such as manual dexterity and the use of methods, materials, tools, and instruments
Innovation	Boosting entrepreneurship, supporting digital transformation of scientific research, and fostering investment in R&D	Technical skills for entrepreneurial skills in digital economy sectors such as e-commerce, e-health, and online education; social behavioral skills such as decision-making, interpersonal skills, and openness to experience
Trust	Ensuring trust through enhanced digital security and protection of private data	Technical skills for R&D on cybersecurity and related public administrative services
Jobs	Examining labor market structure with changing workflows due to increasing teleworking and automation	Technical labor market analysis skills, demand and supply analyses, information technology skills to map teleworking and automation
Society	Addressing the diverse range of social issues created by digital transformation, including questions raised by data-driven health care, disinformation, screen addiction, and many others	Professional skills to address ethical and psychological issues raised; technical skills to ensure the security of private data
Market openness	Ensuring market competitiveness and considering the implications for business dynamics and inclusion as increasingly fewer small and medium-size enterprises access the online world	Entrepreneurship skills, marketing skills, presentation skills, accounting skills, management skills, socioemotional skills

Sources: Original formulations for this publication based on OECD 2019 and World Bank 2016.
Note: ICT = information and communication technology; R&D = research and development.

and teachers in a digital environment (UNESCO-UNEVOC 2020b). The building blocks for expanding school connectivity are as follows:

- Mapping schools to acquire accurate data and identify connectivity gaps
- Identifying affordable, suitable connectivity solutions and assessing school readiness for connectivity
- Building financing models for school connectivity by identifying cost reduction measures and increasing the value of connectivity in communities and among stakeholders
- Increasing access to information and providing high-quality, appropriate, inclusive content through safe, secure platforms to empower learners and instructors and teachers.

TVET has an important role to play in education's digital transformation. TVET is responsible for supplying skilled technicians to expand network connections, building energy and ICT infrastructure in schools, developing software for digital content, and upgrading teacher skills for digital learning environments.

Green industries

COVID-19 is not only a health and economic crisis but also an environmental one. The origins of the pandemic cannot be separated from the environmental challenges it poses, such as climate change and loss of biodiversity. Health and economic measures to mitigate the impact of the pandemic have hurt the environment by increasing water and land pollution and worsening waste management due to single-use materials and medical waste. To address the challenges, many governments have been investing in economic recovery plans that are green and inclusive.

Inclusive green recovery has the "potential to create opportunities for income, jobs, and growth, and at the same time accelerate action on medium and long-term environmental goals, both national and global" (OECD 2020b, 2). For example, the European Commission proposed the European Green Deal to transform the European Union (EU) into a society with a resource-efficient, competitive economy that generates no net emissions of greenhouse gases by 2050 and to decouple economic growth from resource use (European Commission 2020). The Republic of Korea's government launched a New Deal focused on creating jobs in green industries that address climate and environment challenges (Kirk 2020).

Green industries and sectors that are widely discussed and prioritized by the international community include renewable energy, waste management and clean water supply, sustainable agriculture, transport systems, and existing buildings. These fields are important for generating environmentally sustainable economic growth and are expected to create more jobs than conventional industries (table 2.5). Greening projects can be labor intensive. Most of those under way focus on transforming traditional economies into green ones, with the aim of boosting economic efficiency gains over the long term.

The focus on green industries varies by country and depends on their development stage and technological advancement. In Sri Lanka, energy, waste management and water supply, and agriculture seem particularly relevant. The government has committed to expand the share of nonconventional renewable energy to half the total by 2030—supporting electricity generation and developing new manufacturing activities such as production of batteries and transmission equipment (UNDP and ADB 2017). Of the seven sectors in table 2.5, the waste management and water supply sector has experienced the fastest growth and created the most jobs. Between 2014 and 2018, the industry grew 68 percent in economic terms, and its number of workers expanded 165 percent (DCS 2013, 2014, 2015, 2016, 2017, 2018). Finally, the government has made agriculture a priority industry for digitalization and emphasizes its role in exports to EU countries, which place great emphasis on products meeting international standards for sustainable agricultural practices (Government of Sri Lanka 2018).

TVET plays an important role in educating and training young labor market entrants for green sectors and in retraining and reskilling existing workers in traditional sectors. Investing in green industry will inevitably displace jobs and production in traditional sectors, such as those related to fossil fuels. To achieve that, Sri Lanka should define fields of work in green sectors; profile job characteristics; and describe competencies, skills, and work tasks. Such efforts would form the basis for designing training curricula and programs (UNESCO-UNEVOC 2017).

Health care

In 2020, the world spent US$9 trillion—10 percent of global GDP—on health care, with spending steadily growing over recent decades (WHO 2020, 2022). Before the pandemic, the drivers of health care spending were aging populations with increasing chronic diseases and investments in health care infrastructure and technological advances (Deloitte 2020). With the pandemic, the health care sector is expected to expand even faster, so more skilled health workers will be required. In the United States it is projected that related occupations are among the 20 fastest-growing ones (U.S. Bureau of Labor Statistics 2020).

TABLE 2.5 **Green industries and sectors and their potential for creating jobs worldwide and in Sri Lanka**

INDUSTRY OR SECTOR	POTENTIAL FOR JOB CREATION WORLDWIDE	RELEVANCE TO SRI LANKA
Energy: supporting the development and use of renewable energy	Renewable energy jobs are more prevalent than those based on fossil fuels. The International Renewable Energy Agency estimates that the sector will create 40 million new jobs by 2050.	Sri Lanka committed to increase the contribution of NCRE to 50 percent by 2030. It is expected to support the electricity sector and develop new manufacturing industries (such as batteries and transmission equipment).
Waste management and water supply: improving waste management and water quality	Clean technology can make waste a source of energy and materials. Recycling and creating energy using biomass and waste are labor intensive. Investments in R&D for sustainable waste management require high-quality workers.	In Sri Lanka, waste management and water supply had the greatest potential for employment expansion with implications for all sectors over 2013–18.
Agriculture: transforming into sustainable, resilient agriculture	Organic agriculture is more labor intensive than conventional agriculture. It needs complex rotation systems, mixed farming with a higher share of labor-intensive crops (mainly fruits and vegetables), less mechanization, more on-farm processing and trading, and more information.	Sri Lanka has been investing in agricultural R&D institutions and focusing on agricultural products that meet international standards for export to the European Union (organic, pesticide-free, ozone-free). The E-Agriculture plan contains a road map to use ICT and information-sharing technology for agriculture in Sri Lanka. Environmentally friendly farming practices such as precision agriculture, climate-smart farming, and organic farming create market opportunities and green jobs for young people.
Transportation: transitioning into green transport	The expansion of public transport systems and electrification of private transport will create up to 15 million jobs by 2030, with wide cross-sector impacts.	Manufacturing of zero-emissions electric and hybrid vehicles provides job opportunities for young people.
Building: improving the energy efficiency of existing buildings	The International Energy Agency estimates the creation of up to 2.5 million jobs a year as part of efforts to retrofit buildings.	The concept of green building has been gaining popularity, creating jobs such as green building designers, architects, and construction workers.
Forestry: fostering ecosystem restoration	Job-intensive activities are integral to reforestation, management of species, and so on.	For Sri Lanka, afforestation skills and related jobs will contribute to preserving the soil, preventing erosion and landslides, and aiding greening of the environment, among other benefits.
Tourism: promoting ecotourism	Jobs can be created by promoting sustainable tourism and local culture and products.	Sri Lanka's Tourism Development Authority has started encouraging ecotourism in Sri Lanka.

Sources: Summaries from ADB and ILO 2017; DCS 2013, 2014, 2016, 2017, 2018; Government of Sri Lanka 2018, 2020; OECD 2020c; UNDP and ADB 2017; ILO 2020.
Note: ICT = information and communication technology; NCRE = nonconventional renewable energy; R&D = research and development.

By contrast, Sri Lanka's health care industry seems to be static, with little change over time in its workforce composition and production value. Spending on health care did not change much between 2010 and 2018.[5] As discussed, the country's population is aging rapidly, with the share of the population ages 65 and older reaching 17 percent in 2022, up from 11.4 percent in 2010 (World Bank 2021b). In 2017, public investment in health care accounted for just 1.6 percent of GDP—one of the lowest levels in South Asia—and employment and economic value (measured in gross value added, or GVA) in health care remained almost unchanged over the period 2013–21 (figure 2.15, panel a).

Most Sri Lankan health care workers were women (65 percent in 2021) and highly skilled (62 percent in 2021; figure 2.15, panel b). The skills composition has not changed in health care, unlike in other industries, where skills polarization is under way. The population's health profile is becoming similar to that in developed countries, with an aging population and nearly three-quarters of deaths due to noncommunicable diseases (Oxford Business Group 2019).

FIGURE 2.15

Health care as a share of employment and economic production, and skills composition among health care workers in Sri Lanka, 2013, 2015, and 2018

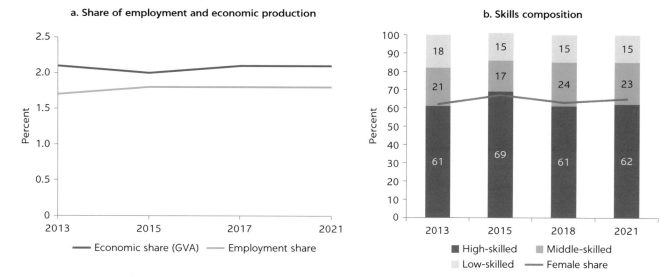

Sources: Original calculations for this publication based on DCS 2013, 2015, 2018, 2021.
Note: GVA = gross value added.

Thus, Sri Lanka needs to transform its health care industry to keep up with changing needs for the elderly—such as geriatric services and long-term care—and people with noncommunicable diseases. It also needs to keep supplying skilled workers in the sector to meet likely rising demand. Doing so would create substantial job opportunities, especially for women.

ANNEX 2A: LABOR MARKET PROGRAMS

Several active labor market programs have been implemented to keep technical and vocational education and training students employed, bring them into employment, increase productivity, and improve functioning of labor markets:

- **National Career Guidance and Counselling Center:** The National Career Guidance and Counselling Center has more than 250 skills development officers/assistants (SDOs) placed at the field (divisional secretariat) level visiting schools and providing career guidance and counseling services to students. These SDOs and instructors are trained by the state ministry. The center runs a website (http://www.youthjobs .lk) where industry players register and which provides information on industry requirements. Students can register by presenting their skills. In addition, several buses converted as Career Guidance Centers are mobilized in some rural areas.
- **Self-Employment Promotion Initiative:** As part of the self-employment promotion, a business development module is included. Based on the proposals submitted, certificate holders can obtain loans of up to LKR 500,000 with a very low interest rate (approximately 1 percent interest).

- **Facilitated and expanded access to training:** A bursary program has been designed to encourage students to register in some fields, such as construction, and to assist vulnerable students.
- **Enhanced access to and relevance of training through industry-based training:** The industry-based training programs designed include Employment Linked Training Agreement / Employment Linked Training Program, on-the-job training, apprenticeship, and so on.
- **Wage subsidies:** A limited number of wage subsidies are provided in the form of attracting youth for less demanded courses and to attract the industry to provide on-the-job training and practical exposure for students.
- **Certifications:** The industry is encouraged to get workers certified through the recognition of prior learning approach. Some of the local firms encourage workers to get certified, and the Foreign Employment Bureau is directing prospective migrant workers to receive National Vocational Qualifications certificates to facilitate better employment opportunities.

However, there are no passive labor market programs, such as unemployment insurance schemes, organized in the sector.

ANNEX 2B: EMPLOYMENT AND LABOR MARKET DECISIONS DURING COVID-19, SELECT COUNTRY CASES

SkillsFuture SG (Singapore)

Supporting companies
Reducing short-term pressures, support transformation through the following activities:

- Job support scheme—wage support
- Loan support—lower-cost loans, enterprise financing, loan insurance, temporary bridging
- Boosters—e-commerce, food delivery, Business Go Digital
- Rental relief.

Supporting workforce
Support livelihoods, upskill for jobs in demand through the following activities:

- Income relief, support grants
- Self-employed persons assistance
- Deferred loan, premium payments
- Job search and skills training support through career centers, place and train, train and place, professional conversion.

Enhanced training support package
Helps companies retain employees, deep skills workforce for recovery through the following activities:

- Tourism, air transport, food and beverage, retail, land transport, arts and culture, aerospace, marine, and offshore sectors, as per need
- Ninety percent enhanced course fee grants, enhanced absentee payroll, and training allowance
- Digital learning workshops, equipment, and broadband access.

Training for essential roles

Rapid scale-up of essential critical roles for national response through the following activities:

- Essential roles in health care, security, cleaning, food services, and safe management
- Limited in-person training, rapid conversion to synchronous online delivery
- Policy adjustment to enable quick scale-up.

Additional details

- Disruptions from COVID-19—sharp increases or decreases in supply and demand of products and services
- New modes for delivery of products and services, interpersonal interactions
- Rapid transformation for business
- Skills and mindset transformation for workers
- Acceleration of need for digitalization.

SGUnited jobs and skills package (Singapore)

Supporting job seekers

The program objectives are to support close to 100,000 job seekers. The package aims to expand job, traineeship, and skills training opportunities to support Singaporeans affected by the economic impact of COVID-19.

Under this program the Ministry of Manpower, Ministry of Education, and Public Service Division will roll out the following initiatives:

- Scale-up job opportunities under SGUnited Job Initiative and Place-and-Train conversion programs
- Expand traineeships through SGUnited Traineeships Program for recent and new graduates, and SGUnited Mid-Career Pathways Program for mid-career individuals
- Strengthen training support through SGUnited Skills Program
- Enhance the hiring incentive under the SkillsFuture Mid-Career Support Package.

Additional details

Enhanced hiring incentive—salary support

- Employers that hire local workers ages 40 and above who had gone through an eligible reskilling program or training can receive salary support of 40 percent for six months, capped at US$12,000 total.
- Employers that hire local workers below age 40 who had gone through an eligible reskilling or training can receive support of 20 percent for six months, capped at US$6,000 total.

This was further replaced by the Jobs Growth Incentive in September 2020 where:

- The government will copay up to 25 percent of salaries for all new local hires for one year with a cap.
- For those ages 40 and above, the copayment will be up to 50 percent.

Comments

This is relevant to the financing of TVET by the government.

Employment safety net and policy under COVID-19 (Republic of Korea)

The program objectives are to (a) keep the current jobs and (b) assist workers who lost their jobs with their livelihood.

Three policy interventions:

- Job retention subsidy—support efforts to keep employees by employers in difficulty.
- Unemployment insurance benefit—help the unemployed keep their livelihood.
- Emergency employment security support—temporary program for workers outside of the unemployment insurance system, aid workers who are in difficulties because of COVID-19.

UNESCO-UNEVOC Medium-Term Strategy III (UNESCO)

The purpose of the project is to mitigate the impact of the COVID-19 pandemic. The objectives of the project are to provide short-term training for workers urgently needed in the post-COVID-19 era; strengthen the capacity of TVET institutions to provide post-COVID-19 reskilling, upskilling, and vocational guidance; support the development of TVET institutions' responsiveness, agility, and resilience to crises; and compile lessons drawn from the COVID-19 experience.

These objectives will be fulfilled through the following activities:

- Mapping immediate local training and mobilizing TVET institutions with the capacity to deliver short-term training
- Developing locally relevant and digitally based capacity-building programs to strengthen institutional services
- Implementing regional peer-learning programs for institutions with a focus on crisis management and digital solutions
- Compiling promising and innovative practices on each of the above.

NOTES

1. According to the UNESCO International Bureau of Education, STEM-related TVET includes the natural sciences (biology, chemistry, and physics) and technology-related subjects including computing and, for example, computer applications technology and mathematics. In Sri Lanka, STEM includes agriculture, mining and quarrying, manufacturing, energy (electricity, gas, and so on), water supply and waste management, construction, ICT, and health care.
2. The "convergence revolution" refers to the merging of virtual, physical, biological, and cognitive technologies with the power of big data, machine learning, and AI. It is fundamentally changing how human beings live, behave, and interact.
3. All else being equal, in economic terms the production possibility frontier (PPF) demonstrates that a nation's economy has reached the highest level of efficiency possible at a given time. The PPF can be moved provided there is progress in increasing and improving multisectoral investments in the human, capital (infrastructure, renewable energy), financial, digital, knowledge, cross-border, governance, and other ancillary domains.
4. A country's Digital Adoption Index (DAI) (People) is the simple average of two normalized indicators from the Gallup World Poll: mobile access at home and internet access at home (World Bank 2016). The DAI (Business) is the simple average of four normalized indicators: the percentage of businesses with websites, the number of secure servers, the speed of downloads, and 3G (third generation) coverage. The DAI (Governments) is the simple average of three normalized subindexes: core administrative systems, online public services, and digital identification.

5. Per capita health spending was US$108 in 2010 and US$157 in 2018 (current prices), making the rate of increase almost the same as inflation.

REFERENCES

Abayasekara, Ashani. 2020. "Girls in STEM: How Is Sri Lanka Faring?" *Talking Economics* (blog), February 11, 2020. https://www.ips.lk/talkingeconomics/2020/02/11/girls-in -stem-how-is-sri-lanka-faring/.

ADB (Asian Development Bank) and ILO (International Labour Organization). 2017. *Sri Lanka: Fostering Workforce Skills through Education—Employment Diagnostic Study*. ADB: Manila, ILO: Geneva. http://dx.doi.org/10.22617/TCS179120-2.

Australian Academy of Science. 2019. *Women in STEM Decadal Plan*. Canberra.

DCS (Department of Census and Statistics). 2013. *Sri Lanka Labour Force Survey Annual Report—2013*. Colombo.

DCS (Department of Census and Statistics). 2014. *Sri Lanka Labour Force Survey Annual Report—2014*. Colombo.

DCS (Department of Census and Statistics). 2015. *Sri Lanka Labour Force Survey Annual Report—2015*. Colombo.

DCS (Department of Census and Statistics). 2016. *Sri Lanka Labour Force Survey Annual Report—2016*. Colombo.

DCS (Department of Census and Statistics). 2017. *Sri Lanka Labour Force Survey Annual Report—2017*. Colombo.

DCS (Department of Census and Statistics). 2018. *Sri Lanka Labour Force Survey Annual Report—2018*. Colombo.

DCS (Department of Census and Statistics). 2019. *Sri Lanka Labour Force Survey Annual Report—2019*. Colombo.

DCS (Department of Census and Statistics). 2020. *Sri Lanka Labour Force Survey Annual Report—2020*. Colombo.

DCS (Department of Census and Statistics). 2021. *Sri Lanka Labour Force Survey Annual Report—2021*. Colombo.

Deloitte. 2020. "The Social Enterprise at Work: Paradox as a Path Forward." Global Human Capital Trends Report. https://www2.deloitte.com/cn/en/pages/human-capital/articles /global-human-capital-trends-2020.html.

Dissanayake, Mihirani. 2020. *Explaining Mismatch between Labor Supply and Demand in Sri Lanka*. Youth and Gender Qualitative Study. World Bank.

European Commission. 2020. "A European Green Deal: Striving to Be the First Climate-Neutral Continent." Brussels. https://ec.europa.eu/info/strategy/priorities-2019-2024/european -green-deal_en.

Government of Australia. 2020. *National Women in STEM Strategy*. Canberra.

Government of Sri Lanka. 2018. "Sri Lanka Digital Economy Strategy Blueprints September 2018." Digital Infrastructure and Information Technology Division, Colombo.

ILO (International Labour Organisation). 2020. "Green Jobs in Sri Lanka: Linkages between Environmental Sustainability and Decent Work." Geneva. https://www.ilo.org/colombo /whatwedo/publications/WCMS_755006/lang--en/index.htm.

International Telecommunications Union. n.d. ICT Price Baskets (database). https://www.itu .int/en/ITU-D/Statistics/Dashboards/Pages/IPB.aspx.

Kearney Advisor Network. n.d. "Regenerative Talent Pools: The 2023 Global Services Location Index." A.T. Kearney, Chicago, IL. https://www.kearney.com/service/digital/gsli/2023 -full-report.

Kirk, Donald. 2020. "Korea Reveals 'New Deal' Designed to Boost Jobs, Revive Sagging Economy." *Forbes*, July 14. https://www.forbes.com/sites/donaldkirk/2020/07/14 /koreas-reveals-new-deal-designed-to-boost-jobs-revive-sagging-economy /#7b17f8423250.

OECD (Organisation for Economic Co-operation and Development). 2019. "Going Digital: Shaping Policies, Improving Lives." Paris. https://doi.org/10.1787/9789264312012-en.

OECD (Organisation for Economic Co-operation and Development). 2020a. "Digital Transformation in the Age of COVID-19: Building Resilience and Bridging Divides." Digital Economy Outlook 2020 Supplement. Paris.

OECD (Organisation for Economic Co-operation and Development). 2020b. "Green Recovery and Job Creation." Paris.

OECD (Organisation for Economic Co-operation and Development). 2020c. "OECD Policy Responses to Coronavirus (COVID-19): Making the Green Recovery Work for Jobs, Income, and Growth." Paris. https://www.oecd.org/coronavirus/policy-responses/making-the -green-recovery-work-for-jobs-income-and-growth-a505f3e7/#section-d1e454.

Oxford Business Group. 2019. "Demographic and Disease Trends Drive Demand for Private Health Care in Sri Lanka." London. https://oxfordbusinessgroup.com/overview/fitter -equilibrium-demographic-and-disease-shifts-drive-demand-private-care.

Portulans Institute. n.d. "Network Readiness Index 2022: Sri Lanka." University of Oxford, Oxford, U.K. https://networkreadinessindex.org/country/sri-lanka/.

SLBFE (Sri Lanka Bureau of Foreign Employment). 2014. *Annual Statistical Report of Foreign Employment 2014*. Battaramulla.

SLBFE (Sri Lanka Bureau of Foreign Employment). 2015. *Annual Statistical Report of Foreign Employment 2015*. Battaramulla.

SLBFE (Sri Lanka Bureau of Foreign Employment). 2016. *Annual Statistical Report of Foreign Employment 2016*. Battaramulla.

SLBFE (Sri Lanka Bureau of Foreign Employment). 2017. *Annual Statistical Report of Foreign Employment 2017*. Battaramulla.

SLBFE (Sri Lanka Bureau of Foreign Employment). 2018. *Annual Statistical Report of Foreign Employment 2018*. Battaramulla.

SLBFE (Sri Lanka Bureau of Foreign Employment). 2019. *Annual Statistical Report of Foreign Employment 2019*. Battaramulla.

SLBFE (Sri Lanka Bureau of Foreign Employment). 2020. *Annual Statistical Report of Foreign Employment 2020*. Battaramulla.

Sosale, Shobhana, Graham Mark Harrison, Namrata Tognatta, Shiro Nakata, and Priyal Mukesh Gala. 2023. *Engendering Access to STEM Education and Careers in South Asia. South Asia Development Forum*. Washington, DC: World Bank. doi:10.1596/978-1-4648-1966-7.

Subasinghe, Shalika, Shobhana Sosale, and Harsha Aturupane. 2023. *Enhancing STEM Education and Careers in Sri Lanka*. International Development in Focus. Washington, DC: World Bank. doi:10.1596/978-1-4648-2004-5.

TVEC (Tertiary and Vocational Education Commission). 2016. *Labour Market Information Bulletin*. Colombo.

TVEC (Tertiary and Vocational Education Commission). 2017. *Labour Market Information Bulletin*. Colombo.

TVEC (Tertiary and Vocational Education Commission). 2018. *Labour Market Information Bulletin*. Colombo.

TVEC (Tertiary and Vocational Education Commission). 2019. *Labour Market Information Bulletin*. Colombo.

TVEC (Tertiary and Vocational Education Commission). 2020. *Labour Market Information Bulletin*. Colombo.

TVEC (Tertiary and Vocational Education Commission). 2021. *Labour Market Information Bulletin*. Colombo.

UGC (University Grants Commission). *Annual Report 2015*. Colombo: Government of Sri Lanka.

UGC (University Grants Commission). *Annual Report 2016*. Colombo: Government of Sri Lanka.

UGC (University Grants Commission). *Annual Report 2018*. Colombo: Government of Sri Lanka.

UGC (University Grants Commission). *Annual Report 2020*. Colombo: Government of Sri Lanka.

UGC (University Grants Commission). *Annual Report 2021*. Colombo: Government of Sri Lanka.

UNDP (United Nations Development Programme) and ADB (Asian Development Bank). 2017. "Assessment of Sri Lanka's Power Sector—100 Percent Electricity Generation through Renewable Energy by 2050." New York.

UNESCO (United Nations Educational, Scientific, and Cultural Organization). 2015. *UNESCO Science Report: Towards 2030*. Paris.

UNESCO (United Nations Educational, Scientific, and Cultural Organization)-UNEVOC (UNESCO International Centre for Technical and Vocational Education and Training). 2017 "Greening Technical and Vocational Education and Training: A Practical Guide for Institutions." Paris.

UNESCO (United Nations Educational, Scientific, and Cultural Organization)-UNEVOC (UNESCO International Centre for Technical and Vocational Education and Training). 2020a. "Boosting Gender Equality in Science and Technology—A Challenge for TVET Programmes and Careers." Paris.

UNESCO (United Nations Educational, Scientific, and Cultural Organization)-UNEVOC (UNESCO International Centre for Technical and Vocational Education and Training). 2020b. "UNESCO–UNEVOC Medium-Term Strategy for 2021–2023." Paris.

United Nations. 2008. "International Standard Industrial Classification of All Economic Activities Revision 4." Statistical papers. Series M No. 4/Rev.4. Department of Economic and Social Affairs Statistical Division. United Nations, New York. https://unstats.un.org/unsd/publication/seriesm/seriesm_4rev4e.pdf.

U.S. Bureau of Labor Statistics. 2020. "Employment Projections: Industries with the Fastest Growing and Most Rapidly Declining Wage and Salary Employment." Washington, DC. https://www.bls.gov/emp/tables/industries-fast-grow-decline-employment.htm.

Vegas, Emiliana. 2020. "School Closures, Government Responses, and Learning Inequality around the World during COVID-19." Brookings Institution, Washington, DC.

WHO (World Health Organization). 2020. *Epidemiology Unit*. Sri Lanka Situation Reports. https://www.epid.gov.lk/web/index.php?option=com_content&view=article&id=225&lang=en&Itemid=0.

WHO (World Health Organization). 2022. *Global Spending on Health: Rising to the Pandemic's Challenges*. Geneva: World Health Organization.

World Bank. 2012a. "Sri Lanka—Demographic Transition: Facing the Challenges of an Aging Population with Few Resources." World Bank, Washington, DC.

World Bank. 2012b. *World Development Report 2012: Gender Equality and Development*. Washington, DC: World Bank.

World Bank. 2016. *World Development Report 2016: Digital Dividends*. Washington, DC: World Bank.

World Bank. 2018. "Sri Lanka Development Update: More and Better Jobs for an Upper Middle-Income Country." World Bank, Washington, DC.

World Bank. 2019. "Sri Lanka Development Update: Demographic Change in Sri Lanka." World Bank, Washington, DC.

World Bank. 2021a. "Sri Lanka Development Update: Economic and Poverty Impact of COVID-19." World Bank, Washington, DC.

World Bank. 2021b. *World Development Indicators 2021*. Washington, DC: World Bank. https://databank.worldbank.org/data/download/GNIPC.pdf.

World Bank. 2022c. "South Asia's Digital Opportunity: Accelerating Growth, Transforming Lives." World Bank, Washington, DC.

3 Education, Training, and Skills Ecosystem

INTRODUCTION

This chapter analyzes Sri Lanka's education system—including its structure and the institutions managing it—and addresses the role of technical and vocational education and training (TVET) in advancing skills. It also discusses how COVID-19 has affected this ecosystem and provides recommendations for strengthening it.

EDUCATION STRUCTURE AND INSTITUTIONS

Sri Lanka has a complex education system (figure 3.1, panel a). The right to a free public education from grade 1 through the university level is enshrined in the country's constitution. In 2021, about 304,000 students entered grade 1 (MoE 2021a),[1] and education is compulsory until grade 11.[2] Education is delivered through a predominantly public system with an extensive, growing network covering 92 percent of schools and employing 94 percent of instructors and teachers in 2021 (MoE 2021a). General education comprises the several levels of education that include primary grades (1–5), junior secondary (6–9), senior secondary (10–11), and collegiate level (12–13) (figure 3.1, panel b).

Children in Sri Lanka start primary school between ages 5 and 6—typically after a year or two of preschool—and remain in the system at least until the end of compulsory education at grade 11. Together with the two years of preschool, Sri Lanka's compulsory education system is for 13 years. Students' access to the collegiate level is contingent on passing the General Certificate of Education (GCE) Ordinary Level (O/L) exam conducted at the end of grade 11. In 2017, the Ministry of Education (MoE) launched a program guaranteeing 13 years of education. In 2021, 74.5 percent of applicants qualified for the GCE Advanced Level (A/L) (DoE 2021b). However, with the introduction of the 13 years of compulsory education, students could pursue collegiate level. Advancing to the university level requires passing the GCE A/L exam at the end of grade 13. In 2021, 64 percent of school students who took the GCE A/L exam became

FIGURE 3.1

Sri Lanka's education and training system

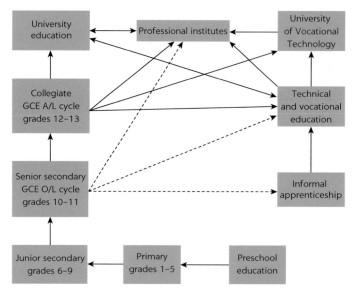

a. Levels of general education

EDUCATION LEVEL		GRADE	ENROLLMENT AGE	
			OFFICIAL	MEDIAN AGE
	ECE	Preparatory	3 to 5	4
Compulsory education	Primary	1	6	6
		2	7	7
		3	8	8
		4	9	9
		5	10	10
	Junior secondary	6	11	11
		7	12	12
		8	13	13
		9	14	14
Extension proposed in 2016	Senior secondary	10	15	15
		11	16	16
	Collegiate	12	17	17
		13	18	19

b. Education and training system

Sources: Original compilation for this publication and Dundar et al. 2017.
Note: A/L = Advanced Level; ECE = Early Childhood Education; GCE = General Certificate of Education; O/L = Ordinary Level.

eligible to apply for university (DoE 2021a). Yet many young people do not access higher education. They also lack the professional qualifications needed to transition from school to work.

In 2021, Sri Lanka had 10,146 public primary and secondary schools, 93 private schools, 30 special schools, and 819 state-funded and managed *pirivenas* (temple) schools. Enrollments were 4.05 million in public schools, 138,828 in private schools, 70,310 in pirivenas, and 2,391 in special schools. There were 241,054 teachers in public schools, 7,776 in private schools, 7,346 in pirivenas, and 499 in special schools (MoE 2021a).

A comparatively large cohort of young people do not get opportunities to access higher education and lack the qualifications needed to productively join the labor force. Entrance into higher education is limited by the relatively few spaces in universities. In 2019, only 22 percent of collegiate students who passed the university entry exam enrolled in public or private higher education. To ensure that students do not drop out of the schooling system, in 2017 the government introduced the new policy of free public TVET (World Bank 2020) and introduced a vocational stream at the collegiate level (World Bank 2018). Thus, access to vocational education needs to be encouraged and enhanced to develop a better-skilled workforce in Sri Lanka.

Further, two education reform programs have facilitated student enrollments in TVET. The first, introduced in 2013, offered streams at the collegiate level for engineering technology and biosystems technology. Initially some 14,000 students enrolled in such training at 252 schools. Of these, nearly 12,700 technology stream students sat for the GCE A/L exam for the first time in 2015 (7,882 in engineering and 4,815 in biosystems); just over half of the students qualified for university. In 2021, approximately 61.77 percent of engineering technology and 73.38 percent of biosystems technology school students became eligible for university entrance (DoE 2021a). Separate faculties in public universities and university colleges were established to provide opportunities for students to receive further educational opportunities. University colleges were put under the purview of the University of Vocational Technology (UNIVOTEC). Some of the students who could not join the universities became attracted to vocational training.

The second reform, introduced in 2017, sought to provide skills to students who do not have strong enough grades to continue to the GCE A/L. The reform introduced vocational streams at the collegiate level. Students who do not pass the GCE O/L could continue to attend school by following the vocational stream and remain in school until year 13. The National Institute of Education (NIE) and the Tertiary and Vocational Education Commission (TVEC) collaborated to prepare the vocational courses. The vocational stream included three components to develop general skills, specific vocational and technical skills, and provide industrial training (box 3.1). The program was initiated in 42 schools in 2017. The number of schools offering the vocational stream increased to 192 in 2018, 311 in 2019, 421 in 2020, and 519 in 2021. Partnership agreements or a memorandum of understanding was signed with partner vocational training institutes. For example, practical training was offered in 100 public and private vocational training institutes in 2019.

BOX 3.1

Structure of Sri Lanka's vocational education stream

The vocational education stream has three main components:

1. *General component.* The National Institute of Education (NIE) has designed subjects to develop general skills and subjects, including in first language (Sinhala or Tamil), business English and communications, aesthetic appreciation, information and communication technology (ICT), citizenry, health and life skills for social well-being, entrepreneurship, career guidance, and extracurricular activities such as sports and societies. These subjects, common for all students, are offered during the first year of the General Certificate of Education Advanced Level.

2. *Applied subjects (vocational and technical skills).* The NIE has identified 26 applied vocational subjects under seven clusters as electives, with four modules per subject. The clusters and subjects identified are as follows:

- *Health and social services*: child psychology and care, health and social care, and physical education and sports

- *Sociocultural studies*: performing arts, event management, and arts and crafts
- *Designing*: interior design, fashion design, graphic design, art and design, website design, and landscaping
- *Agricultural and food technology studies*: applied horticulture, livestock production, food processing, aquatic resources, and plantation production
- *Technical studies*: construction, automobiles, electricity and electronics, textiles and apparel, metal fabrication, aluminum fabrication, and software development
- *Tourism and hospitality*: tourism and hospitality
- *Environmental studies*: environmental studies.

The State Ministry of Skills Development, Vocational Education, Research and Innovations (SMSDVERI) helps students identify public and private vocational training institutes that provide training in the selected subject area.

3. *Industrial skills training.* The selected training institutes and the SMSDVERI help students with information and options for industry work experience.

Source: NIE 2018.

About 9,600 students benefited from the program. Of the 1,545 students enrolled in the vocational stream in 2017, 1,143 completed the training in 2019. Some 12,200 students—4,615 of them women—of 182,572 students followed the vocational stream in GCE A/L classes in 2019. The NIE trained 1,237 teachers who now teach the common curriculum, and 250 teachers who teach the vocational subjects. In addition, in 2018, 898 new graduate teachers were recruited to teach the vocational subjects.

After completing the three components satisfactorily, students receive an Advanced Certificate in Vocational Education (ACVE). The MoE has discussed equating the ACVE to a National Vocational Qualification (NVQ) level 4 (see figure 3.3 later in the chapter). The Subcommittee on Vocational Stream at the MoE has conducted a review of this initiative and has identified a few gaps such as introduction of labor market–demanded courses, lack of qualified and experienced teachers, lack of career guidance provided to students in selecting appropriate courses, and so on. The main goal of exploring this option is to enable students to apply for jobs and to provide options for further studies.

The review of the vocational stream resulted in discontinuation of software design and web design and introduction of computer hardware and networking and manufacturing as vocational stream subjects offered for students in 2021.[3] Further review of its subjects, teaching resources, physical resources, and on-the-job training provider feedback will be used to improve it. The vocational stream applications are called to send applications indicating the courses and names of schools offering such courses.

Institutional aspects

The MoE formulates education policies and provides policy guidance to relevant state ministries, including the State Ministry of Skills Development, Vocational Education, Research and Innovations (SMSDVERI). The NIE is responsible for curricula and teacher development for schools. The National Education Commission (NEC) advises the president and residents on education policies for preschool, school, tertiary, and vocational training and higher education. TVET and university education comprise tertiary education in Sri Lanka.

Tertiary and vocational education and training

TVEC is responsible for formulating policies, planning, quality assurance, coordination, and development of tertiary and vocational education. Vocational training institutes are public, private, nongovernmental, and charity based. The Tertiary and Vocational Education Act 20 of 1990 makes it mandatory for all TVET institutions to obtain TVEC registration to provide tertiary education or vocational training. Although most institutions obtain registration, some fail to renew their registrations or do not register at all. Private training providers are concentrated in information and communication technology (ICT), construction, professional and scientific activities, tourism, and catering. Most nongovernmental organizations (NGOs) are voluntary or religious organizations that offer crafts training targeting unemployed youth, rural women, school dropouts, and semi- or unskilled workers. Most NGOs charge nominal or no fees as the NGOs have agreed with their sponsoring agency.

University education

The Higher Education Division of the MoE is responsible for delivering, managing, and coordinating higher education and policy making. The University Grants Commission (UGC) is responsible for allocating funds to higher education institutions, planning and coordinating university education, maintaining academic standards, and regulating administration of and admission of students to these institutions through the Quality Assurance and Accreditation Council. Nonstate degree-awarding institutes are managed by the nonstate division of the Ministry of Higher Education.

In December 2021, Sri Lanka had 17 public universities, 8 higher education institutes, and 11 postgraduate institutes under the direct supervision of the UGC (UGC 2021). In December 2021, it had 25 nonstate institutes that awarded 153 bachelor's degree programs recognized by the UGC (UGC 2021). There are also several other public tertiary education institutions such as advanced technological institutes and private institutions offering overseas university degrees. Some private institutes offer courses without any official recognition. The Sri Lanka Institute of Advanced Technological Education (SLIATE) has 18 advanced technological institutes that award higher national diplomas.[4]

Funding aspects

General education includes public, private, and special schools. Of the 10,155 schools, 373 national ones are administered and directly funded by the MoE (along with 816 pirivenas and 30 special schools). The administration of only general education is largely devolved to provincial governments, but not TVET. The other 96 percent—public primary and secondary schools covering about 80 percent of public students—are administered at the provincial level.

Most provincial school funding comes from the central government through grants to provincial councils, over which provinces have budgetary autonomy. In 2021, 18.4 percent of province-specific grants were allocated to education (MoF 2021). Education grants range from 15.8 percent in the North Central Province to 20.6 percent in the Eastern Province. Some provinces, especially the Western Province, also collect revenue to fund education.

TVET providers include public, private, and nongovernmental institutes. Publicly funded TVET training institutes receive funds from the central government through the respective ministry and are allowed to charge fees from commercial-oriented courses such as cosmetology. Since the government introduced free TVET in 2017, the income collected from student fees has fallen. Similarly, higher education institutes receive funds from the central government through the UGC.

Developing higher-level skills is crucial to Sri Lanka's economic transformation and global competitiveness. Demand for such skills to boost productivity continues to rise due to economic, technological, and demographic changes in the country. With GDP per capita of US$3,815 in 2021, Sri Lanka became a lower-middle-income country (CBSL 2022). As the country moves forward, human capital will remain critical for modernizing agriculture, deepening industrial development, and expanding services.

At the same time, rapid technological progress lends urgency for a skills delivery system that keeps pace with the changing nature of work. Sri Lankan workers must gain the technical competencies and higher-order cognitive skills to meet needs in domestic and foreign markets and remain globally competitive. Demographic changes also have important implications for skills training and workforce development. Sri Lanka is confronted with a dwindling demographic dividend: the share of young people entering the workforce is falling, while that of the older workforce is rising. These structural changes in the workforce call for efforts to upgrade skills for new and existing workers to support Sri Lanka's economic transformation.

TVET issues

TVET in Sri Lanka involves multiple providers of skills training (figure 3.2). Public skills training is provided by 24 national and state ministries and several statutory bodies (annex 3A). In 2020, public sector training accounted for 79 percent of TVET enrollments, and the other 21 percent was provided by private institutions and NGOs (TVEC 2020). TVEC sets policies and guidelines, registers vocational training centers, and shares guidelines and plans. The large number of public and private institutes creates a challenge for coordination and monitoring to ensure quality—challenges that likely create inefficiencies and complicate overall implementation of skills development.

In December 2021, about 1,064 TVET institutions were registered with TVEC (roughly 45 percent public, 50 percent private, and 5 percent NGO). Public TVEC institutions are overseen by several ministries, creating significant challenges for program coordination and accreditation. TVEC is unable to specify the exact numbers of students enrolled in the accredited TVEC institutions. By December 2021, TVEC had accredited more than 2,889 courses: 2,275 for public institutions (79 percent), 472 for private ones (16 percent), and 142 for NGOs (5 percent). Most public TVET institutes are large providers and offer TVEC-accredited courses. Most private institutes are small providers and offer courses

FIGURE 3.2

Governance structure of TVET in Sri Lanka

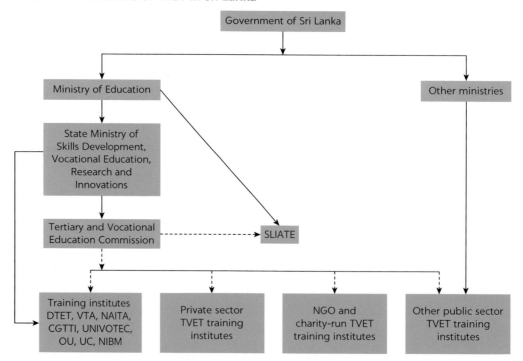

Source: Original figure for this publication.
Note: CGTTI = Ceylon–German Technical Training Institute; DTET = Department of Technical Education and Training; NAITA = National Apprentice and Industrial Training Authority; NGO = nongovernmental organization; NIBM = National Institute of Business Management; OU = Ocean University; SLIATE = Sri Lanka Institute of Advanced Technological Education; TVET = technical and vocational education and training; UC = university colleges; UNIVOTEC = University of Vocational Technology; VTA = Vocational Training Authority.

without receiving TVEC accreditation; courses are offered based on regional student or industry demand.

The public TVET system comprises statutory bodies and training institutes under several ministries. The SMSDVERI is the main ministry responsible for TVET (see figure 3.2). Other ministries impart training through affiliated training institutes. For example, the Ministry of Ports and Shipping trains port workers through the Mahapola Ports and Maritime Academy, while the State Ministry of Rural Housing, Construction, and Building Materials Industries Promotion provides training to operate construction equipment through the Construction Equipment Training Center. Although the president aims to consolidate TVET in a single system, many issues stand in the way. These include the fragmentation of TVET providers and providers' lack of continuous registration under TVEC, failure to seek accreditation for courses offered, and inability to offer certificates linked to the NVQ system or Sri Lanka Qualifications Framework (SLQF).

A strategy for developing skills and ensuring steady governance is crucial for shaping Sri Lanka's future workforce. TVET responsibilities and functions are not anchored in a central ministry but are under a state ministry, with standards and accreditation of institutions vested with TVEC. Responsibility for skills development has shifted under successive ministries. For instance, during 2014–20 the Skills Sector Development Division was moved across nine ministries. Further, rotating secretaries in parent ministries are barred from opposing political factions, leaving skills development orphaned. This haphazard decision-making and implementation have hampered the development of a quality workforce.

The movement of responsibility for skills development and TVET has resulted in the secretary being responsible for many activities not directly relevant to TVET. Since mid-2020 the SMSDVERI has been responsible for 15 activities including TVET, and in January 2021 its mandate was expanded by adding three more responsibilities (box 3.2).

The SMSDVERI's priority activities are conducted by the departments and other statutory bodies that it oversees. In December 2020, there were eight main agencies under the SMSDVERI (box 3.3). TVEC is also mapped under the state ministry as the vocational training policy-making body.

Tertiary and Vocational Education Commission

TVEC was established by the Tertiary and Vocational Education Act 20 of 1990 and subsequent amendments in 1999. Its mandate includes making policy, planning, ensuring quality, coordinating, and developing training. Most of its board members represent employer associations and private entrepreneurs. Its main activities are as follows:

- *Policy making.* In 2018, TVEC, in coordination with the NEC, developed the National Policy on Technical and Vocational Education.
- *Planning.* TVET plans are prepared for growing industry sectors in provinces. TVEC has prepared 17 such plans, for textiles and garments, gems and jewelry, printing, construction, hotels and tourism, automobile repair and maintenance, office management, food and beverages, rubber and plastics, leather and footwear, plantations, electricity and electronics, metal and light engineering, hairdressing and beauty, ceramics and glassware, health, and ICT. A vocational education and training (VET) plan is intended to identify an industry's staffing and training needs, assess training supply, analyze gaps and surpluses between the demand for and supply of skills, and introduce

BOX 3.2

Responsibilities of Sri Lanka's State Ministry of Skills Development, Vocational Education, Research and Innovations

- Initiating a program to provide technical and vocational education and training (TVET) without regard for educational qualifications
- Subjecting all TVET institutions to systematic evaluations, effecting a complete physical and curriculum modification to suitable institutions, and networking them under the "One TVET" concept and transferring them into institutions awarding technology degrees
- Establishing a network of technical and technical university colleges across the island
- Expanding Ceylon's German Technical Training Institute
- Increasing the scheme of 7 levels of National Vocational Qualification to 10 and amending the Sri Lanka Qualifications Framework accordingly
- Providing opportunities to pursue vocational education up to postgraduate levels
- Amending curricula to integrate vocational education and entrepreneurship by including information and communication technology (ICT) as well as English and other languages
- Providing vocational education focused on domestic and foreign job markets by coordinating with the Ministry of Foreign Employment Promotion and Market Diversification
- Establishing information technology (IT) entrepreneurship
- Developing Sri Lanka as an innovation hub by maximizing use of the Internet of Things, artificial intelligence, biotechnology, robotics, augmented reality, cloud computing, nanotechnology, and 3-D printing

- Making more efficient the system for issuing patents to researchers for their innovations and to secure ownership of their research designs
- Providing facilities for domestic research institutions to collaborate with international research institutions
- Providing tax relief to private enterprises contributing to research
- Luring domestic or foreign investors required to manufacture innovative products under a domestic brand
- Formulating an efficient mechanism to channel innovations and research results to investors and relevant users
- Taking actions to establish city universities as degree-level higher education institutes by giving priority to improving their physical resources—while giving due consideration for the technical colleges, technical universities, and institutions falling under their purview—with a focus on skills development targeting employment opportunities related to the sector-specific production needs of each district
- Taking steps to establish the National Institute of Innovations in accordance with the 2019 National Innovation Agency Act 22
- Introducing mobile technology education services to promote the potential of TVET for entrepreneurship and income generation, to bring it closer to people and create opportunities to access it across the island.

Sources: Department of Government Printing 2020, 2021.

interventions to provide the required human resources. VET plans are updated regularly in consultation with industry, and training providers are expected to consult the plans. In addition to industry VET plans, TVEC has prepared eight provincial plans (except for the Western Province).

- *Quality assurance.* This function entails registering institutes and accrediting training courses. By December 30, 2021, approximately 1,064 training providers had been registered with TVEC, and just over 2,889 courses had

BOX 3.3

Main public TVET providers under the State Ministry of Skills Development, Vocational Education, Research and Innovations

Department of Technical Education and Training (DTET). Established in 1893, DTET was the first formal technical training institute established in Sri Lanka. Its main functions are to direct, supervise, and coordinate delivery of technical education programs. DTET comprises 29 technical colleges and 9 colleges of technology, with 1 in each province.

Vocational Training Authority (VTA). The VTA was established by the Vocational Training Authority of Sri Lanka Act 12 of 1995 to facilitate self-employment and supply skills, specifically for the informal sector, through employment-oriented short courses. The VTA operates 8 national training institutes, 22 district vocational training centers, and 186 rural vocational training centers. Its mandate is to provide technical and vocational education and training (TVET), conduct trade tests, offer career guidance and counseling programs, conduct research and development, help trained youth obtain further training and provide employment or self-employment opportunities, foster self-employment for trained youth by facilitating funding through bank loans to help them start small-scale projects, and coordinate with national and international public and private entities to achieve its goals.

National Apprentice and Industrial Training Authority (NAITA). Established in 1990, NAITA's main task is to boost job skills through industry-based training, promoting apprenticeships for young people in TVET and those undergoing on-the-job training at the university level. NAITA arranges on-the-job training for university engineering undergraduates, issues National Vocational Qualification (NVQ) certificates by recognition of prior learning for informally skilled and trained craftspeople, conducts entrepreneurship development programs, interacts with industry to develop curricula, and sets national competency standards for vocational training.

Ceylon–German Technical Training Institute (CGTTI). The CGTTI was established in 1959 to provide training in automobile engineering and allied trades. This institute originated as a result of an agreement between the governments of the Federal Republic of Germany and Sri Lanka to supply training assistance in maintaining the bus fleet, which belonged to the Transport Board. The CGTTI was under the Ministry of Transport until 2004, then was transferred to the Ministry of Skills Development Vocational and Technical Education.

Sri Lanka Institute of Printing (SLIOP). Established by Parliament in 1984, SLIOP's mission is to develop printing and digital arts skills. The institute offers study programs leading to advanced diplomas in printing and visual communications technology.

Ocean University. Created by Parliament in 2014 to expand the scope of the National Institute of Fisheries and Nautical Engineering, Ocean University is registered under the Tertiary and Vocational Education Commission (TVEC) to offer vocational courses and the University Grants Commission (UGC) to offer degree courses. The university has eight regional colleges, with some specializing in vocational courses.

University of Vocational Technology (UNIVOTEC). Established by Parliament in 2008, UNIVOTEC offers TVEC-accredited courses and NVQ level 7 courses—equivalent to a university degree. The degrees offered by UNIVOTEC are recognized by the UGC and the Ministry of Public Administration.

University colleges (UC). Set up by Parliament in 2014, university colleges are affiliated with UNIVOTEC and offer NVQ levels 5 and 6. The courses are offered free of charge and, when students have completed them they are eligible to follow degree programs offered by UNIVOTEC. There are six university colleges spread over several provinces.

Sources: CGTTI, DTET, NAITA, OU, SLIOP, UNIVOTEC, and VTA websites: http://www.cgtti.lk/; http://www.dtet.gov.lk/en/; http://www.naita .gov.lk/; http://ocu.ac.lk/about-us/; https://sliop.edu.lk/about/; http://univotec.ac.lk/; https://www.vtasl.gov.lk/ (accessed March 13, 2021). There are separate websites for each University College.

been accredited. Registration lasts two years; at the end of that period, training providers are expected to reregister. Accredited courses must comply with national competency standards and physical infrastructure, teaching, and learning systems. Students who complete them can obtain an NVQ.

- *Establishing standards for TVET institutions.* TVEC has developed a Quality Management System, based on international standards, to assess the services provided by TVET institutes.[5] TVEC has certified 242 training institutions. The Quality Management System was assessed in 2017—resulting in the development of a stronger Quality Improvement System that has helped foster a culture of quality assurance. The Quality Improvement System rates training institutions using "stars." The National Coordination Committee recommends the number of stars to be awarded to the TVET institution. The institutions are likely to receive three, four, or five stars; one or two stars will not be awarded to any institution. Excellence in quality is denoted by five stars. By the end of 2020, the system had issued certificates to 232 training centers—with 114 receiving three stars, 118 receiving four stars, and none of the centers awarded five stars. The quality award competitions are organized at the provincial and national levels to encourage centers to develop and maintain quality.
- *Labour Market Information System.* TVEC publishes a biannual *Labour Market Information Bulletin* and an annual *Skills Report*. Both documents include useful information for policy makers, researchers, and industry.

TVET in provinces and districts

TVEC and the SMSDVERI have implemented several initiatives to strengthen skills and coordinate activities with stakeholders. TVET functions have not been constitutionally devolved to provincial councils. Most head offices for TVET centers and colleges are in Colombo, whereas TVET centers are distributed across provinces, districts, and divisional secretariats. Still, regional centers can propose and implement courses demanded by local employers. Regional centers are encouraged to source part-time instructors and encourage on-the-job training by coordinating with local employers.

TVEC's first initiative was to develop provincial and industry-based TVET plans to guide public, private, and NGO training institutes. The provincial plans were compiled with the participation of industry associations, employers, and TVET providers. Industry associations and employers have also contributed to industry-based vocational education plans in sectors such as construction, electricity and electronics, health, hotels and tourism, and food and beverages.

The second initiative by the SMSDVERI involved its Vocational Training Division reactivating district coordinating committees to engage them in social marketing and career guidance activities at the district level. This move was made to maximize training capacity across agencies through rationalization and resource sharing. The committees have also offered locally relevant training programs in consultation with local employers.

The SMSDVERI's third initiative was to encourage all vocational training institutes to develop center management plans. These plans assess each center's resources, the demand for courses offered, local employers' requests in different subject areas, staffing, employment rates, and other information. All centers preparing such plans must work with local chambers of commerce, employers, and business associations to understand the demand for skills and develop courses to meet it. As part of the plans, the centers are encouraged to sign memoranda of understanding with employers. In addition, the plans include a section to demonstrate centers' social responsibility to contribute to local communities. This initiative commenced in 2015, when 20 centers prepared such plans. By the end of 2020, about 128 centers had prepared plans and 116 had implemented them.

Another SMSDVERI initiative involves organizing an annual competition to recognize the achievements of vocational training institutes by size (small, medium, and large) and region (district, provincial, and national). District winners compete to be provincial winners, then provincial winners compete to be national winners. The selection panel comprises a committee of assessors who review applications and visit institutions. An annual award ceremony is held to reward all winning training institutes.

Quality Management System

TVEC has developed the Quality Management System (QMS) based on standards developed by the International Organization for Standardization (ISO), Sri Lanka Standards Institution, and International Workshop Agreement. The QMS follows ISO 9001:2008, and training institutes are required to adopt six procedures:[6]

1. Maintain documents of training processes.
2. Maintain records of training processors.
3. Be subject to internal audit and management reviews.
4. Demonstrate how control of nonconformities (deficiencies and variations identified) are exercised.
5. Maintain evidence of corrective actions taken to correct deviations.
6. Maintain evidence of preventive actions taken.

The QMS helps to promote a culture of quality within the training institutes. Therefore, the ownership of the entire process is vital. Two main tasks include (a) the appointment of focal staff members (head of quality, quality management staff, quality review committee, internal quality auditing staff) and (b) the preparation of documents (quality plan, preparation of quality manual). TVEC will review these documents and undertake a site visit of the training institutes prior to awarding QMS certificates.

The QMS was reviewed in 2017. The review highlighted that the main deficiency of the QMS is that it is more about reports and less about promoting the culture of quality enhancement within the training centers. Based on the review, the program was positioned as "Quality Is Fun," and the QMS amalgamated and developed the Quality Improvement System (QIS). It includes three levels and three-star-level certificates. The QMS installation grew from 2013 to 2018.

NVQ system

The NVQ system has helped unify TVET and build an internationally competitive workforce (table 3.1). This system has been used to link vocational qualifications to the Sri Lanka Qualifications Framework—introduced in 2012—and to set minimum standards for workers seeking foreign employment. National skills standards were prepared by National Industrial Training Advisory Committees. Subsequently, sector skills councils were established for construction, ICT, manufacturing and light engineering, and tourism. These councils have reviewed and updated the NVQ standards, which have

TABLE 3.1 **National Vocational Qualification levels in Sri Lanka**

LEVEL	RESULTING QUALIFICATION	DESCRIPTION
1	Certificate in building career skills	Introduces students to basic skills that facilitate employment, including communication skills in English, cognitive skills, and social attitudes that enable employees to work with others and understand systems and routines and apply relevant knowledge.
		Level 1 provides entry-level skills.
2	Certificate in developing career skills and basic competencies for professions	Develops communication skills in English and advanced cognitive skills, including time and task management, prioritization, and organization. Basic work competencies enable workers to function effectively under qualified supervisors.
3	Certificate in specific careers	Introduces students to specific sectors and competencies in a range of occupations for productive employment. Develops understanding of basic requirements for careers with knowledge of fundamentals in such areas and positive attitudes for career development. Competent workers learn how to fulfill routine tasks in specific fields and to work efficiently under qualified supervisors.
4	Certificate in specific occupations	Trains professionals to work independently and head teams.
5	National diploma	Fosters professional competencies to work independently, make administrative decisions, and supervise processes at the middle-management level.
6	Advanced diploma	Trains professionals in problem solving who manage processes at the middle-management level.
7	Bachelor's degree	Trains professionals to manage processes in a specific field and with the flexibility to develop capacities in other areas of work.

Sources: TVEC 2016b, 2021b.

Note: The Tertiary and Vocational Education Commission (TVEC) is adopting the International Labour Organization international occupational classification for the labeling qualifications at levels 1–4 for international comparability. For National Vocational Qualification levels 5, 6, and 7, the European Credit Transfer and Accumulation System is used. One credit is equivalent to 25 notional hours, and the learning objectives must be satisfied within the time frame. Direct learning (direct contact with instructors, teachers, and trainers) and self-directed learning time doing assignments and assessments are considered in calculating notional hours.

been used to train instructors, teachers, and assessors how to conduct programs and assessments using a competency-based approach.

TVEC is adopting the International Labour Organization international occupational classification for the labeling qualifications at levels 1–4 for international comparability. For NVQ levels 5, 6, and 7, the European Credit Transfer and Accumulation System is used. One credit is equivalent to 25 notional hours, and the learning objectives must be satisfied within the time frame. Direct learning (direct contact with instructors, teachers, and trainers) and self-directed learning time doing assignments and assessments are considered in calculating notional hours.

The NVQ system was initially implemented only for TVET. It was then incorporated into the Sri Lanka Qualifications Framework (SLQF) to gain popularity, facilitate lateral mobility in vocational education, and permit vertical mobility to higher education. The University Grants Commission (UGC) has developed and implemented the NVQ. This applies to all higher education institutions that provide postsecondary education, both public and private, and was developed and implemented by the UGC. NVQ courses are more practical, whereas SLQF courses are more theoretical (figure 3.3). The mapping of NVQ to SLQF provides confidence to employers and students to recognize either qualification framework as an educational qualification for recruitment purposes.

The pathways created since the introduction of the SLQF have helped raise awareness and recognition of NVQ courses. As a result, more students have been gaining NVQ certificates over the years (figure 3.4). Yet fewer women receive NVQ certificates, as evidenced in TVET enrollments and completion rates.

Approximately 304,000 to 340,000 students enter grade 1 each year. The share of students who took the GCE O/L increased from 79 percent to 102 percent as a

FIGURE 3.3

Sri Lanka Qualifications Framework and National Vocational Qualification system

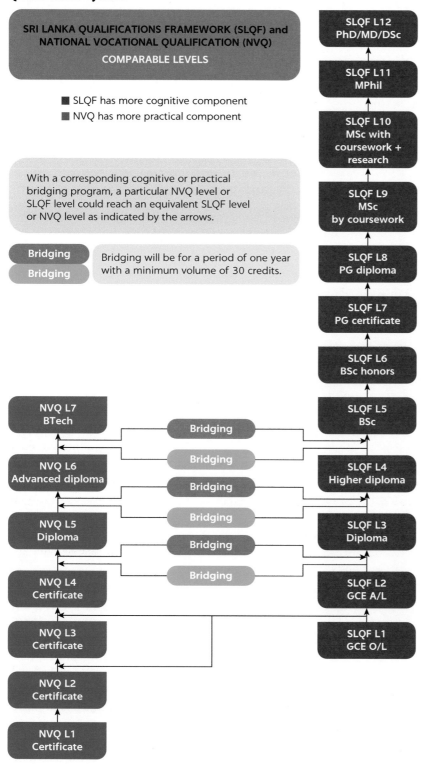

Note: A/L = Advanced Level; BSc = bachelor of science; BTech = bachelor of technology; DSc = doctor of science; GCE = General Certificate of Education; L = level; MD = doctor of medicine; MPhil = master of philosophy; MSc = master of science; NVQ = National Vocational Qualification; O/L = Ordinary Level; PG = postgraduate; PhD = doctor of philosophy; SLQF = Sri Lanka Qualifications Framework.

FIGURE 3.4

NVQ certificate recipients in Sri Lanka, by gender, 2011–21

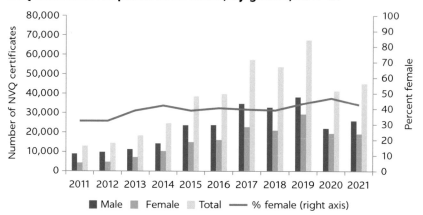

Source: Sri Lanka TVEC administrative database.
Note: NVQ = National Vocational Qualification; TVEC = Tertiary and Vocational
Education Commission.

percentage of grade 1 enrollments from 2012 to 2021. Among students who took the GCE O/L and GCE A/L exams in 2019, approximately 55 percent registered for public TVET. Similarly, the share of students who sat for GCE A/L as a percentage of grade 1 enrollments increased from 57 percent to 78 percent from 2012 to 2021. Between 2012 and 2019, the number of TVET students registered in public TVET institutions as a percentage of grade 1 enrollments rose from 30 percent to 55 percent, and completion rose from 23 percent to 38 percent. However, due to the COVID-19 pandemic the public sector TVET enrollment and completion percentages decreased from 2019 to 2020 (table 3.2). Total TVET enrollments increased from 44 percent to 75 percent relative to grade 1 enrollments and dropped to 39 percent in 2020. Again, in 2021, total TVET enrollment slightly increased to 48 percent. Because TVET enrollments include students of various age groups and those in the workforce, the exact number of students who have sat for GCE O/L or GCE A/L exams and then enrolled in TVET could be less than 75 percent in 2019, less than 39 percent in 2020, and less than 48 percent in 2021.

The number of students registered in full-time public TVET programs increased between 2012 and 2021, as did the number of full-time students and NVQ certificate holders (figure 3.5). The share of full-time students rose from 66 percent in 2012 to 78 percent in 2021, the total number of public sector participants increased by 11 percent during the period, and the number of full-time students increased by 29.8 percent. During the same period, the number of NVQ certificates issued increased to 145 percent. The greatest growth occurred from 2012 to 2019. However, due to COVID-19 lockdowns, the total number of students registered, number of full-time students, and NVQ certificate recipients decreased drastically in 2020 and further reduced in 2021.

When considering only those training institutes under the SMSDVERI, which includes data from the training institutes under the State Ministry of Skills, the share of full-time students increased 58 percent, and the number of NVQ certificate holders jumped 281 percent between 2012 and 2019 (figure 3.6). The number of total participants rose by 37 percent from 2012 to 2019. However, during the COVID-19 pandemic, the total number of participants reduced by approximately 27 percent from 2019 to 2021, and the percentage of full-time students fell from 86 percent to 80 percent. Similarly, the number of NVQ certificate holders fell by 47 percent.

TABLE 3.2 **School enrollments, exams, and TVET data for Sri Lanka, 2012–21**

EDUCATION LEVEL	2012 DATA	%	2015 DATA	%	2018 DATA	%	2019 DATA	%	2020 DATA	%	2021 DATA	%
Grade 1 (government schools)	339,142		334,877		328,632		333,074		319,415		304,105	
Number of students who took the GCE O/L examination	268,995	79	273,410	82	296,029	90	305,427	92	308,134	96	311,321	102
Number of students who took the GCE A/L examination (school candidates)	194,448	57	210,340	63	218,191	66	235,550	71	251,168	79	236,035	78
TVET enrollments (public sector)	102,609	30	117,321	35	148,085	45	183,312	55	98,313	31	123,825	41
TVET completion (public sector)	79,236	23	84,552	25	99,735	30	125,721	38	57,335	18	58,329	19
TVET enrollments (total)	148,131	44	173,421	52	186,042	57	250,690	75	124,419	39	144,319	48
TVET completion (total)	105,585	31	115,453	34	127,826	39	176,080	53	74,928	23	72,803	24

Sources: DoE 2012a, 2012b, 2015a, 2015b, 2018a, 2018b, 2019a, 2019b, 2020a, 2020b, 2021a, 2021b; MoE 2012, 2015, 2018, 2019, 2020, 2021a; TVEC 2012, 2015a, 2018, 2019, 2020, 2021a.
Note: A/L = Advanced Level; GCE = General Certificate of Education; O/L = Ordinary Level; TVET = technical and vocational education and training.

FIGURE 3.5

Public sector TVET training profile in Sri Lanka, 2012–21

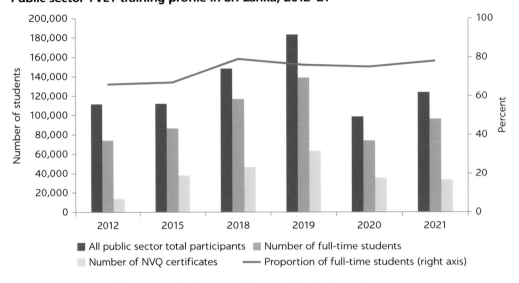

Sources: TVEC administrative data and original compilation for this publication.
Note: NVQ = National Vocational Qualification; TVEC = Tertiary and Vocational Education Commission;
TVET = technical and vocational education and training.

FIGURE 3.6

**Student registration, share of full-time students, and National Vocational Qualification
certificates in training institutes under SMSDEVRI, 2012–21**

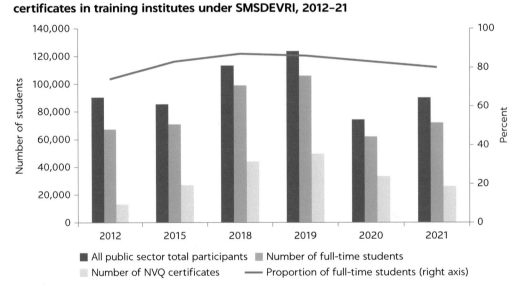

Sources: TVEC administrative data and original compilation for this publication.
Note: Includes data from training institutes that are under the State Ministry of Skills Development,
Vocational Education, Research and Innovations. NVQ = National Vocational Qualification; TVEC = Tertiary
and Vocational Education Commission.

TVET enrollments and completion in public and private sector institutions

Enrollments in public TVET institutes increased 47 percent between 2013 and
2017. With the introduction of free public TVET in 2017, enrollments fell from
165,238 in 2017 to 148,085 in 2018, and then increased to 183,312 in 2019. This is
a 23 percent enrollment increase from 2018 to 2019. But over 2013–19, enrollments increased from 112,569 to 183,312, which is a 63 percent increase from
2013 to 2019. With the introduction of the free TVET policy in 2017, the number
of students enrolled and dropped out during the initial period increased.
Therefore, total enrollments in 2018 decreased from 2017. In 2013, 75 percent of

students completed public TVET programs—implying that nearly 25 percent dropped out. The completion rate fell to 69 percent in 2019, suggesting a 31 percent dropout rate. However, enrollments in 2020 decreased due to COVID-19: the midyear student intake was halted, and the students enrolled only in the January 2020 semester.

The COVID-19 pandemic hit Sri Lanka in March 2020, and the government imposed immediate lockdown. The first wave of the pandemic lasted until June 2020. Since then, students have faced disruption in learning, especially those who had commenced their programs in January 2020. Because their education was disrupted, the government decided to eliminate enrollments for the second batch of students for year 2020 (figure 3.7, panel a). Enrollments increased by 26 percent from 2020 to 2021. Completion rates were consistently higher for women during 2013–19. However, this trend reversed in 2020 and 2021, with less than 50 percent of female students completing (figure 3.7, panel b).

By the end of 2020 there were 621 private TVET institutions and 54 other nonpublic TVET institutes in Sri Lanka. The number of private registered TVET institutions reduced to 540, but the number of other training institutions remained the same at the end of 2021.[7] As in the public sector, student enrollments fluctuated during 2013–19 in the private sector institutions, but in the opposite direction. With the introduction of free public TVET in 2017, there was a 23 percent decline in private enrollments between 2017 and 2018, from 49,057 to 37,957, although enrollments then increased to 67,398 in 2019. The fluctuations in private and public sector enrollments can be attributed to the introduction of free TVET policy in 2017. Students seem to have been actively assessing the quality of public versus private TVET education by initially enrolling in public sector institutions and dropping out within a short period of time. Their numbers were not being actively tracked to determine the uptake for programs. However, due to COVID-19, the number of enrollments declined to 26,106 in 2020. Enrollments decreased by 60 percent from 2019 to 2021 (figure 3.8, panel a). The drop in enrollment from 2017 to 2018 was due to public perceptions about accessing free TVET in the public sector. All private institutions providing TVET charge fees.

FIGURE 3.7

Enrollments and completion rates for public TVET institutes in Sri Lanka, 2013–21

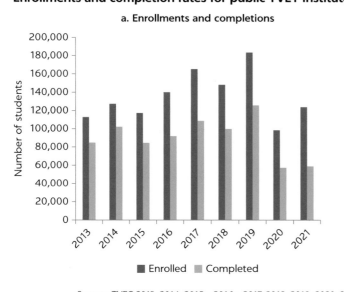
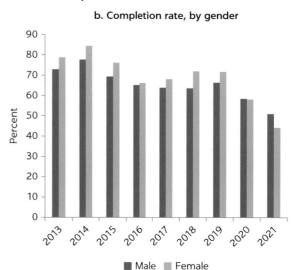

Sources: TVEC 2013, 2014, 2015a, 2016a, 2017, 2018, 2019, 2020, 2021a.
Note: TVET = technical and vocational education and training.

FIGURE 3.8

Enrollments and completion rates for private TVET institutes in Sri Lanka, 2013–21

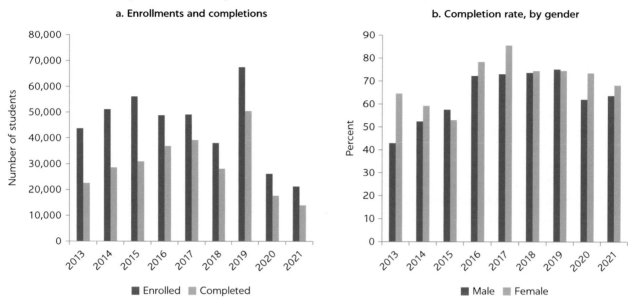

Sources: TVEC 2013, 2014, 2015a, 2016a, 2017, 2018, 2019, 2020, 2021a.
Note: TVET = technical and vocational education and training.

Enrollments of women in private TVET fell from 60 percent in 2013 to 46 percent in 2019 and slightly increased to 53 percent in 2020. In 2013, only 51 percent of students completed private programs, implying that 49 percent dropped out. By 2019, the completion rate was 75 percent. Completion rates for women rose considerably during 2013–19, from 43 to 75 percent. Due to the COVID-19 pandemic and lockdowns, the completion rate of women dropped to 62 percent, and thereafter slightly increased to 64 percent in 2021 (figure 3.8, panel b).

Student enrollments and completion rates in public and private TVET institutes vary considerably over time and across provinces (figure 3.9). During the 2017–21 period, across Sri Lanka the number of graduates with O/L school leaving certificates increased by about 7 percent (figure 3.9). However, during the same period, there was a decrease in both public sector (25 percent) and private sector (57 percent) TVET enrollments. Further, TVET completion rates also decreased by an average of 46 percent in public sector TVET institutions and a significant 65 percent in private sector ones. There were year-on-year variations between 2017–21 due to the types of programs being offered by the TVET institutions—short-term (three to six months) and long-term (some spanning one to two years). The increase in enrollments and completion numbers were always lower than during the base year 2017.

Public institutions for TVET

In 2019, in total 250,690 students were enrolled in public and private registered TVET institutions, and public institutions covered 73 percent of students enrolled in TVET. However, the total number of students enrolled reduced to 124,219 in 2020 due to the COVID-19 pandemic, and public institutions covered 79 percent of students enrolled. From 2015 to 2019, the share of public sector enrollment in public institutions increased 56 percent as the

FIGURE 3.9

GCE O/L completion and enrollments and completion rates for public and private TVET institutions in Sri Lanka, 2017–21

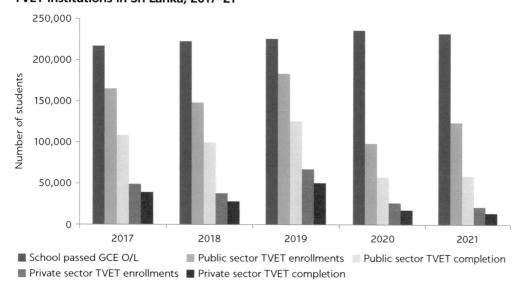

Sources: TVEC administrative information and original compilation for this publication; DoE 2021b; TVEC 2017, 2018, 2019, 2020, 2021a.
Note: GCE = General Certificate of Education; O/L = Ordinary Level; TVEC = Tertiary and Vocational Education Commission; TVET = technical and vocational education and training.

enrollments increased from 117,321 to 183,312. During the same period, the share of public sector enrollments increased from 68 percent to 73 percent. The total number of enrollments rose from 173,421 to 250,690 (45 percent) between 2015 and 2019; however, the public sector TVET expansion was higher than the total TVET enrollment expansion (figure 3.10). The number of public sector TVET graduates increased from 84,552 to 125,721 (49 percent) between 2015 and 2019, which is less than the percentage of public TVET enrollment expansion. There are several reasons for the reduction in the number of graduates:

- Public TVET institutions run longer programs.
- Students sought jobs before finishing TVET and so did not complete courses during this period.
- Students dropped out for various reasons (financial, family, and so on).

The central government supports more than 20 public TVET institutions—including the National Youth Services Council and the National Youth Corps—seven of which are financed by the SMSDVERI. Training agencies have centers scattered across the country.[8] In addition, provincial and local government agencies support a small number of regional centers across the country.

The seven main public institutions engaged in TVET are the Department of Technical Education and Training (DTET), National Apprentice and Industrial Training Authority (NAITA), Vocational Training Authority (VTA), Ceylon-German Technical Training Institute (CGTTI), Ocean University, University of Vocational Technology (UNIVOTEC, which includes university colleges), and Sri Lanka Institute of Printing (SLIOP). Of these, two—Ocean University and UNIVOTEC—were established recently. Four of the seven institutions grew between 2015 and 2019, with a 49 percent total increase in the number of

FIGURE 3.10

Enrollments in and graduates of public TVET institutions in Sri Lanka, 2012–21

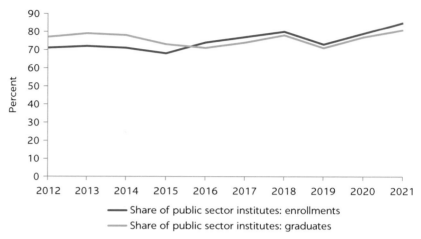

Sources: Original calculations for this publication based on TVEC 2012, 2013, 2014, 2015, 2016, 2017, 2018, 2019, 2020, 2021.
Note: TVET = technical and vocational education and training.

enrollments (table 3.3). UNIVOTEC expanded the most, with enrollments jumping 296 percent between 2015 and 2019 (although from a small base). University college enrollments increased 153 percent during that period. However, due to the COVID-19 pandemic, the TVET institutions were closed along with other educational institutions in 2019–20. Total enrollments dropped by 7 percentage points between 2019 and 2020, reflecting the effects of the COVID-19 pandemic. During the period 2015–21, enrollments increased on average by only 5 percentage points, signaling the skepticism in the quality and outcomes of the skills development system.

Provincial-level enrollments and completion in public and private sector TVET institutions

Student enrollments and completion rates in public and private TVET institutes vary considerably across provinces (figures 3.11a and 3.11b). The Western Province has the highest average percentage of students enrolled in both public (32 percent) and private (61 percent) TVET institutions, with the trend continuing from 2017 to 2020. During this period, the Western Province also registered the highest enrollments in private institutions. The Eastern, North Central, Sabaragamuwa, and Uva Provinces registered less than 2 percent of private TVET enrollments. Based on the number of students passing the GCE O/L, TVET enrollment and completion slightly increased in the public sector but decreased in the private sector institutions from 2020 to 2021. Overall, during the 2017 to 2021 period, enrollments in TVET public sector institutions decreased by 25 percent, with the Western Province also registering a 25 percent decline and the North Central Province registering a 35 percent drop.

The TVET public sector ecosystem also witnessed low completion rates over the 2017–21 period, with an average of 46 percent (figure 3.11c). The North Central Province registered a huge 66 percent decrease in completion rate; the North Western Province followed with a 60 percent drop, and the Western Province also saw a decline at 30 percent completion rate. The trend partly signaled the emerging post-COVID-19 pandemic problems:

TABLE 3.3 **Number of students in public TVET institutions in Sri Lanka, 2015–21**

INSTITUTION	NUMBER OF STUDENTS							TREND	% CHANGE, 2015–19	% CHANGE, 2019–20	% CHANGE, 2015–21
	2015	2016	2017	2018	2019	2020	2021				
Department of Technical Education and Training	19,864	26,591	39,910	32,151	42,657	24,950	25,550		115	−42	29
National Apprentice and Industrial Training Authority	22,555	31,907	32,668	32,327	29,989	14,210	16,977		33	−53	−25
Vocational Training Authority	28,745	31,585	36,695	36,654	37,936	24,604	33,375		32	−35	16
Ceylon-German Technical Training Institute	4,025	600	3,949	600	1,169	1,197	1,994		−71	2	−50
Ocean University (formerly National Institute of Fisheries and Nautical Engineering)	918	1,052	575	609	116	114	1,002		−87	−2	9
Sri Lanka Institute of Printing	1,113	901	1,084	967	930	—	—		−16	—	—
University of Vocational Technology (including university colleges)	799	1,781	2,927	3,093	3,161	1,904	2,999		296	−40	275
Total	**78,019**	**94,417**	**117,808**	**106,401**	**115,958**	**66,979**	**81,897**		**49**	**−42**	**5**

Sources: TVEC 2015, 2016, 2017, 2018, 2019, 2020, 2021.
Note: The TVEC *Labor Market Information Bulletin* for 2020 and for 2021 does not include enrollment data for the Sri Lanka Institute of Printing.
— = not available; TVET = technical and vocational education and training.

delays in graduation, increased time for TVET graduates to find jobs, and slower than anticipated return to students' physical attendance in the TVET public system.

In private sector TVET institutions, there was a 57 percent decrease in enrollments from 2017–21 (figure 3.11b). In the North Central and Northern Provinces, enrollments fell by 68 percent, whereas in the Southern Province alone, the average increase was a resounding 163 percent increase from 2017 to 2021. Private sector TVET institution enrollments decreased from 2019 to 2020 in all provinces except in the Northern Province, which showed an increase of 12 percent, especially during the height of the pandemic lockdowns in 2019 and 2020. Overall, completion rates in the private sector TVET institutions declined by 65 percent: The largest decline was in the Central and Northern Provinces (69 percent), closely followed by the North Western and Western Provinces, respectively (figure 3.11d). The Sabargamuwa Province seems to have fared well with completion rates, registering a decline of only about 12 percent. The Southern Province registered an improvement in completion by 208 percent from 2017 to 2021.

FIGURE 3.11

TVET public and private sectors: Enrollments and completions in Sri Lanka, by province, 2017–21

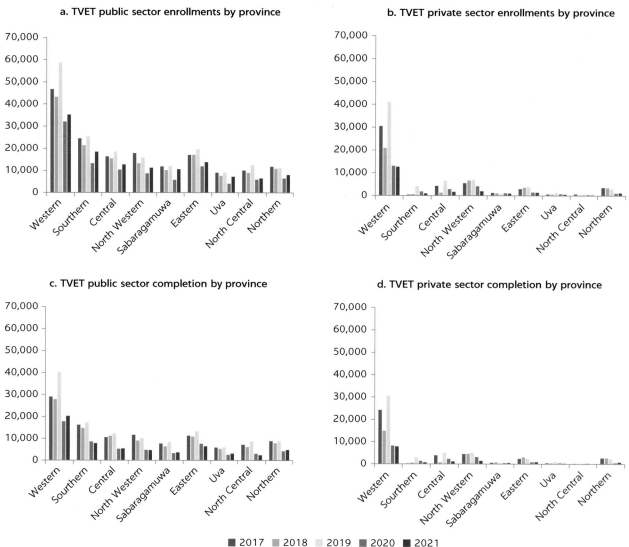

Spatial-level analysis of TVET enrollments and completion rates in Sri Lanka point to considerable disparities, with the Western Province matriculating the largest numbers and the Northern Province the fewest. This is likely due to the population spread of school-age children. The number of graduates with O/L school leaving certificates increased across the country except in the Northern Province, where it remained somewhat constant. The Western Province had the largest number of graduates with O/L certificates, followed by the Southern, Central, North Western, Sabaragamuwa, Eastern, Uva, North Central, and Northern Provinces (figure 3.12a).

Figure 3.11a shows the distribution of graduates with General Certificate in Examination (GCE) O/L by province. The O/L examinations link to five or more subjects, and the GCE O/L pass rates by province indicate that, in general, most students who take up the GCE O/L examination tend to pass the examination (figure 3.12b). However, the Southern and Western Provinces have the highest pass rates, whereas the Northern and North Central Provinces have slightly lower pass rates. All students, whether they pass the GCE O/L or not, are eligible to enroll in TVET programs, not just the matriculating numbers of students.

FIGURE 3.12

GCE O/L completion in Sri Lanka, by province, 2017–21

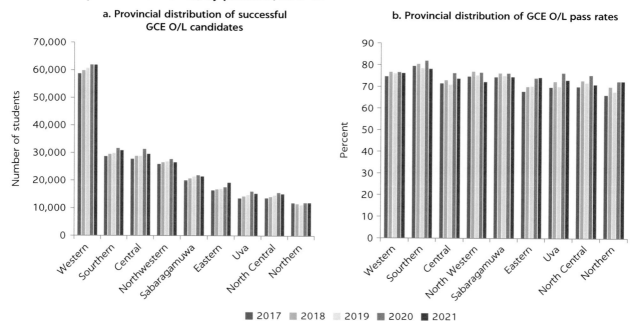

Bringing it all together

Overall, the public sector TVET landscape in Sri Lanka is characterized by fewer, larger, and more stable institutions; greater number of students enrolled; higher number of students; and TVET education being free. In comparison, the private sector TVET landscape has a different profile: more, smaller, and less stable institutions from a registration perspective; fewer students enrolled; fewer students graduating; and tuition fees. The quality of TVET education varies between the public and private sector institutions. Spatial analysis shows that TVET education at the provincial level shows significant variation: the largest numbers enrolled in the public sector institutions are in the Western Province, and the lowest are in the Northern Province. The same pattern is observable in the private sector institutions, except that the graduates are fewest in the North Central Province. The overall decline in enrollments and completion rates signal a growing crisis in Sri Lanka. With significant unutilized capacity in the existing public and private sector institutions, it would be appropriate for the government to take steps to introduce fundamental systemic reforms to transform the ecosystem to rescript the skill development policies to foster inclusion, facilitate recovery, and build resilience for the future. Future pandemic preparedness will depend on a new and robust ecosystem for skill development.

THE SHOCK OF THE COVID-19 PANDEMIC

Skills development is an essential medium-term imperative to mitigate the effects of COVID-19 on workers and their families. A key finding from the 2018 World Bank Sri Lanka Economic Update was that the Northern and Eastern Provinces have lower employment rates. At the time, there appeared to be no quick fixes. But a key recommendation was that to the extent that skills and access to finance are key constraints to households and firms, the same agenda as on the rest of the island should apply to the Northern and Eastern Provinces;

that is, investing in human and physical capital will raise productivity and better connect workers to more productive jobs.

As early as 2012, Sri Lanka's labor market was becoming polarized—with a decline in middle-skill occupations intensive in cognitive and manual skills and an increase both in high-skill occupations intensive in nonroutine cognitive and interpersonal skills and in low-skill occupations intensive in nonroutine manual skills. The number of direct jobs created by digital technologies is modest, but the number enabled by them can be large (World Bank 2016).

This finding is borne out by the challenges precipitated by COVID-19, which are demanding the sudden, intensive use of digital technologies and applications for delivering services such as education, health care, social protection, e-government, and financial services and banking.

The COVID-19 pandemic affected the entire education sector and the labor market. Although there was a gradual shift to offer online education, the learning losses remained very high. Student enrollments in TVET courses in all sectors decreased by nearly 50 percent, and completion was down by 57 percent (table 3.4). The human health and social work activities–related courses had the smallest reduction in enrollments, and completion rates were greatest in the wholesale, retail, and repair of motor vehicles and motorcycles courses.

As a result of the COVID-19 pandemic, enrollments in private sector TVET institutions decreased by almost 61 percent compared to public sector enrollments, which experienced a decline of 46 percent from 2019 to 2020 (table 3.5). Compared to 2019, both private and public sector enrollments further declined in 2021, and there were more men (51 percent) in private sector training institutes (66 percent) in 2020 than in 2019. However, these institutes could not attract more students. Also, compared to 2019, in 2020 more women than men (59 percent versus 56 percent) did not complete the courses for which they had enrolled. A similar pattern of reduction in completion could also be observed from 2019 to 2021. Similarly, more women in private sector training institutes did not complete courses (63 percent versus 57 percent in public sector training institutes).

TABLE 3.4 **Performance of TVEC–registered public and private sector training institutes in Sri Lanka, by industry sector, 2019 and 2020**

FIELD OF STUDY	REGISTERED			COMPLETED		
	2019	2020	% REDUCTION	2019	2020	% REDUCTION
Information and communication technology	53,144	25,079	53	40,044	15,293	62
Education	47,298	18,821	60	32,320	9,685	70
Construction	37,771	20,462	46	23,693	10,135	57
Manufacturing	21,432	12,988	39	15,858	9,151	42
Other service activities	18,900	10,105	47	15,240	6,716	56
Accommodation and food service activities	17,162	6,365	63	13,675	5,055	63
Professional, scientific, and technical activities	17,109	10,454	39	10,108	6,198	39
Wholesale and retail trade; repair of motor vehicles and motorcycles	17,089	10,049	41	9,843	6,268	36

continued

TABLE 3.4, *continued*

FIELD OF STUDY	REGISTERED			COMPLETED		
	2019	2020	% REDUCTION	2019	2020	% REDUCTION
Administrative and support service activities	5,155	2,260	56	4,027	1,792	56
Human health and social work activities	5,044	3,273	35	3,435	2,106	39
Agriculture, forestry, and fishing	4,980	2,987	40	3,037	1,261	58
Transportation and storage	4,467	1,095	75	3,958	851	78
Water supply, sewerage, waste management, and remediation activities	—	125	—	—	115	—
Activities of households as employers	—	108	—	—	58	—
Electricity, gas, steam, and air conditioning supply	—	25	—	—	25	—
Financial and insurance activities	422	—	—	422	—	—
Activities of extraterritorial organizations and bodies	363	16	96	89	3	97
Arts, entertainment, and recreation	354	207	42	331	216	35
Total	**250,690**	**124,419**	**50**	**176,080**	**74,928**	**57**

Sources: TVEC 2019, 2020; UN 2008.

Note: Industry sectors based on International Standard Industrial Classification of All Economic Activities (ISIC), Rev. 4 (UN 2008; see https://unstats.un.org/unsd/publication/seriesm/seriesm_4rev4e.pdf). — = data not available for the industry sector for the given year. TVEC = Tertiary and Vocational Education Commission.

TABLE 3.5 **Performance of TVEC-registered public and private sector training institutes in Sri Lanka, by gender, 2019–21**

TVET INSTITUTE CATEGORY	ENROLLMENT						COMPLETION					
	% REDUCTION, 2019–20			% REDUCTION, 2019–21			% REDUCTION, 2019–20			% REDUCTION, 2019–21		
	MALE	FEMALE	TOTAL	MALE	FEMALE	TOTAL	MALE	FEMALE	TOTAL	MALE	FEMALE	TOTAL
Public sector	46	47	46	41	20	32	53	57	54	55	51	53
Private sector	66	56	61	73	64	69	67	63	65	75	69	72
Total	**51**	**49**	**50**	**51**	**49**	**50**	**56**	**59**	**57**	**56**	**59**	**57**

Sources: TVEC 2019, 2020, 2021a and original compilation for this publication.

Note: TVEC = Tertiary and Vocational Education Commission; TVET = technical and vocational education and training.

THE FUTURE—AND CHALLENGES—OF DEVELOPING SKILLS IN SRI LANKA

In mid-2020, the president of Sri Lanka declared 2021–30 as the Decade of Skills Development. There is anticipation that this "would herald a transformational phase of educational reform and skills development for the nation in line with the government's national policy framework, *Vistas of Prosperity and Splendour*" (GoSL 2019).[9] The road map envisaged is to provide multiple reentry points into education pathways that encourage lifelong learning. *Vistas of Prosperity and Splendour* places significant emphasis on citizens' knowledge, skills, and capabilities as drivers of Sri Lanka's economic and social progress. The framework sets out the need to develop and execute an action plan on education that engineers the "creation of an environment that provides our youth and local entrepreneurs with new opportunities, gives everyone new hope and a sense of pride, where people can use their skills, talents and business acumen to be the world leaders in any field of their choice" (NEC 2022).

The president also launched the National Skills Passport on World Youth Day 2020. Youth with NVQ-level training and at least one year of related employment experience will receive the passport, which is a smart card linked to a dedicated online platform (nsp.gov.lk). The platform brings together employees, employers, qualification bodies, and labor market intermediaries. The passport is intended to address the long-standing issue of recognizing skilled workers with certified experience through a central online database. In addition, a Presidential Task Force on Sri Lanka's Education Affairs has been created to review the education system in line with national policies and develop an action plan for transformation.

Confronted with rapidly changing skills demands, Sri Lanka faces new challenges of skills shortages and mismatches in the labor market. Systemic issues contribute to skills constraints. Seven are discussed below.

- *Contradictions in policy intent and practice—the quantity-quality tradeoff.* As noted, in 2017, the government introduced free TVET in public institutions, creating a temporary surge in enrolled trainees. However, many dropped out within the first few weeks when learning expectations did not match the program content being offered. Therefore, the reported enrollments decreased, but many were not dedicated to completing their programs. Moreover, a chronic shortage of assessors has led to long wait times for assessments. Meanwhile, many students who have completed their programs have moved on to jobs without undertaking their final assessments. Free public TVET was intended to extend continuous education and lower entry barriers to employment. Instead, it has led to scarce resources being expended across a larger number of students. While economies of scale and scope might have been achieved to some extent, there might not be commensurate positive impact on TVET learning outcomes.

- *Disconnect between curricula in TVET institutes and job market demands.* Weak links with employers and industry—especially in designing curricula, developing training programs, fostering instructors' and teachers' professional development, establishing apprenticeships, and visiting with industry—explain part of the difference between the demand for and supply of skills. Although TVEC has taken steps to increase the market relevance of courses, there is a long way to achieve the full outcomes. Steps such as curricular updates and teacher development taken to enhance market relevance are a continuous process. More investments are needed in this sector to make all courses market relevant.

- *Lack of appropriately skilled workers.* With Sri Lanka's economic growth since 2009, the challenge of skills shortages has been exacerbated and will likely deepen as the country aspires to move toward high-income status. About 1 in 6 firms surveyed view the lack of well-trained workers as a major barrier to their productivity and growth (Dundar et al. 2017). Almost a third considered TVET skills to be most important when recruiting for mid-level and high-level technical positions. Yet few workers enter the job market with appropriate skills training.

Among the 450,000 students who take the GCE A/L exam each academic year, only 20 percent move on to higher education and only about a third enroll in TVET programs (Dundar et al. 2017). Those data indicate that almost half of students leave secondary schools with no opportunity for further education or training. In addition, female workforce participation was only about 35 percent in 2019 and further declined to 32 percent in 2020, further limiting the supply of trained labor and the prospects for higher returns from training and employing women (DCS 2019, 2020). Finally, the TVET system has failed to signal the importance of technical education to students and parents, who often undervalue technical skills in favor of general academic ones.

- *Nonalignment of training standards and competencies with labor market needs.* Progress on alignment has been very slow, further weakening the TVET system's links with employers' needs.
- *Shortage of qualified trainers.* TVET suffers from serious shortages of qualified instructors and teachers, especially those with industrial experience. Incentive structures for instructors' and teachers' career development and performance undermine their motivation and make it difficult to attract quality instructors and teachers. Moreover, the lack of modern equipment and facilities makes the teaching-learning environment challenging.
- *Nascent quality assurance system for private providers.* Many private TVET providers and courses are unregistered, unaccredited, or both.
- *Absence of systematized graduate tracer studies.* Regular tracking of TVET graduate outcomes and feedback mechanisms are largely missing.

RECOMMENDATIONS

Global evidence on short- and long-term TVET programs provides valuable insights for potential reforms of Sri Lanka's TVET system (Sánchez Puerta and others 2016; World Bank 2015). All skills development programs are different, with significant heterogeneity in content, duration, participant profiles, and contexts. Still, some factors are key to successful outcomes that make programs responsive to labor demand: high-quality content, flexible delivery modes, strong links with employers, and supportive labor market conditions. For quality, technical training combined with soft and life skills training contribute to the likelihood of program success. For delivery modes, combining classroom and workplace or practical training offers greater potential for success, as does training combined with support services for trainees—specifically, career counseling, mentoring, monitoring, job search, and placement assessment assistance.

For Sri Lanka to become globally competitive, young people require skills in three areas. The first is good working knowledge of English. A major factor that has shaped schooling in Sri Lanka has been the abolishment of English as a medium of instruction in schools since independence in 1948. Unlike in many Asian countries, most students in Sri Lanka—including those from the upper-middle classes—pursue general education in public schools in the national or vernacular language—Sinhala for the majority and Tamil for the minority (Aturupane and Little 2020). The second is digital skills, a key driver of economic growth and competitiveness in the 21st century. The third is good soft skills or transferable skills (SEAMEO 2014).

The Skills Development Program (SDP) supports both public and private education providers. With support from the government and development partners, the supply of skilled workers increased through the nine institutions overseen by the SDP. Although there was a decline in the number of TVET graduates in 2018, the figure was still higher than in the baseline year (2014) throughout the SDP implementation period—indicating an overall increase in the supply of skilled workers. However, it was COVID-19 that affected the TVET education system and the labor market.

Short- to medium-term recommendations are as follows:

- Promote TVET as a learning option for students at an early stage. Provide all students, parents, and society at large with the opportunities created and career paths for students. Communicate to all that skilling and reskilling are continuous processes.
- Enhance access to TVET by introducing and promoting all options to achieve qualifications and experience to become a productive worker.
- Further develop systems for the public, private, NGO, and workplace-based training providers to offer micro credentials or full certification to receive NVQ certification.
- Map the industry-demanded qualification systems for NVQ and SLQF.
- Further develop micro credentials and flexible learning options.
- Integrate English language, digital, and soft skills programs as part of all curricula.
- Give TVEC greater responsibility in registering centers, accrediting courses, and implementing "one TVET."
- Map all public sector TVET courses to NVQ and SLQF to facilitate lateral movement.
- Review teacher recruitment, development, and career path development options to promote teachers with more industrial experience.
- Continue to prepare Center Management Plans for all TVET training institutes to attract more students, maximize utilization of resources, enhance quality of courses, attract industry collaboration, and so forth.

ANNEX 3A: SNAPSHOT OF GOVERNANCE OF PUBLIC SECTOR VOCATIONAL TRAINING INSTITUTES

TABLE 3A.1 **Snapshot of governance of other public sector vocational training institutes**

NO.	NATIONAL OR STATE MINISTRY	INSTITUTE
1	State Ministry of Skills Development, Vocational Education, Research and Innovations	Department of Technical Education and Training, Vocational Training Authority, Ceylon–German Technical Training Institute, National Apprentice and Industrial Training Authority, Ocean University, university colleges, University of Vocational Technology
2	Ministry of Youth and Sports	National Youth Services Council, National Youth Corps
3	Ministry of Agriculture	District Agriculture Training Centers and other agricultural schools
4	State Ministry of Primary Health Care, Epidemics, and COVID Disease Control	Department of Social Services runs vocational training centers for people with special needs
5	Ministry of Tourism	Sri Lanka Institute of Tourism and Hotel Management
6	State Ministry of Foreign Employment Promotion and Market Diversification	Bureau of Foreign Employment

continued

TABLE 3A.1, *continued*

NO.	NATIONAL OR STATE MINISTRY	INSTITUTE
7	State Ministry of Rural Housing, Construction and Building Material Industries	Centre for Housing Planning and Building, Heavy Equipment Operator Training Center
8	Ministry of Labour	National Institute of Occupational Safety and Health
9	Ministry of Irrigation and Water Resources Management	International Training Institute of Irrigation and Water Management
10	Ministry of Shipping	Mahapola Ports and Maritime Academy
11	State Ministry of Batik, Handloom, and Local Apparel Products	Sri Lanka Institute of Textile and Apparel
12	State Ministry of Gem and Jewellery Related Industries	Gem and Jewellery Research and Training Institute
13	State Ministry of Provincial Councils and Local Government (Colombo Municipal Council)	Abdul Hameed Vocational Training Centre, Public Assistant Department Training Centre
14	Ministry of Power	Ceylon Electricity Board Technical Training Center
15	State Ministry of Provincial Councils and Local Government	Various provincial councils run small-scale carpentry training institutes
16	State Ministry of Provincial Councils and Local Government (Provincial Ministry of Education)	Various provincial schools run computer resource centers
17	State Ministry of Coconut, Kithul, Palmyrah and Rubber Cultivation Promotion and Related Industrial Product Manufacturing and Export Diversification	Coconut Development Training Center
18	State Ministry of Cooperative Services, Marketing Development and Consumer Protection	National Institute of Co-operative Development
19	Ministry of Plantation	National Institute of Plantation Management
20	Ministry of Wildlife and Forest Conservation	Sri Lanka Forestry Institute
21	Ministry of Transport	Sri Lanka German Railway Technical Training Centre
22	State Ministry of Samurdhi, Household Economy, Micro Finance, Self Employment, Business Development and Underutilized State Resources Development	National Institute of Social Development
23	Ministry of Defence	Army Service Corp Training School, Sri Lanka Army Volunteer Force Training Center, In-Service Training Institute
24	Ministry of Industries	Industrial Development Board

Sources: Tertiary and Vocational Education Commission and original compilation for this publication.

NOTES

1. This includes students who entered public and private schools. Data for pirivena schools' admissions for grade 1 are not available.
2. The Cabinet of Ministers approved the minimum age for employment to 16 years of age and for hazardous work minimum age to 18 years of age (https://www.dailynews.lk/2021/09/29 /political/260543/cabinet-decisions).
3. Per review of original list of subjects in call for applications in 2021, as announced in "Application: GCE A/L Vocational Stream 2021," https://www.guruwaraya.lk/2021/10 /application-gce-al-vocational-stream.html.
4. For more information about SLIATE, see http://www.sliate.ac.lk/ (accessed December 26, 2021).
5. ISO 9001:2008 and SLS IWA 2: 2007. Guidelines for the Application of ISO 9001:2008 in Education.
6. The Sri Lanka Standards Institution and International Workshop Agreement 2:2007 *Guidelines for the Application of ISO 9001:2008 in Education* sets forth required procedures for training institutes.
7. See https://www.tvec.gov.lk/?page_id=2764 (accessed December 31, 2021).

8. For example, the Department of Technical Education and Training (DTET) has 38 training colleges and colleges of technology in 23 districts. The Vocational Training Authority has 216 training centers (8 national vocational training centers, 22 district training centers, and 186 rural training centers).

9. See https://www.un.int/srilanka/news/president-declares-2021-%E2%80%93-2030 -decade-skills-development and https://sundaytimes.lk/online/news-online/2021-2030 -declared-as-the-decade-of-skills-development/2-1122216.

REFERENCES

Aturupane, H., and Angela Little. 2020. "General Education in Sri Lanka." In *Handbook of Education Systems in South Asia*, edited by P. M. Sarangapani and R. Pappu. Springer Nature Singapore. https://doi.org/10.1007/978-981-13-3309-5_18-1.

CBSL (Central Bank of Sri Lanka). 2022. *Annual Report*. Colombo. https://www.cbsl.gov.lk/en /publications/economic-and-financial-reports/annual-reports/annual-report-2020.

DCS (Department of Census and Statistics). 2019. *Labour Force Survey Report 2019*. Colombo.

DCS (Department of Census and Statistics). 2020. *Labour Force Survey Report 2020*. Colombo.

Department of Government Printing. 2020. *Extraordinary Gazette 2196/27-6 October 2020*. Colombo.

Department of Government Printing. 2021. *Extraordinary Gazette 2209/14-4 January 2021*. Colombo.

DoE (Department of Examination). 2012a. *GCE Ordinary Level: Performance of Candidates Report 2012*. Battaramulla, Sri Lanka.

DoE (Department of Examination). 2012b. *GCE Advanced Level: Performance of Candidates Report 2012*. Battaramulla, Sri Lanka.

DoE (Department of Examination). 2015a. *GCE Ordinary Level: Performance of Candidates Report 2015*. Battaramulla, Sri Lanka.

DoE (Department of Examination). 2015b. *GCE Advanced Level: Performance of Candidates Report 2015*. Battaramulla, Sri Lanka.

DoE (Department of Examination). 2017a. *GCE Ordinary Level: Performance of Candidates Report 2017*. Battaramulla, Sri Lanka.

DoE (Department of Examination). 2017b. *GCE Advanced Level: Performance of Candidates Report 2017*. Battaramulla, Sri Lanka.

DoE (Department of Examination). 2018a. *GCE Ordinary Level: Performance of Candidates Report 2018*. Battaramulla, Sri Lanka.

DoE (Department of Examination). 2018b. *GCE Advanced Level: Performance of Candidates Report 2018*. Battaramulla, Sri Lanka.

DoE (Department of Examination). 2019a. *GCE Ordinary Level: Performance of Candidates Report 2019*. Battaramulla, Sri Lanka.

DoE (Department of Examination). 2019b. *GCE Advanced Level: Performance of Candidates Report 2021*. Battaramulla, Sri Lanka.

DoE (Department of Examination). 2020a. *GCE Ordinary Level: Performance of Candidates Report 2020*. Battaramulla, Sri Lanka.

DoE (Department of Examination). 2020b. *GCE Advanced Level: Performance of Candidates Report 2021*. Battaramulla, Sri Lanka.

DoE (Department of Examination). 2021a. *GCE Advanced Level: Performance of Candidates Report 2021*. Battaramulla, Sri Lanka.

DoE (Department of Examination). 2021b. *GCE Ordinary Level: Performance of Candidates Report 2021*. Battaramulla, Sri Lanka.

Dundar, Halil, Benoît Millot, Michelle Riboud, Mari Shojo, Harsha Aturupane, Sangeeta Goyal, and Dhushyanth Raju. 2017. *Sri Lanka Education Sector Assessment: Achievements, Challenges, and Policy Options*. Directions in Development. Washington, DC: World Bank. doi:10.1596/978-1-4648-1052-7.

GoSL (Government of Sri Lanka). 2019. *Vistas of Prosperity and Splendour.* Colombo: Ministry of Finance, Treasury of Sri Lanka.

MoE (Ministry of Education). 2012. *Annual School Census of Sri Lanka: Final Report 2021.* Battaramulla, Sri Lanka.

MoE (Ministry of Education). 2015. *Annual School Census of Sri Lanka: Final Report, 2015.* Colombo.

MoE (Ministry of Education). 2018. *Annual School Census of Sri Lanka: Final Report, 2018.* Colombo.

MoE (Ministry of Education). 2019. *Annual School Census of Sri Lanka: Final Report, 2019.* Colombo.

MoE (Ministry of Education). 2020. *Annual School Census of Sri Lanka: Final Report 2020.* Battaramulla, Sri Lanka.

MoE (Ministry of Education). 2021a. *Annual School Census of Sri Lanka: Final Report, 2021.* Battaramulla, Sri Lanka.

MoE (Ministry of Education). 2021b. "Advanced Level Vocational Stream: Call for Applications for Grade 12 Admissions—2021." Battaramulla, Sri Lanka.

MoF (Ministry of Finance). 2021. *Budget Estimates.* Book III. Colombo, Sri Lanka.

NEC (National Education Commission). 2022. *National Education Policy Framework (2020–2030).* Colombo, Sri Lanka.

NIE (National Institute of Education). 2018. "Proposed New Educational Reforms and Related Opinion Survey 2018." Department of Research and Development, National Institute of Education. Maharagama, Colombo.

Sánchez Puerta, Maria Laura, Alexandria Valerio, and Marcela Gutiérrez Bernal. 2016. *Taking Stock of Programs to Develop Socioemotional Skills: A Systematic Review of Program Evidence.* Directions in Development. Washington, DC: World Bank. doi:10.1596/978-1-4648-0872-2.

SEAMEO (Southeast Asian Ministers of Education Organization). 2014. "Integration of Transferable Skills in TVET Curriculum, Teaching-Learning, and Assessment." Final Report of the Workshop Organised by SEAMEO VOCTECH in collaboration with the British Council, British High Commission Singapore, and UNESCO Bangkok. https://www .voced.edu.au/content/ngv%3A65805.

TVEC (Tertiary & Vocational Education Commission). 2012. *Labour Market Information Bulletin.* Volume II. Colombo.

TVEC (Tertiary and Vocational Education Commission). 2013. *Labour Market Information Bulletin.* Vol. II. Colombo.

TVEC (Tertiary and Vocational Education Commission). 2014. *Labour Market Information Bulletin.* Vol. II. Colombo.

TVEC (Tertiary and Vocational Education Commission). 2015a. *Labour Market Information Bulletin.* Vol. II. Colombo.

TVEC (Tertiary and Vocational Education Commission). 2015b. *Sri Lanka Qualifications Framework.* Colombo: University Grants Commission.

TVEC (Tertiary and Vocational Education Commission). 2016a. *Labour Market Information Bulletin.* Vol. II. Colombo.

TVEC (Tertiary and Vocational Education Commission). 2016b. *National Vocational Qualifications of Sri Lanka: Operations Manual.* 2016 update. Colombo.

TVEC (Tertiary and Vocational Education Commission). 2017. *Labour Market Information Bulletin.* Vol. II. Colombo.

TVEC (Tertiary and Vocational Education Commission). 2018. *Labour Market Information Bulletin.* Vol. II. Colombo.

TVEC (Tertiary and Vocational Education Commission). 2019. *Labour Market Information Bulletin.* Vol. II. Colombo.

TVEC (Tertiary and Vocational Education Commission). 2020. *Labour Market Information Bulletin.* Vol. II. Colombo.

TVEC (Tertiary and Vocational Education Commission). 2021a. *Labour Market Information Bulletin.* Vol. II. Colombo.

TVEC (Tertiary and Vocational Education Commission). 2021b. *National Vocational Qualifications of Sri Lanka: Operations Manual.* Colombo.

UGC. (University Grants Commission). 2015. *Sri Lanka Qualifications Framework.* Nugegoda: Government of Sri Lanka, University Grants Commission. https://www.eugc.ac.lk/qac/downloads/SLQF_2016_en.pdf.

UGC. (University Grants Commission). 2021. *Annual Report.* Colombo.

UN (United Nations). 2008. "International Standard Industrial Classification of All Economic Activities (ISIC), Rev. 4." *Statistical Papers* (4): Rev.4. New York: United Nations. https://unstats.un.org/unsd/publication/seriesm/seriesm_4rev4e.pdf.

World Bank. 2015. "Labor Market Impacts and Effectiveness of Five Skills Development Programs in India: Assam, Andhra Pradesh, Madhya Pradesh, Odisha, Rajasthan." Report no. 94682-IN. World Bank, Washington, DC. https://documents1.worldbank.org/curated/en/798601468034846280/pdf/94682-Change-in-Title-Final-Revised-Output-Skill-Report-5-States.pdf.

World Bank. 2016. *World Development Report 2016: Digital Dividends.* Washington, DC: World Bank. https://www.worldbank.org/en/publication/wdr2016.

World Bank. 2018. "Sri Lanka—General Education Modernization Project." World Bank, Washington, DC. https://documents.worldbank.org/curated/en/480271524967257414/Sri-Lanka-General-Education-Modernization-Project.

World Bank. 2020. "Sri Lanka—Skills Development Project." World Bank, Washington, DC. https://documents.worldbank.org/curated/en/160691592858430513/Sri-Lanka-Skills-Development-Project.

4 Governance, Quality Assurance, and Relevance of Technical and Vocational Education and Training

INTRODUCTION

This chapter assesses a range of policies, regulations, strategies, and challenges for advancing technical and vocational education and training (TVET) in Sri Lanka. Ensuring the quality and promoting the relevance of TVET are key regulatory powers vested with the Tertiary and Vocational Education Commission (TVEC). TVEC was established by the Tertiary and Vocational Education Act 20 of 1990, as amended in 1999. The commission has three main mandates:

- Planning, coordinating, and developing TVET at all levels in keeping with Sri Lanka's human resource needs;
- Developing nationally recognized systems for granting tertiary education awards and vocational education awards including certificates and other academic distinctions; and
- Maintaining academic and training standards in TVET institutes, agencies, and all other establishments providing it.

As one of the main steps toward fulfilling these mandates, the National Vocational Qualifications (NVQ) framework was established in 2004 as the unified qualification system for TVET. The framework

- Serves as a unified qualification framework that is recognized domestically and understood internationally;
- Responds to industry competency needs;
- Enhances the quality, relevance, performance, effectiveness, efficiency, and transparency of TVET;
- Develops progressive qualifications for career advancement;
- Provides convenient, flexible access to TVET for potential training seekers;
- Improves international links and recognition; and
- Promotes an education and training culture focused on responsiveness and excellence.

TVEC is responsible for developing and implementing the NVQ framework with the active participation of all public and private TVET providers (see chapter 3). The main components of NVQ implementation are as follows:

- Developing national competency standards (NCS) in consultation with industry counterparts
- Developing competency-based training (CBT) curricula based on NCS
- Delivering training based on those curricula using appropriate resources (physical and human), infrastructure, environment, training methods, and technology
- Assessing student performance (formative assessment)
- Conducting competency-based assessment (summative assessment)
- Issuing NVQ certification.

These processes undergo quality assurance protocols. Implementing such a system across the entire TVET system gives rise to many issues that need to be addressed.

POLICIES FOR ENSURING TVET QUALITY AND RELEVANCE

Several policies, materials, and guidelines for TVET quality and relevance were reviewed:

- *Tertiary and Vocational Education Act 20 of 1990 and 1999 amendment.* The Tertiary and Vocational Education Act 20 of 1990, as amended in 1999, defines the statutory provisions for quality assurance of TVET on which many programs and systems have been developed and implemented to ensure quality training. The Development Plan 887/8 of 1995 specifies the criteria, conditions, and procedures for registering training institutions under the act. In addition, people who provide training courses can register with TVEC under the same provisions. Registered institutions are required to submit training information to TVEC twice a year for planning and development purposes.
- *National Vocational Qualifications operations manual of 2009* (TVEC 2009). The operations manual was published in 2005 and was amended in November 2009, 2016, and 2021. It sets general policy related to implementation of the NVQ framework as the unified qualification certification system for TVET in Sri Lanka. The manual describes the policy for developing NCS, preparing curricula, preparing assessment materials, conducting competency-based assessments, installing quality management systems, and implementing the NVQ framework.
- *National Policy Framework on Higher Education and Technical and Vocational Education of 2009 and Tertiary and Vocational Education Policy of 2018.* Policies and strategies on quality assurance, assessment, and accreditation for TVET are defined in part III of the National Policy Framework on Higher Education and Technical and Vocational Education. The policy emphasizes the adoption of good practices for delivering TVET including training of training center managers and grading of centers. The policy requires all training providers to be registered with TVEC to ensure quality TVET. For accreditation of courses, it requires that all TVET institutions establish an accreditation and quality assurance framework.

The policy requires that institutions be "recognized" to make them eligible to conduct competency-based assessments for the award of NVQ certificates. Development of NCS based on labor market indicators is also in progress—paving the way to accredit courses and assess competencies for awarding NVQ certificates. Awarding of NVQ certificates through the recognition of prior learning (RPL) by experienced workers is also progressing but needs to be expanded.

NCS and curriculum development

NCS specify the competencies that a person must acquire to get qualified and obtain NVQ for a job in a specific industry sector. Because NVQ is the unified qualification in TVET, many public and private sector training institutions—as well as those related to foreign employment—request the NVQ certificate. Training institutions also request accreditation in keeping with the NVQ framework for their programs and courses. Yet, NCS and curricula for many occupations and industry sectors are not available to cater to these demands. NCS and curricula are supposed to be updated regularly to keep abreast of technologies and labor market demands. However, for logistical reasons, it takes a long time to develop new or revise existing standards and curricula.

Under the 2009 NVQ operations manual (TVEC 2009), TVEC identifies occupations to develop NCS, and the National Apprentice and Industrial Training Authority (NAITA) develops them. NAITA develops draft standards, validates them through National Industrial Training Advisory Committees (NITACs, known as skills councils), and forwards them to TVEC for endorsement. The University of Vocational Technology (UNIVOTEC) is responsible for developing competency-based training curricula. The university conducts task analysis workshops, develops curricula, and forwards them to NITAC for validation. By August 2023, TVEC had developed and published 427 national competency standards under the NVQ framework. The list of NCS included 335 level 1 to 4 and 92 level 5 to 6 standards, with the largest number of competency standards (77) being in the manufacturing sector.

National competency standards are developed for occupations identified based on the labor market demands. The standards describe the knowledge, skills, and attitudes needed to perform in a particular occupation and are essential to developing competency-based standard curricula and competency-based assessment resources.

Multiple issues and challenges are involved in these processes:

- Due to the thorough analysis of competency profiles, it takes a long time to develop and revise NCS and curricula.
- Because NCS and curricula are developed by two institutions and two industry panels, there are mismatches between curricula for NCS and competency-based standards.
- Only core technical competencies are included in NCS. Competencies including soft skills and employability skills have not been adequately identified.
- There are difficulties in obtaining services resource persons for services representing a cross-section of industry—from micro to large enterprises—for NCS and curriculum development.

Policy development and implementation goals

The National Policy on Technical and Vocational Education of 2018 includes several policy directives for enhancing relevance and quality of TVET programs. Under Policy 28, development and revision processes for NCS need to be analyzed and mechanisms developed to shorten the time period for development and revision. International best practices could inform the processes. Under Policy 29, institutions responsible for developing curricula for NCS and competency-based standards need to be broadly based and have good links to industry. These institutions must be assigned the capacity to oversee these needs in addition to NAITA and UNIVOTEC.

Policy strategies

Strategies for implementing these policies include the following:

- Developing guidelines for NCS and curricula for process management and facilitation based on international best practices.
- Strengthening the capacity of state training institutions for developing NCS and curricula.
- Delegating the development of NCS and curricula to institutions with clear guidance and sound monitoring systems.
- Harmonizing the duration of courses at the same level. Minimum durations need to be introduced for at least NVQ level 4 courses.
- Including employability modules such as entrepreneurship, green concepts, communication skills, and information technology (IT) for all training programs.

POLICIES FOR COMPETENCY-BASED ASSESSMENTS AND NVQ CERTIFICATION

Competency-based assessments gather evidence and make judgments on whether applicants have achieved the knowledge, skills, and attitudes specified by the NCS. Assessments are conducted by trained, registered NVQ assessors. With the rising demand for NVQ assessments and certificates, the existing pool of assessors cannot keep up with the need for assessments of public and private institutions. Demand for NVQ through RPL is also growing, exerting more pressures and leading to delays and, sometimes, inconsistencies in assessments. Issues include the following:

- Nominating assessors to conduct assessments takes a long time, causing delays. There are also delays in payments to assessors, leading some to refuse to conduct them. Moreover, some institutions and assessors do not submit results in a timely way, and there are 3- to 12-month delays in issuing certificates.
- There is a lack of a common procedure for submitting applications that recognize prior learning.
- Some assessors are not sufficiently updated on NCS assessment rules and regulations.
- The assessor database is not up-to-date, so some inactive assessors are still in it.

- Assessors are not available for some occupations in the language of assessment (Tamil and English) and in some geographic areas.
- Assessment materials are insufficiently developed, improved, and updated.
- Institutions have to pay large fees to TVEC for exams at the end of semesters.
- There is no proper mechanism for obtaining recognized certificates (records of achievement) for certain units of NCS. In addition, there is no mechanism for obtaining full NVQ certification for people who have obtained records of achievement.
- Some assessors conduct common theory tests instead of eligibility tests for competency-based assessments.
- Assessments are inconsistent, with unclear data on the number of students and units assessed per day and no mechanism for verifying and auditing assessments.

Policy development and implementation goals

The National Policy on Technical and Vocational Education of 2018 includes several policy directives for enhancing relevance and quality of TVET programs. Under Policy 28, development and revision processes for NCS need to be analyzed and mechanisms developed to shorten the time period for development and revision. International best practices need to be sought. Under Policy 29, institutions responsible for developing curricula for NCS and competency-based standards need to be broadly based and have good links to industry. These institutions need to be assigned the capacity to oversee these needs in addition to NAITA and UNIVOTEC.

Policy strategies

Efforts on competency-based assessments and NVQ certification could accomplish the following goals:

- Establish a system for verifying formative assessment results and auditing competency assessments to improve the validity and reliability of the assessments.
- Create systems to conduct assessment-related administrative and coordination activities efficiently and effectively.
- Increase the number of competency-based assessors, based on the demand by occupation, medium of assessment, and geographic distribution of training programs.
- Take steps to increase the share of industry-based assessors from 20 to 80 percent over the next five years.
- Prepare computerized assessor selection software that enables training institutes to select assessors as needed.
- Develop an annual assessment calendar based on available training programs.
- Foster sound mechanisms for monitoring, verifying, and auditing assessments.
- Prepare questions and conduct theory tests, if required, to ensure consistent assessments.

- Develop guidelines for preparing portfolios of evidence required to assess RPL.
- Formalize records of achievement to increase recognition.
- Create procedures for people with records of achievement to obtain full NVQ certification.

REGULATIONS FOR ENSURING TVET QUALITY AND RELEVANCE

The three main regulatory tools that TVEC uses to ensure TVET relevance and quality are registering training institutions, accrediting courses, and installing quality management systems. Although it is mandatory for TVET institutions to register with TVEC, some providers conduct training programs without doing so—putting trainees at a disadvantage because unregistered providers are not legally accepted.

The Tertiary and Vocational Education Act 20 of 1990 requires that institutions register with TVEC if they provide TVET, including training (section 14); courses in tertiary and vocational education, including training specified by the government (section 15); or examination conferment or granting of TVET certificates or training awards (section 16). Public and private providers of tertiary education, TVET, and training are expected to comply with these regulatory requirements. An institute can award NVQ if all three criteria have been satisfied and accepted by TVEC. These regulatory processes are required to be clearly formulated, unambiguous, and efficiently executed for training institutes to comply with the requirements.

In recent years the number of institutes having registered and received accreditation from TVEC has fallen. Several prevalent issues need to be resolved for proper implementation of quality assurance measures:

- Weak guidelines for registration, accreditation, and quality management systems
- Cumbersome procedures for renewal of registration
- Delays in new registration and accreditation processes that demoralize TVET providers
- Training providers and instructors consider quality management systems a burden due to the complexity of the process
- Inadequate public awareness of registered institutions and accredited courses
- Lack of a proper mechanism to assign accreditation assessors based on subject specialty
- Closing registered institutions and moving to other locations or complete discontinuation of courses or programs.

Regulation development and implementation goals

Under Policy 32, TVEC is required to implement regulatory processes in a simple but effective, fair way. Under Policy 33, TVET institutions are required to conduct employment-oriented courses with accreditation and issue NVQ certificates when relevant standards are available. Under Policy 34, a legal environment needs to be established to facilitate implementation of the NVQ framework.

Regulation strategies

Regulations on TVET quality and relevance are required to do the following:

- Work with local governments to identify unregistered TVET institutions.
- Introduce a legal framework for a prior registration system, where a potential training provider can seek registration from TVEC before establishing itself.
- Encourage and facilitate accreditation of TVET courses.
- Introduce a code of practice for quality assurance systems and inculcate a quality culture in TVET.
- Strengthen the accreditation of assessors based on subject specialty.
- Enact legal provisions for effective implementation of the NVQ framework.

FURTHER DEVELOPMENT OF THE NVQ FRAMEWORK

The NVQ framework, with seven levels of qualifications, was established in 2004 under the provisions of the Tertiary and Vocational Education Act. The framework's qualification descriptors were adopted from New Zealand's Qualifications Framework. All supporting systems were created for competency standard development, curriculum development, competency-based training, and assessment of competencies. In 2009, the Sri Lanka Qualifications Framework (SLQF) was developed to cover all qualifications—from general education to doctoral degrees— and the NVQ framework was mapped to the SLQF. The SLQF was revised in 2015 and transfer of programs and learners from the NVQ framework to the SLQF and vice versa were clearly established. Students can move from NVQ level 7, which is equivalent to SLQF degree level, on to a master's program.

Processes for the NVQ framework's operations were established early on and evolved to cater to developing TVET requirements. The system needs to be continuously enhanced to reflect the country's emerging human resource development needs.

The NVQ framework consists of four certificate levels, two diploma levels, and one bachelor's degree (see chapter 3). To receive the two diplomas, students must earn 60 and 120 European Credit Transfer and Accumulation System (ECTS) credits[1]; the bachelor's degree requires 180 credits. Certificates do not use a credit system, and the duration of training for different occupations may vary for different certificate levels.

Two types of groups (in addition to school leavers) seek employment-oriented education and training. The first are employed workers seeking formal vocational qualifications through the NVQ without disrupting their employment. This group is required to be given the opportunity to accumulate competencies and obtain qualifications, whether certificates, diplomas, or a degree. The second group is diploma or degree holders in other disciplines— such as arts and humanities—who wish to acquire employment-oriented education and training that matches their education level. These study programs may be shorter but need to comply with more advanced learning descriptors.

Policy development and implementation goals

Under Policy 35 of TVET Policy 2018, mechanisms and procedures in the NVQ framework are required to be established to award all levels of qualifications using a modular approach for workers employed in the industry involved. Under Policy 36, the NVQ framework needs to be amended, where appropriate, to award certificates or similar qualifications for higher NVQ levels.

Strategies for policy implementation

- Training centers are required to offer training programs on a modular basis and at convenient times for workers.
- The knowledge component of training needs to be delivered through open and distance learning.
- Mechanisms and procedures need to be established for issuance of records of achievement and the award of the final qualification.
- The NVQ framework needs to be amended—in line with international best practices—to award certificates or similar qualifications leading to higher NVQ levels (diplomas and degree). Annex 4A provides examples from Australia and India.
- A campaign needs to be launched to attract graduates with fewer employment opportunities to pursue employment-oriented, higher-level TVET.

OTHER EFFORTS ON QUALITY ASSURANCE

TVET quality assurance functions comprise many components, several of which are discussed above and others below: policy development and planning, industry relations, registration of training institutions, accreditation of courses, monitoring of institutions, student assessments, NCS and learning resources, and quality audits (see also chapter 3).

Policy development and planning

The National Education Commission has a mandate to prepare all education policies and advise the president of Sri Lanka. The State Ministry of Skills Development, Vocational Education, Research and Innovations (SMSDVERI), in charge of vocational education and skills development, helps prepare quality assurance policies. TVET quality assurance is governed by policies, plans, and guidelines such as the following:

- The NVQ manual of 2005, as revised in 2009, 2016, and 2021 (the 2016 version was not published; the revised version was published in 2021)
- The TVET Development Plan of 1995 (the amended version of 2020 was not published)
- The Quality Management System manual
- Provincial vocational education training plans
- Industry-based vocational education plans
- Guidelines and circulars on registration, assessment, RPL, and issuance of NVQ, among other aspects.

Industry relations

Close collaboration between TVET and employers is required to make training more relevant to industry needs. Industry input is sought to develop and validate

NCS, identify training needs, facilitate on-the-job training for students, and design apprenticeship options for work-study. To foster training and industry collaboration, TVEC has initiated two formal approaches to enhance quality:

- *Industry skills councils.* Four industry skills councils were created under the Companies Act (2007) in construction, tourism and hospitality, information and communication technology (ICT), and manufacturing and engineering. In addition, the health and automobile industries are setting up skills councils.
- *National Industrial Training Advisory Committees (NITACs).* These councils are constituted as interfaces or links between NAITA and different industry sectors. Each NITAC has a governing council. There are 27 such councils. The councils are required to have at least 60 percent industry representation and to help develop competency standards; validate course materials; and prepare standardized assessments, question banks, and evaluation materials.

Registration of training institutions

Registration of institutions with TVEC is the first step in ensuring the quality of TVET. Under the Tertiary and Vocational Education Act 20 of 1990, training providers are required to register if they offer tertiary or vocational education (clause 14), courses in tertiary or vocational education (clause 15), or examinations conferring or granting certificates or awards (clause 16). The Development Plan of 1995 covers policies, procedures, and criteria for the registration of training institutions.

Before providing training, training institutions are required to obtain a preregistration letter from TVEC. The application can be submitted through TVEC's website. Registration applications need to include details on the

- Management of the institution;
- Basic facilities and physical resources;
- Selection and guidance processes for students;
- Teaching process, including courses, curricula and syllabi, teaching methods, equipment, tools and materials, number of instructors and teachers, their qualifications, and testing and certification requirements; and
- Factors influencing internal and external efficiency of training programs.

Application processing fees are LKR 1,500 (about US$7) for public training institutes and twice that for private, nongovernmental organization (NGO), and other training institutes. Documentation is reviewed by evaluation panels appointed by TVEC and, if it is deemed satisfactory, the panels visit sites. Any deficiencies identified are communicated to the applicants for them to submit amended applications. Once satisfied, evaluation panels prepare evaluation reports to TVEC for approval. Registration certificates are valid for two years. Renewal applications are required to be sent to TVEC at least three months before registration certificates expire. Institutions that fail to renew registrations before the expiration date are shown as having expired registrations on TVEC's website. Thus, the number of registered training institutes varies over time (figure 4.1).

Data for February 2022 through December 2022 show the variation in the number of registered public, private, and other (NGO, charity) training institutes (figure 4.2). Approximately 45 percent of public, 50 percent of private, and 5 percent of other agencies own active registered training institutes as of December 2022.

FIGURE 4.1

Number of registered training institutes in Sri Lanka, 2013–22

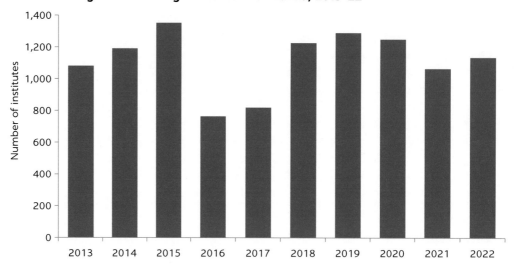

Source: Tertiary and Vocational Education Commission administrative data.

FIGURE 4.2

Number of registered training institutes in Sri Lanka, by type of institute, February–December 2022

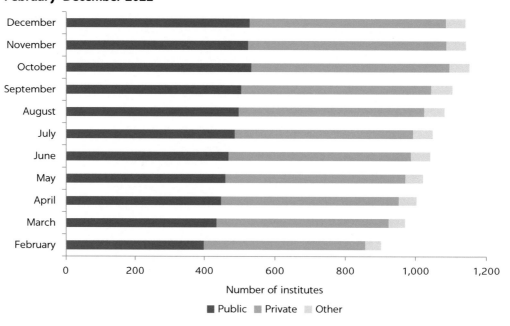

Source: Tertiary and Vocational Education Commission administrative data.
Note: Data reported are as of month end.

When considering the last 25 years, approximately 3,460 institutes have registered with TVEC. However, as of August 2023, there were approximately 1,371 training institutes with active registration. The number of registered training institutes is highest in the Western Province and lowest in the Uva Province, followed by the North Central Province (figure 4.3, panel a). A similar pattern can be seen among active registered institutions, with the highest number of active institutes in the Western Province, followed by the Central Province. The lowest number of active registered training centers was in Uva Province, followed by the North Central Province (figure 4.3, panel b).

The analysis of training institutes continuing to maintain active registration status indicates that the highest number of discontinuations was in the Western Province followed by the Southern Province. The highest discontinuation was in the private sector training institutions (figure 4.4). The reasons for inactivity

FIGURE 4.3

Registered training institutes in Sri Lanka, by province and ownership

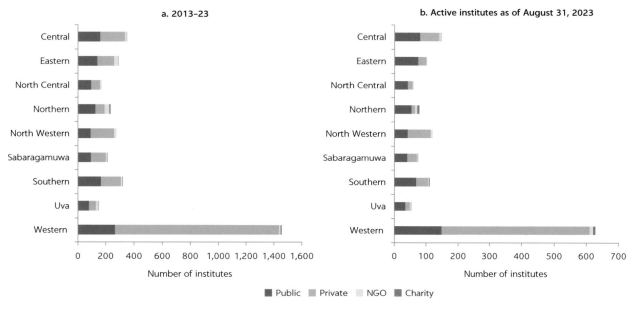

Source: Tertiary and Vocational Education Commission administrative data.
Note: NGO = nongovernmental organization.

FIGURE 4.4

Number of inactive registered training institutes in Sri Lanka, by province and type of institute, 1995–2023

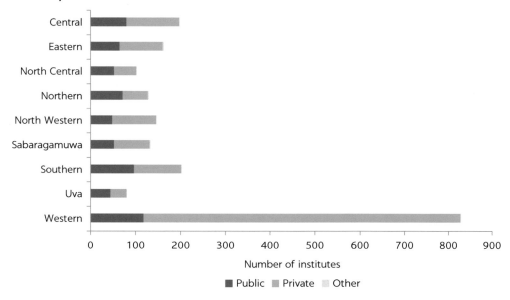

Source: Tertiary and Vocational Education Commission administrative data.

include discontinuation of vocational training course offerings, closing of the training institute, delay in reregistration, and suspension of registration due to complaints.

Enforcing the compliance for registration by training institutes can be challenging. Training centers in some areas do not apply for registration. Moreover, registrations are often not renewed in a timely manner after they expire. The TVEC Act needs amendments to close loopholes on registration and compliance.

Courses offered in collaboration

Courses can be offered in collaboration with foreign training institutions and industry. Some training institutes offer Sri Lankan students foreign qualifications recognized by foreign countries by signing memoranda of understanding (MOUs) with foreign institutes. The foreign institutes can also register with TVEC for joint monitoring of course delivery. The competency standards of the foreign training course can be mapped to TVEC's NCS to allow students to receive either the NVQ certificate or the certificate issued by the foreign training institute, for example, an MOU to offer Cisco Systems network training courses at the Vocational Training Authority (VTA). Training institute information pertaining to courses includes course descriptions, purposes, and assessment methods.

Accreditation of courses

All registered training institutes are required to apply for accreditation of courses. The number of courses accredited by TVEC has varied over time (figure 4.5).

TVEC is responsible for accrediting training courses. Courses that fulfill criteria in the NVQ operations manual are accredited. Accreditation requires that TVEC receive evidence of

- Availability of appropriate, adequate facilities,
- Training delivery at a satisfactory level (based on a simple set of criteria) and review of full content,

FIGURE 4.5

Accredited courses in registered training institutes in Sri Lanka, 2013–22

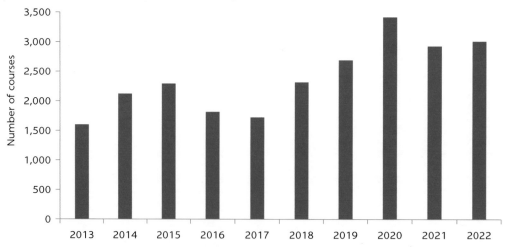

Source: Tertiary and Vocational Education Commission administrative data.

- Availability of trained academic staff to deliver the specified courses,
- An institute conducting formative assessment with proof of positive feedback,
- Opportunities provided for job training, and
- Conformity with the NVQ framework.

Accreditation is provided for courses that meet the competencies set out in the NCS leading to NVQ and courses that meet the competencies of one or more units from a national competency standard in a single or range of learning areas that culminate in a record of achievement.

Training institutions are required to be accredited to commence student enrollment. Accreditation requires that the institution has at least one accredited course. However, once the institution is accredited, it can offer myriad other courses that are not accredited. Most public training institutes have applied for course accreditation, but many private ones have neither applied for it nor meet the required standards. The course accreditation is awarded by a review committee. The award of NVQ or RPL certificate requires registered training institutes to offer accredited courses. A registered training institute can offer a combination of accredited and nonaccredited courses without losing TVEC registration. The number of courses accredited between July 2021 and May 2022 indicates that there is interest in maintaining accreditation levels (figure 4.6). About 78 percent of accredited courses are offered by public training institutions, 18 percent by private ones, and just 4 percent by NGO and charity training institutes.

FIGURE 4.6

Accredited courses in registered training institutes in Sri Lanka, by type of institute, July 2021–May 2022

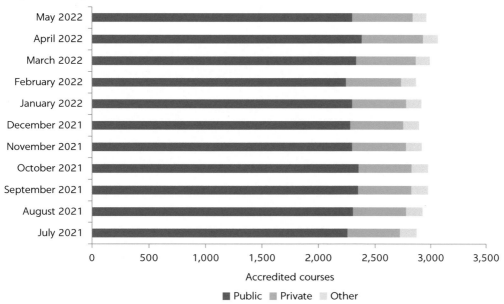

Source: Tertiary and Vocational Education Commission administrative data.
Note: Data reported are as of month end.

Student assessments

As noted, TVEC is responsible for designing the NVQ framework. As part of those efforts, TVEC has developed assessment policies and guidelines. The guidelines are usually issued as circulars. Assessments include both formative and summative assessments. Training institutes are responsible for conducting formative assessments as part of continual assessments and to issue records of achievement. TVEC is responsible for conducting summative assessments to issue NVQ certificates as well as endorsing assessment resources prepared by NAITA with the assistance of skills councils or NITACs. Assessment resources may include descriptions and outlines of problems to be solved or skills needed at the workplace, tools and equipment required or made available to solve those problems or provide needed workplace skills, assessment tools (test items and specifications) to assess underpinning knowledge, and descriptions to justify methods for solving workplace problems or their application.

TVEC maintains a database of assessors competent in assessing NCS. Level 1–4 assessors are registered for occupations, and level 5–6 assessors are for specific fields. Assessors receive a five-day training program designed by UNIVOTEC. Between 2014 and 2021, UNIVOTEC trained 1,527 assessors.

To assess the knowledge of students before assessment, most written exams are conducted by the Department of Examinations, which is responsible for conducting all exams—General Certificate of Education Ordinary Level (GCE O/L), GCE Advanced Level (A/L), and recruitment for various services—across the island. Exams are conducted based on requests from industry or industry skills councils. In addition, written exams are conducted to equate National Certificates in Technology and National Certificates for Industrial Technicians with the NVQ framework. TVEC devises questions, conducts knowledge assessments, and announces grades. Most requests for applications to sit for written exams are posted on TVEC's website.

Preassessment is conducted to check and verify evidence of continuous assessment and to assess the readiness of institutions and students. During preassessment, training institutes provide evidence of the assessment marks and materials used for continuous assessment. In addition, discussions are held with candidates to inform them about the type of assessment and documents they will be given to complete before the final assessment. The institute and candidates are informed of the date of the final assessment and the materials, equipment, and tools required for it. This is important for candidates planning to obtain NVQ certification through RPL (see below).

Final summative assessments are conducted by panels of assessors with at least two members. Feedback is shared with students, and outcomes are shared with training institutes and TVEC. Ratings are based on the competency level (competent or not yet competent). To ensure the quality of NVQ certificates, TVEC continues to be involved in student assessment even though it is the responsibility of training institutes. As required, training institutes develop their own sets of final assessments to award records of achievement.

RECOGNITION OF PRIOR LEARNING

To help workers have their skills assessed and certified, many countries have developed policies that recognize prior learning—formal and informal—to acquire qualifications or credits without going through a formal education or training program (ILO 2018a). This approach is used to provide economic opportunities, empower people to acquire knowledge by signing up for modular programs that build on their skills, and promote lifelong learning.

In Sri Lanka, TVEC and NAITA have different definitions for RPL. TVEC (2009; 2021b) defines RPL as "a process that recognizes a learner's current competencies which may have been achieved through means that include any combination of formal or informal training and education, work experience or general life experience." NAITA (n.d.) defines it as "an assessment process that assesses the person's competencies acquired through informal, non-institutional learning to determine the extent to which that person has achieved the required competencies as set out in the relevant National Skills Standard leading to a qualification of the NVQ framework." This definition has not been amended or adapted over time. Thus, RPL has evolved over time in tertiary and vocational education as a concept to recognize workers' competencies in Sri Lanka. A singular definition combining the key elements of the TVEC and NAITA definitions might serve the system better, avoid duplication, and provide greater recognition for recipients of RPL certification.

Development of the RPL concept in Sri Lanka

In Sri Lanka, the RPL and certification processes commenced with the World Bank's 1981 Construction Industry Project (World Bank 1981). That project sought to train construction workers by providing knowledge and skills through modular curricula and introduced a system of trade testing to assess the competence of construction employees according to skills standards (World Bank 1988). The National Apprenticeship Board was in charge of test assessments, certifications, and registrations. National trade tests considered workers' experience, and the issuance of trade certificates helped enhance careers (World Bank 1986, 1996).

In 1990, under the Tertiary and Vocational Education Act 20 of 1990, NAITA was established with a wider mandate to replace the National Apprenticeship Board, enabling NAITA to conduct trade tests and other agencies to do the same under the direction of NAITA. National trade test certificate requirements continued.

In 2004, the NVQ framework was introduced with assistance from the Asian Development Bank's Skills Development Project, and in 2005, the government issued a circular on the guidelines for implementing the framework and directing all training institutions to use competency-based tests and the framework (ADB 2008). As a result, all policy decisions were made by TVEC's governing board, and operational and implementation issues were discussed by the NVQ Steering Committee. TVEC communicated all policy decisions and guidelines through circulars (ADB 2011). The NVQ framework certifies competencies acquired, and certificates are issued to workers who have acquired such competencies through training or employment. TVEC developed the NVQ manual to operationalize the NVQ framework. The manual covers the awarding of certificates through RPL (TVEC 2009). There is no difference between NVQ certificates issued through traditional competency-based training methods and RPL.

NVQ is a requisite for recruiting workers. In 2009, the Ministry of Public Administration and Home Affairs issued a circular recognizing NVQ as part of the public sector recruitment. The Salaries and Cadres Commission specified salary scales for such NVQ levels. NVQ level 1 was considered unskilled, NVQ levels 2 and 3 were considered semiskilled, and NVQ level 4 was considered skilled.

In 2012, the NVQ framework was integrated with the Sri Lanka Qualifications Framework (SLQF), offering lateral mobility within the SLQF (Ministry of Higher Education 2012). The SLQF integrates the NVQ framework developed by TVEC, and the pathways of lateral mobility between the vocational education sector and the higher education sector have also been identified. NVQ levels 2 and 3 were made equivalent to SLQF 1 and NVQ level 4 to SLQF 2 (see chapter 3). In 2012, the National Human Resources and Employment Policy recognized school leavers entering industry directly and acquiring NVQ certificates through RPL and SLQF links with the NVQ framework (Secretariat for Senior Ministers 2012).

The importance of RPL continued, and based on decisions by the NVQ Steering Committee, several guidelines were issued in 2013 and 2017 to provide further guidance to assessors and authorized training providers. The draft NVQ manual prepared in 2016 and 2021 also covered RPL. Also in 2016, the Ministry of Public Administration and Management issued a circular equating the qualifications for GCE O/L to NVQ level 3 and GCE A/L to NVQ level 4 for public positions in technical and technological industries.

The National Education Commission's (NEC's) 2018 TVET Policy highlighted the importance of recognizing prior learning, with several policies focused on encouraging it (NEC 2018). Policy 30 highlighted that the "processes involving assessment and certification should be analyzed and streamlined for valid, reliable, quality assured and speedy issue of NVQ certificates to those who have completed pre-employment training and for those who are assessed through [RPL]" (p. 24). Policy 46 noted the importance of strengthening competencies obtained through foreign employment to provide RPL certificates under the NVQ framework. In 2020, TVEC prepared a draft TVET action plan that reviewed policies and suggested several actions to popularize RPL. The NVQ framework operations manual (TVEC 2021b) provided clear roles and responsibilities and steps to follow in providing NVQ certificates through RPL.

The president's 2019 *Vistas of Prosperity and Splendour* (GoSL 2019) states that he wants to reduce the number of low-skilled workers in Sri Lanka's workforce. This goal can only be achieved by training and retraining workers and by encouraging all workers to seek qualifications through RPL.

Establishing skills assessments for recognition of prior learning

TVEC can grant permission to institutions to conduct assessments that recognize prior learning. Initially, NAITA and the VTA were authorized to conduct such assessments. In 2017, TVEC issued a circular confirming the VTA, NAITA, and Department of Technical Education and Training (DTET) as the agencies legally authorized to conduct them. In addition, TVEC published a circular with guidelines to candidates and assessors.

According to the 2009 NVQ operations manual, the three training agencies must follow 12 steps to offer certificates based on RPL (table 4.1). Although the manual defines the role of a coordinator for RPL, those functions are performed by the authorized training agencies, with the 13th step—issuance of an NVQ certificate—performed by TVEC.

TABLE 4.1 **Activities and responsibilities for issuing certificates in RPL in Sri Lanka**

STEP	ACTIVITY	RESPONSIBILITY
1	Provide information on RPL to prospective candidates.	TVEC and authorized training agencies (NAITA, VTA, DTET) (RPL coordinator appointed by each agency)
2	Complete application and forward it to the authorized training agency along with any supporting documentation and evidence.	Applicants
3	Assign and approve panel of assessors and verifier.	TVEC
4	Forward copy of application and other documentation and evidence to assessor.	Authorized training agency (NAITA, VTA, DTET)
5	Contact student to commence assessment process and prepare assessment plan.	Assessor and authorized training agency (NAITA, VTA, DTET)
6	Provide evidence of competence.	Candidates
7	Assess students' record of achievement outcomes.	Assessors appointed by TVEC
8	Provide feedback to students on assessment outcomes and obtain signed acknowledgments from candidates.	Assessors appointed by TVEC
9	Return completed assessment to authorized training agency (NAITA, VTA, DTET).	Assessors appointed by TVEC
10	Forward all related documents and records to verifier.	Authorized training agency (NAITA, VTA, DTET)
11	Review and verify assessment decision and return to authorized training agency (NAITA, VTA, DTET).	Verifier
12	Forward completed form to TVEC for issuance of qualification.	Authorized training agency (NAITA, VTA, DTET)
13	Issue NVQ certificate.	TVEC

Sources: TVEC 2009, 2021b.
Note: The TVEC 2021 operations manual presents step 3 as two activities. DTET = Department of Technical Education and Training; NAITA = National Apprentice and Industrial Training Authority; NVQ = National Vocational Qualification; RPL = recognition of prior learning; TVEC = Tertiary and Vocational Education Commission; VTA = Vocational Training Authority.

Age requirement

The 2009 and 2021 NVQ operations manuals do not specify any age limits for candidates to apply for NVQ certification through RPL. During implementation, the NVQ Steering Committee felt the need to stipulate guidelines, so TVEC circular NVQ/2017/04 provided guidelines for candidates' minimum age to apply. For NVQ levels 2 and 3, applicants must be at least 18. That requirement is also applicable to students who have taken technical subjects at school. Candidates with NVQ 2 qualifications applying for NVQ 3 level are required to be at least 20, and those with NVQ 3 level qualifications applying for NVQ level 4 must be at least 21. Candidates applying directly for NVQ level 4 are required to be at least 23.

Industrial experience

The 2009 NVQ operations manual states that the minimum industrial exposure requirement to become eligible for RPL is 18 months for NVQ levels 2 and 3. Over the years, that amount of experience remained unchanged. But in 2017, non-NVQ certificates from TVEC registered institutions were acknowledged. The amount of industry experience required for candidates with non-NVQ certificates changed depending on the duration of courses taken. The NVQ Steering Committee has developed additional guidelines for the industrial experience required for NVQ 4 in several ways: candidates with NVQ 2 qualifications require three years of industry experience after obtaining NVQ 2, those with NVQ 3 qualifications require two years of industry experience, and those applying directly for an NVQ 4 certificate require four years of work experience. The 2021 NVQ operations manual does not specify the minimum industrial exposure requirement. Instead, TVEC is authorized to communicate to institutions through circulars about such requirements. These guidelines will likely need to be reviewed and updated to conform to the needs of a 21st-century skills strategy.

Documentation and evidence

The documentation required as evidence for work experience varies depending on the NVQ level applied for. Candidates need to send documentary evidence for industry experience along with their applications. The type of documentary evidence required varies depending on the employment type, NVQ level, and other factors:

- Formally employed workers are required to submit a service certificate.
- Self-employed workers need to present a business registration certificate.
- Informal workers are required to submit a letter from a village-level government officer certified by the divisional secretary.
- When applying directly for NVQ level 4, formally employed workers need to submit a service certificate along with their pension numbers or provident fund contribution numbers.
- Workers with foreign experience are required to present copies of their passports, visas, and service certificates. In addition, records of work done (portfolios, photographs, videos), samples of products, testimonials, evidence of successful completion of courses, project reports, and completed assignments can be submitted.
- Certified copies of identity cards and all other documentary evidence are required to be submitted to the authorized training agency.

The regulations for documentary evidence also require review and simplification to foster skilling, reskilling, and upskilling.

Application

Applicants interested in receiving NVQ through RPL can complete and submit applications designed by the authorized training agency (DTET, NAITA, VTA). If a candidate is in a rush to obtain certificates recognizing prior learning, they can submit their applications directly to TVEC, which then forwards the applications to one of the authorized training centers to conduct assessments at accredited training centers. VTA and DTET only conduct assessments recognizing prior learning in their own training centers. NAITA can do so in one of its own training centers, training centers owned by other accredited training agencies, and within industries.

Application fees, usually around LKR 20,000 (approximately US$65 in June 2023 exchange), cover registration, the written exam, practical assessment, assessment center costs, the use of materials, and issuance of the certificate. Fees per applicant vary depending on whether the assessment is conducted for an individual applicant or a group. (Costs are lower when the assessment is conducted for a group because the costs of materials and assessments are divided among applicants.) Fees also vary depending on the training agency, trade, and type of assessment. The authorized training center reviews applications for eligibility by checking on the documentary evidence submitted before asking TVEC to appoint an assessor.

Assessors

TVEC appoints registered assessors with the technical competency to assess students at the NVQ levels. The TVEC database enables it to appoint assessors without human intervention to be impartial when choosing assessors. Assessors must follow a code of conduct to assess candidates fairly and transparently. Assessors take a five-day professional development course on assessment capabilities at UNIVOTEC.

Assessment

Assessors interview candidates before assessments and confirm that the documentary evidence they have submitted is valid and genuine. If satisfied with the evidence, confirmation of applications and evidence need to be sent to TVEC within seven days of the interview. Once the applications and evidence are considered legitimate, applicants are interviewed and advised on their qualification packages and relevant competency units, eligibility for the NVQ-level qualification application, preparation of further evidence for the final assessment, and any other information required. Interview questions help plan for the final assessment and determine its date.

Some NVQ certifications require knowledge assessments and, based on the NVQ level, can last from 30 minutes to 2 hours. Written exams are conducted by TVEC/DTET according to a schedule prepared by the Examination Board or as and when required. The authorized training centers are responsible for submitting the candidates' applications to TVEC and for taking exams.

The final assessment is likely to be scheduled within 3 to 30 days of the interview. During the interview, if candidates require a beginner's course module, they are directed to achieve the competencies involved. The assessment is conducted according to the assessment plan using materials, tools, and equipment stipulated for the relevant competency standard. Assessments need to be conducted based on the criteria, guidelines, and methodologies defined by TVEC. Variety in methods of assessment is encouraged. Demonstrations of skills, attestations from formal groups, interviews, and evaluations of work samples or projects can be used. Although there had been a delay in processing assessor fees, TVEC now processes them within two weeks of submission of assessment documents.

Based on the competency level, a record of achievement can be given to applicants; thereafter, candidates can obtain the relevant competency by attending a training program or working in the relevant industry. Repeat assessments can be requested along with records of achievement to complete the rest of the units to demonstrate competency and receive the relevant NVQ certificate.

Establishing a skills assessment mechanism to recognize prior learning for returning migrant workers

In 2009, TVEC developed guidelines to offer NVQ certificates for RPL through skills gained overseas. Since 2016, the Sri Lanka Bureau of Foreign Employment and TVEC have been collaborating to harmonize occupational classifications and encourage migrant workers to obtain certificates (ILO 2018b). In 2017, TVEC expanded guidelines for workers with four years of overseas experience to receive NVQ level 4.

Because of COVID-19, NAITA introduced an initiative to get a list of returning migrant workers and to offer them the option of getting NVQ certificates through RPL (TVEC 2021a). In addition, TVEC Policy 46 (2018) highlighted that competencies obtained through foreign employment need to also be considered through RPL under the NVQ framework. The activities suggested were to obtain details of returnees from the Sri Lanka Foreign Employment Bureau and the Department of Emigration and Immigration, launch a program to raise awareness on the RPL system of NVQ certification and its benefits, and help returnees obtain NVQ certification through RPL.

The State Ministry of Foreign Employment Promotion and Market Diversification has drafted an action plan for 2020–23 that presents core policy areas and employment opportunities for skilled and semiskilled migrant workers in the domestic and foreign economies. Items highlighted include establishing and strengthening country-specific skill standards for occupations and facilitating RPL. The draft policy highlights strengthening of national, district, and divisional secretariat officials to create awareness of RPL and skills development options for migrant workers and returnees.

Pros and cons for RPL

RPL offers many advantages toward NVQ certification. Qualifications gained through it help workers. Because NVQ levels obtained through competency-based training and RPL are the same, there is no discrimination against workers who obtained them through RPL. Mechanisms to recognize NVQ certificates as part of recruitment and salary scales are developed based on qualification levels.

The receipt of a certificate based on industrial experience and demonstration of competencies helps workers enter the formal education system. NVQ 4 is a prequalification for NVQ 5 and 6, then proceeds to NVQ 7 (equivalent to an undergraduate degree).

Several negative perceptions and misconceptions exist about RPL in the TVET system. For example:

- If applicants need to receive certificates quickly and select the individual approach for assessment, they must bear the full cost.
- NVQ certificates can be obtained more quickly through RPL than by completing a traditional center-based training program.
- Receiving NVQ certificates through RPL is easy, if applicants can afford to pay fees.
- People who receive NVQ through RPL go through only short courses; they do not internalize theoretical concepts because their focus is to pass their exams and obtain certificate.

The complex nature of the process is not well understood, and there are institutional challenges linked to the organizational processes required for RPLs. For instance, the documentation required for enrolling and accounting for candidates seeking RPL may be cumbersome.

Trends in RPL

The number of certificates granted through RPL has increased, with the most certificates issued in 2015 (figure 4.7). Between 2007 and 2021, the number of NVQ certificates issued through RPL was 74,962, with 54,040 for men and 20,922 for women—so, more than 70 percent of such NVQ certificates were issued to men.

Between 2007 and 2021, NAITA issued the most NVQ certificates through RPL, acting as the authorized training agency for 84 percent of such certificates. The VTA issued 15 percent and DTET, less than 1 percent. DTET commenced RPL assessments only after the 2017 TVEC circular. However, DTET is also renting its training centers to conduct assessments for NAITA. During the same period about 60 percent of NVQ level 3 certificates were issued through RPL, while interest in receiving level 1 certificates was minimal (figure 4.8). The second most popular certification was NVQ level 4 (33 percent).

NVQ certificates issued through RPL, by industry

By the end of 2021, about 15 percent of NVQ certificates had been issued through RPL (table 4.2). The highest numbers were in electricity, gas, and water supply, followed by manufacturing. The largest shares were in education, followed by transport, storage, and communications. Only one such certificate was issued for financial intermediaries and for fisheries.

FIGURE 4.7

Number of NVQ certificates issued through RPL in Sri Lanka, by gender of recipients, 2007–21

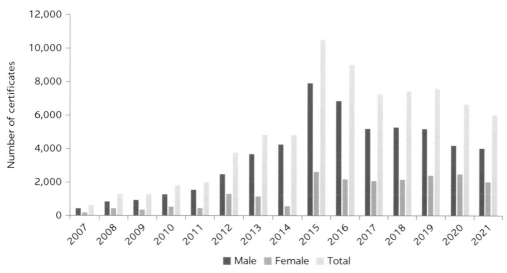

Source: Tertiary and Vocational Education Commission administrative data.
Note: NVQ = National Vocational Qualification; RPL = recognition of prior learning.

FIGURE 4.8

Number of NVQ certificates issued through RPL in Sri Lanka, by level, 2007–21

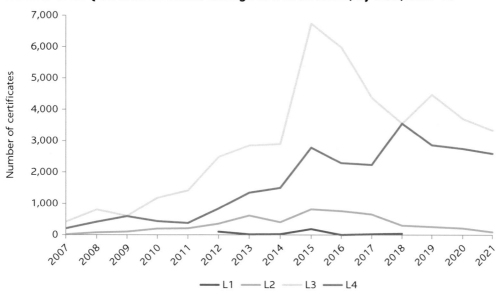

Source: Tertiary and Vocational Education Commission administrative data.
Note: L = level; NVQ = National Vocational Qualification; RPL = recognition of prior learning.

TABLE 4.2 **NVQ certificates issued in Sri Lanka, by industry and type, December 2021**

INDUSTRY	NUMBER				PERCENTAGE			PERCENTAGE RPL OF TOTAL NVQ
	CBT	EBT	RPL	TOTAL	CBT	EBT	RPL	
Transport, storage, and communications	1,821	8	2,483	4,312	42	0	58	0
Education	2,082	159	3,280	5,521	38	3	59	1
Electricity, gas, and water supply	36,613	193	13,717	50,523	72	0	27	3
Construction	36,552	7,935	10,371	54,858	67	14	19	2
Agriculture, hunting, and forestry	7,804	69	1,206	9,079	86	1	13	0
Other community, social, and personal service activities	61,536	60	12,210	73,806	83	0	17	2
Manufacturing	81,967	851	13,540	96,358	85	1	14	3
Wholesale and retail trade	37,209	1,355	5,179	43,743	85	3	12	1
Health and social work	6,924	663	1,003	8,590	81	8	12	0
Real estate, renting, and business activities	103,839	676	10,382	114,897	90	1	9	2
Hotels and restaurants	14,939	989	1,290	17,218	87	6	7	0
Common competencies/skills	27,962	0	308	28,270	99	0	1	0
Financial intermediaries	2,038	6	1	2,045	100	0	0	0
Public administration	49	0	22	71	69	0	31	0
Fishing	224	0	1	225	100	0	0	0
Total	**421,559**	**12,964**	**74,993**	**509,516**	**83**	**3**	**15**	**15**

Source: TVEC 2021a.
Note: CBT = competency-based training; EBT = enterprise-based training; NVQ = National Vocational Qualification; RPL = recognition of prior learning.

TABLE 4.3 **Number of NVQ certificates issued in Sri Lanka through RPL, by occupation, 2007–21**

OCCUPATION	NUMBER OF NVQ THROUGH RPL	TOTAL NUMBER OF NVQ	PERCENTAGE RPL OF NVQ HOLDERS BY OCCUPATION
Electrician	11,759	39,530	30
Beautician	7,507	31,917	24
Computer application assistant	6,109	54,234	11
Construction craftsperson (masonry)	5,737	19,825	29
Automobile mechanic	2,961	19,826	15
Hairdresser	2,411	18,037	13
Clerk	2,242	4,955	45
Plumber	1,798	6,669	27
Wood craftsperson (furniture)	1,485	8,825	17
Tailor	1,759	9,050	19
Telecommunications assistant	1,188	1,583	75

Source: Tertiary and Vocational Education Commission administrative data.
Note: NVQ = National Vocational Qualification; RPL = recognition of prior learning.

Among occupations, 75 percent of telecommunications assistants have received NVQ certificates through RPL, as have close to one-half of clerks (table 4.3). In addition, nearly a quarter of electricians, beauticians, plumbers, and construction craftspeople (masonry) have received NVQ through that approach.

National competency standards

The number of NCS used for NVQ certificates serves as the basis for issuing RPL certification. While the competency standards have been increasing in number, from 106 in 2016 to 173 in 2021, the bases for RPL certifications have been decreasing, from 83 of 106 in 2016 to about 75 of 173 in 2021. In 2016, NVQ certificates were offered through RPL for about 78 percent of the competency standards, whereas in 2021 it was only about 43 percent, showing a steady decline over time (table 4.4). RPL will likely constitute an important signaling mechanism in the job market for a 21st-century skills strategy, for reskilling and upskilling requirements.

NVQ certificates

Approximately 80 percent of NVQ courses are offered by the public active training institutes, and only 17 percent are offered by private training institutes. The most active training institutes in the Western Province offer NVQ courses. The fewest NVQ courses are offered in the North Central Province, and only a marginally greater number are offered in the Uva Province (figure 4.9).

TABLE 4.4 Number of NCS for NVQ and RPL and percentage of standards for RPL in Sri Lanka, 2016–21

YEAR	NCS USED FOR NVQ	NCS USED FOR NVQ THROUGH RPL	PERCENTAGE
2016	106	83	78
2017	107	72	67
2018	135	83	61
2019	147	96	65
2020	162	80	49
2021	173	75	43

Source: Tertiary and Vocational Education Commission administrative data.
Note: NCS = national competency standards; NVQ = National Vocational Qualification; RPL = recognition of prior learning.

FIGURE 4.9

NVQ course offerings in active training institutes in Sri Lanka, by province and type of institute, June 2022

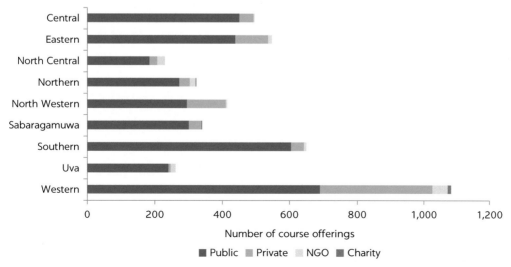

Source: Tertiary and Vocational Education Commission administrative data.
Note: NGO = nongovernmental organization; NVQ = National Vocational Qualification.

CONCLUSION

The mandate of the TVEC is critical for skill development in Sri Lanka and for planning, coordinating, and developing TVET across all levels of skilling as well as for contributing to the development of human resources in the country. The credibility of the TVET system lies in certification and other academic distinctions. TVEC's role is crucial for standardizing and maintaining academic and training standards across TVET agencies through the NVQ framework. The review and analysis of several policies, materials, and guidelines for TVET quality and relevance has revealed the following:

- Since the NVQ framework is the unified qualification system in TVET, public and private sector training institutions and those related to foreign employment view the NVQ certificate as legitimate, signifying that graduates with the certificate have received a level of quality training.
- The regulatory system is well established. TVEC identifies occupations to develop NCS based on labor market demand, and NAITA develops the standards.
- NAITA develops draft standards, validates them through national industrial training advisory committees (known as skills councils), and forwards them to TVEC for endorsement.
- The competency-based assessments in Sri Lanka require a system with assessors who are sufficiently updated on NCS assessment rules and regulations. There is a need for assessors who conduct both theory and eligibility tests for competency-based assessments. Further, assessments need to be consistent, with clear data on the number of students and units assessed per day and a mechanism for verifying and auditing assessments.

Competency-based assessments and NVQ certification require the establishment of a system for verifying formative assessment results and auditing competency assessments to improve the validity and reliability of the assessments. They also require the following systems and resources:

- Creation of systems to conduct assessment-related administrative and coordination activities efficiently and effectively
- Additional competency-based assessors based on demand (by occupation, medium of assessment, and geographic distribution of training programs)
- Greater numbers of industry-based assessors
- Computerized assessor selection software
- An annual assessment calendar
- Mechanisms for monitoring, verifying, and auditing assessments
- Preparation of question banks for assessments
- Guidelines for preparing portfolios of evidence to assess RPL
- Formalization of achievement records to increase the recognition of competencies
- Creation of procedures for citizens with records of achievement to open pathways for them to obtain full NVQ certification.

To achieve the results, appropriate levels of financing and expertise would be necessary to rationalize, develop, or adapt regulations to emerging circumstances, and to codify the standards and certifications to new skill requirements for the economy.

ANNEX 4A: INTERNATIONAL EXAMPLES OF QUALIFICATION FRAMEWORKS

Australian Qualification Framework

The Australian Qualification Framework (AQF) provides a single framework for qualifications from Senior Secondary Certification to PhD. The qualifications are grouped to the three educational sectors responsible for their accreditation: secondary school, vocational education and training (VET), and higher education. The organizing framework for the AQF is a structure of levels and qualification types, each of which is defined by a taxonomy of learning outcomes. The taxonomic approach is designed to enable consistency in the way in which qualifications are described and clarity about the differences and relationships between qualification types. Table 4.A1 describes the qualification types and levels. Further, Australia also has the Australian Quality Training Framework, a national set of agreed standards and conditions with which training providers must comply to ensure nationally consistent, high-quality training and assessment in the VET system.

India National Skills Qualifications Framework

The India National Skills Qualifications Framework (NSQF) qualifications are organized according to a series of levels of knowledge, skills, and aptitudes (table 4.A2). These levels are defined in terms of learning outcomes, which the learner must possess regardless of whether they were acquired through formal, nonformal, or informal learning. Some elements of the NSQF include national principles for skill proficiency and competencies at different levels that are

TABLE 4.A1 **Australian Qualification Framework qualification types and levels**

LEVEL	QUALIFICATION TYPE	LEVEL
1	Certificate I	Graduates at this level will have knowledge and skills for initial work, community involvement, and/or further learning
2	Certificate II	Graduates at this level will have knowledge and skills for work in a defined context and/or further learning
3	Certificate III	Graduates at this level will have theoretical and practical knowledge and skills for work and/or further learning
4	Certificate IV	Graduates at this level will have theoretical and practical knowledge and skills for specialized and/or skilled work and/or further learning
5	Diploma	Graduates at this level will have specialized knowledge and skills for skilled/paraprofessional work and/or further learning
6	Advanced diploma / associate degree	Graduates at this level will have broad knowledge and skills for paraprofessional/highly skilled work and/or further learning
7	Bachelor's degree	Graduates at this level will have broad and coherent knowledge and skills for professional work and/or further learning
8	Bachelor honors degree / graduate certificate / graduate diploma	Graduates at this level will have advanced knowledge and skills for professional highly skilled work and/or further learning
9	Master's degree	Graduates at this level will have specialized knowledge and skills for research, and/or professional practice and/or further learning
10	Doctoral degree	Graduates at this level will have systematic and critical understanding of a complex field of learning and specialized research skills for the advancement of learning and/or professional practice

Source: Australian Qualification Framework Council 2013, 18.

TABLE 4.A2 **Process by qualification types and levels in India**

LEVEL	QUALIFICATION TYPE	PROCESS
1	Grade IX	Prepares person to carry out processes that are repetitive, on a regular basis, and require no previous practice.
2	Grade X	Prepares person to carry out processes that are repetitive, on a regular basis, with little application of understanding more of practice.
3	Grade XI/diploma	Person may carry out a job that may require limited range of activities routine and predictable.
4	Grade XII /diploma	Person works in a familiar, predictable, routine, situation of clear choice.
5	Advanced diploma / bachelor's degree	Job requires well-developed skills, with clear choice of procedures in familiar context.
6	Advanced diploma / bachelor's degree	Demands a wide range of specialized technical skills, clarity of knowledge, and practice in broad range of activity involving standard and nonstandard practices.
7	Advanced diploma / bachelor's degree	Requires a command of wide-ranging, specialized theoretical and practical skills, involving variable routine and nonroutine contexts.
8	PG diploma / master's degree	Comprehensive, cognitive, theoretical knowledge and practical skills to develop creative solutions to abstract problems. Undertake self-study, demonstrate intellectual independence, analytical rigor and good communication.
9	PG diploma / master's degree	Advanced knowledge and skill. Critical understanding of the subject, demonstrating mastery and innovation, completion of substantial research and dissertation.
10	Degree / doctorate	Highly specialized knowledge and problem-solving skill to provide original contribution to knowledge through research and scholarship.

Source: National Skill Development Agency 2013, 9.

equivalent to international standards, progression pathways defined in the framework, opportunities to promote lifelong learning and skills development, partnership with employers from the industry, an accountability mechanism, multiple entry and exit between vocational education, skills training, general education, technical education and job markets.

NOTE

1. The European Credit Transfer and Accumulation System (ECTS), or the ECTS Grading Scale, is an evaluation system of the European Commission. The evaluation framework has been created to support students to facilitate student exchange from one college to another. It provides a common reviewing platform. The framework permits and facilitates local and international grades to be utilized interchangeably. The evaluations are arranged from alphabet grades A to F. The ECTS is created to encourage students in their studies and to transfer credits from one college to the next by giving due acknowledgment to the program(s) or course(s) of study completed there. To calculate the ECTS for a particular subject, the credit hours for the subject in a week are multiplied by the total number of weeks for the subject. Finally, the figure is to be divided by 30 hours. One ECTS is equivalent to 30 hours. That would be the total ECTS for the subject. The ECTS is not to be utilized exclusively, or as a sole decision to interpret grade transfers between institutions.

REFERENCES

ADB (Asian Development Bank). 2008. *Skills Development Project: Completion Report.* Manila.

ADB (Asian Development Bank). 2011. *National Qualifications Framework for Skills Training Reform in Sri Lanka.* Manila.

Australian Qualifications Framework Council. 2013. *Australian Qualifications Framework* (2nd ed.). Australian Qualifications Framework Council, South Australia. https://www.aqf .edu.au/framework/australian-qualifications-framework.

GoSL (Government of Sri Lanka). 2019. *Vistas of Prosperity and Splendour.* Colombo: Ministry of Finance, Sri Lanka.

ILO (International Labour Organization). 2018a. *Recognition of Prior Learning (RPL): Learning Package.* Geneva.

ILO (International Labour Organization). 2018b. *Skills Recognition of Sri Lankan Migrant Workers.* Colombo.

Ministry of Education. 2013. *National Skills Qualification Framework.* National Skill Development Agency. Government of India, New Delhi. https://www.education.gov.in /sites/upload_files/mhrd/files/NSQF%20NOTIFICATION.pdf.

Ministry of Higher Education. 2012. *Sri Lanka Qualifications Framework.* Colombo. https://www.tvec.gov.lk/wp-content/uploads/2019/05/Policy-Book-English-web.pdf.

NAITA (National Apprentice and Industrial Training Authority). n.d. *RPL: The Easiest Pathway to Obtain NVQ Certificate for Persons with Knowledge, Skills, Capabilities, and Experience.* Rajagiriya, Sri Lanka.

NEC (National Education Commission). 2018. *National Policy on Technical and Vocational Education.* Colombo.

Parliament of the Democratic Socialist Republic of Sri Lanka. 2007, March 23. Companies Act, No. 07 of 2007. Gazette of the Democratic Socialist Republic of Sri Lanka. Colombo. https://www.drc.gov.lk/en/wp-content/uploads/2018/04/Act-7-of-2007-English.pdf.

Secretariat for Senior Ministers. 2012. *National Human Resources and Employment Policy.* Colombo.

TVEC (Tertiary and Vocational Education Commission). 2009. *National Vocational Qualifications Framework of Sri Lanka: Operations Manual.* Colombo.

TVEC (Tertiary and Vocational Education Commission). 2017. *Circular 2017/04.* Colombo.

TVEC (Tertiary and Vocational Education Commission). 2021a. *Labour Market Information Bulletin.* Vol. II. Colombo.

TVEC (Tertiary and Vocational Education Commission). 2021b. *National Vocational Qualifications Framework of Sri Lanka: Operations Manual.* Colombo.

World Bank. 1981. *The Construction Industry Project: Staff Appraisal Report.* Report No. P2996. Washington, DC. https://documents.worldbank.org/curated/en/473861468301520870 /Sri-Lanka-Construction-Industry-Project.

World Bank. 1986. *The Second Vocational Training Project: Staff Appraisal Report.* Report No. 5958. Washington, DC. https://documents.worldbank.org/curated/en/801421468301522160 /Sri-Lanka-Second-Vocational-Training-Project.

World Bank. 1988. *The Construction Industry Project: Implementation Completion Report.* Report No. 7560. Washington, DC. https://documents.worldbank.org/curated /en/762361468303073940/Sri-Lanka-Construction-Industry-Project.

World Bank. 1996. *The Second Vocational Training Project: Implementation Completion Report.* Report No. 5958-CE. Washington, DC. https://documents1.worldbank.org/curated /fr/928941567089949234/pdf/Sri-Lanka-Second-Vocational-Training-Project.pdf.

5 Financing for Technical and Vocational Education and Training

INTRODUCTION

Studying financing for technical and vocational education and training (TVET) in Sri Lanka is challenging because of its complexity, frequently changing governance structure—involving many public and private entities—and lack of consistent financial recordkeeping and monitoring (Dundar et al. 2014). For example, this challenge is reported in the World Bank's Implementation Completion and Results Report (ICR) on the Skills Development Project (SDP), which took place in 2014–20 (World Bank 2020). The ICR states that reporting responsibilities involved eight ministries that had subsequent changes in leadership during the project, as well as at the implementing agency. Further, the 2022 triple crisis (fuel, food, fiscal) resulted in significant depreciation of the Sri Lanka Rupee (LKR) against the US dollar, creating moving targets for currency conversion.

Acknowledging the challenges, this chapter first analyzes the public spending on and trends in TVET, analyzes the cost-effectiveness of the most recent Skills Sector Development Program (SSDP), and summarizes good practice examples of TVET financing system in the Republic of Korea. Private spending is not analyzed here due to data limitations and availability at the time the analysis was conducted. Government budget and spending are shown in LKR, whereas the rate of return to TVET and skills development are calculated in US dollars, taking into account inflation.

PUBLIC SPENDING ON TVET

This section provides an overview of government spending on education and the sector's governance; analyzes public TVET institutions; analyzes TVET spending by the State Ministry of Skills Development, Vocational Education, Research and Innovations (SMSDVERI) and other ministries; and describes initiatives financed by foreign development partners.

Spending on education and its governance

In 2018, the government of Sri Lanka invested 2.1 percent of GDP in education (figure 5.1, panel a). Public spending on education grew substantially between 2010 and 2016, when it reached 3.4 percent of GDP, but it fell over the next two years. Relative to other countries in South Asia in 2016–18, Sri Lanka's education investment fell at the low end of the distribution, ahead of only Bangladesh—while the South Asia average was 3.5 percent of GDP (figure 5.1, panel b). Nepal had the region's highest investment in education, spending 5.1 percent of GDP, followed by 4.5 percent in Malaysia and 4.3 percent in Korea.

Many ministries are involved in education in Sri Lanka. After parliamentary elections in August 2020, roles and responsibilities for the education sector were brought under the Ministry of Education (MoE). In addition, several state ministries were created to focus on subsectors. The MoE is responsible for general education (primary and secondary) and higher education. For general education, the MoE and the State Ministry of Women and Child Development, Preschool and Primary Education, School Infrastructure, and Education Services (MoWCD) have relevant activities and programs. The MoWCD is responsible for early childhood development and education. Higher education is the responsibility of the MoE and the State Ministry of Education Reforms, Open Universities, and Distance Learning Promotion. The SMSDVERI is responsible for TVET. The Tertiary and Vocational Education Commission (TVEC), the TVET policy-making body, and more than eight other TVET training institutes are mapped under SMSDVERI.[1] In addition, based on the technical specialization, there are TVET institutes mapped under other ministries.[2]

In 2020, the government allocated approximately LKR 14.3 billion—0.1 percent of GDP—to skills development and TVET. This was less than 9 percent of the total education expenditure (table 5.1). Budgets for general education and

FIGURE 5.1

Government spending on education in Sri Lanka, 2010–18, and other South Asian and select Southeast Asian countries, 2018

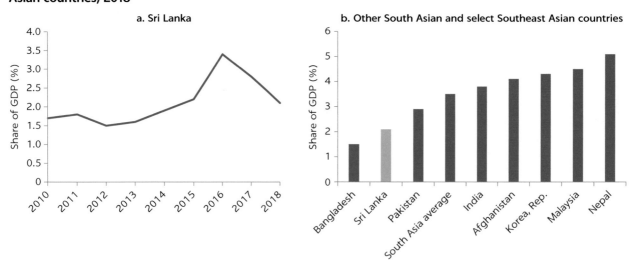

Sources: World Bank Data Portal; United Nations Educational, Scientific, and Cultural Organization Institute for Statistics, 2010–18.
Note: In panel b, countries are listed by percentage of GDP spent on education. Years vary depending on the availability of data. Bangladesh data are for 2016, Sri Lanka 2018, Pakistan 2017, South Asia 2017, India 2013, Afghanistan 2017, the Republic of Korea 2016, Malaysia 2018, and Nepal 2018.

TABLE 5.1 **Public education spending in Sri Lanka, 2020–23**

LKR (thousands)

TYPE OF SPENDING	2020			2021			2022 (ESTIMATE)			2023 (PROJECTION)		
	GENERAL EDUCATION (PRIMARY AND SECONDARY)	HIGHER EDUCATION	TVET	GENERAL EDUCATION (PRIMARY AND SECONDARY)	HIGHER EDUCATION	TVET	GENERAL EDUCATION (PRIMARY AND SECONDARY)	HIGHER EDUCATION	TVET	GENERAL EDUCATION (PRIMARY AND SECONDARY)	HIGHER EDUCATION	TVET
Recurrent	60,557,776	51,506,171	10,407,759	63,228,960	56,473,000	12,475,400	89,932,500	59,755,000	12,350,650	66,601,550	64,478,000	12,783,385
Capital	16,718,678	22,614,507	3,925,585	22,299,247	20,919,000	6,354,780	16,191,000	17,741,000	4,777,600	17,141,100	25,850,000	3,106,470
Total	**77,276,454**	**74,120,678**	**14,333,344**	**85,528,307**	**77,392,000**	**18,830,180**	**106,123,500**	**77,496,000**	**17,128,250**	**83,742,650**	**90,328,000**	**15,889,855**
% of total education spending	47.0	45.0	8.6	47.0	43.0	10.0	53.0	39.0	9.0	44.0	48.0	8.0
% of GDP	0.5	0.5	0.1	0.5	0.4	0.1	0.4	0.3	0.1	—	—	—
Financing												
Foreign funding	999,116	4,696,358	1,121,147	3,183,000	7,571,424	511,900	2,435,500	6,562,000	180,000	4,891,000	12,715,000	590,000
% foreign funding	1.0	6.0	8.0	4.0	10.0	3.0	2.0	8.0	1.0	6.0	14.0	4.0

Sources: Ministry of Finance 2022a, 2022b; World Bank World Development Indicators (https://databank.worldbank.org/source/world-development-indicators#).
Note: Only direct program and project spending in each area are included. The ministry's administrative and establishment-related spending is excluded due to the complications of government structures. — = not available; GDP = gross domestic product; LKR = Sri Lanka rupees; TVET = technical and vocational education and training.

higher education were more than five times that, at approximately LKR 77.3 billion and approximately LKR 74.1 billion, respectively. The 2023 projection is estimated to be approximately LKR 15.8 billion, only 10.5 percent over the 2020 allocation for skills development and TVET. This amount is only about 8 percent of total education expenditure. The estimated budgets for general and higher education are significantly more, at 44 percent (fivefold) and 48 percent (sixfold) respectively. The share of public spending on TVET was less than 10 percent in 2021.

Reliance on foreign financing was highest for TVET, at 8 percent. General education had the lowest reliance on foreign sources. In 2022 the estimated share decreased further, to 1 percent, and in 2023 the projected share is estimated to be 4 percent (that is, one-half of the support from the 2021 actual spending). This amount factors the foreign financing disbursement for the achievement of the final SSDP indicator for preparing the new TVET Strategy. The SSDP closed in June 2023.

Spending by the SMSDVERI

In 2020 and 2021, major TVET activities in Sri Lanka were administered by the SMSDVERI, although the governance structure and responsibilities had changed slightly during the period. Total spending on programs for skills development and vocational training was estimated to be approximately LKR 9.8 million, and LKR 13.0 million for DTET (figure 5.2). Whereas DTET is funded entirely by domestic sources, foreign financing is an important source for skills development and vocational training. In 2020, the share of foreign financing in skills development and TVET reached 10 percent (figure 5.2).

FIGURE 5.2

Spending on skills development and vocational education in Sri Lanka, by program and financing source, 2015–22

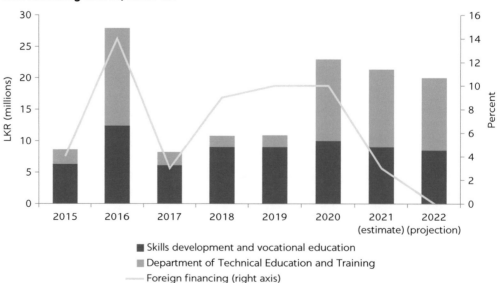

Sources: Ministry of Finance 2016, 2017, 2018, 2019, 2020, 2021.
Note: Includes program activities under the main ministry responsible (State Ministry of Skills Development, Vocational Education, Research and Innovations) as of 2020. LKR = Sri Lanka rupees.

Public spending on TVET has been inconsistent, although the budget allocated—especially for skills development and vocational education—tends to be closely correlated with the share of foreign financing (figure 5.2). Total spending, especially for skills development and vocational education, is expected to fall as foreign financing dropped to 3 percent of the total in 2021 and close to 0 percent in 2022.

Activities in skills development and vocational education are split into operational and development activities and, for each activity, recurrent and capital spending. Operational activities include regular recurrent items (such as staff salaries and spending on operations and maintenance), financial incentives for lecturers, stipends for students, and financing for vocational training authorities and institutions such as TVEC, VTA, NAITA, CGTTI, UNIVOTEC, and Ocean University. Development activities include various development programs funded through multilateral sources (Asian Development Bank and the World Bank) and bilateral sources (Australia, Austria, Germany, U.S. Agency for International Development). From 2017 to 2021, operational activities accounted for 62–68 percent and development activities for 32–38 percent of spending on skills development and vocational education, depending on the year and amount of the foreign financing (table 5.2). The foreign financing has varied from 4 to 17 percent of financing.

TABLE 5.2 Spending on skills development and vocational education in Sri Lanka, 2017–23
LKR (thousands)

TYPE OF SPENDING	2017	2018	2019	2020	2021 (REVISED)	2022 (ESTIMATE)	2023 (FORECAST)	TREND
Operational								
Recurrent	3,658,453	4,531,738	4,632,770	4,526,045	5,264,300	5,410,100	5,583,760	
Capital	531,392	1,198,370	990,550	10,043	100,000	30,000	30,930	
Subtotal	4,189,845	5,730,108	5,623,320	4,536,088	5,364,300	5,440,100	5,614,690	
Development								
Recurrent	243,134	80,000	77,000	56,671	560,000	1,000,000	1,000,000	
Capital	1,735,243	3,199,202	3,298,000	2,114,249	2,419,500	2,720,000	743,000	
Subtotal	1,978,377	3,279,202	3,375,000	2,170,920	2,979,500	3,720,000	1,743,000	
Total	**6,168,222**	**9,009,310**	**8,998,320**	**6,707,008**	**8,343,800**	**9,160,100**	**7,357,690**	
% operational	68	64	62	68	64	59	76	
% development	32	36	38	32	36	41	24	
Financing								
Foreign funding	219,650	996,202	1,169,000	1,121,147	511,900	180,000	590,000	
% foreign funding	4	11	13	17	6	2	8	

Source: Original calculations for this publication based on Ministry of Finance 2018, 2019, 2020, 2012, 2022a, 2022b. This excludes expenditures incurred for the Department of Technical Education and Training.
Note: The skills development and vocational training program budget was under the Ministry of Finance and Ministry of National Policies, Economic Affairs, Resettlement and Rehabilitation, Northern Province Development, Vocational Training and Skills Development and Youth Affairs in 2019 and the State Ministry of Skills Development, Vocational Education, Research and Innovations in 2020. LKR = Sri Lanka rupees.

Between 1994 and 2021, DTET financed all 39 colleges (9 colleges of technology and 30 technical colleges) that came under the department. All the department's spending is domestically sourced, and operational activities accounted for approximately 87 percent in 2017, increasing to 93 percent in 2020. Development activities accounted for about 13 percent in 2017, decreasing to only 7 percent in 2020. Capital spending fluctuated drastically over the time period (table 5.3). Compared to the skills development and vocational education budget, DTET spending was largely increased over this period.

Nearly two-thirds of spending for skills development and vocational and technical education programs is allocated to the six public institutions, with recurrent spending accounting for 81 percent of the total (table 5.4). In 2018, the cost per student at these institutions averaged LKR 65,000, although with large variations. The highest per capita cost was LKR 420,000, at UNIVOTEC, and the lowest was LKR 45,000, at NAITA.

This variation was due to the amount of capital spending allocated to each institution. Newer institutions, such as Ocean University (established in 2014) and UNIVOTEC (established in 2009), have higher capital costs. Both have relatively large shares of capital spending: 39 percent at Ocean University and 47 percent at UNIVOTEC, compared with 11 percent at DTET and 23 percent

TABLE 5.3 **DTET spending on technical education and training in Sri Lanka, 2017–23**

TYPE OF SPENDING	2017	2018	2019	2020	2021 (REVISED)	2022 (ESTIMATE)	2023 (PROJECTION)	TREND
A. Operational activities (OA)								
Recurrent spending	1,800,861	1,850,559	1,853,795	1,983,057	2,387,400	2,200,000	2,285,690	
B. Development activities (DA)								
Capital spending	275,847	226,711	204,661	155,578	542,700	310,000	361,530	
Total	**2,076,708**	**2,077,270**	**2,058,456**	**2,138,635**	**2,930,100**	**2,510,000**	**2,647,220**	
% OA	87	89	90	93	81	88	86	
% DA	13	11	10	7	19	12	14	

TABLE 5.4 **Public recurrent, capital, and per capita spending on public TVET institutions in Sri Lanka, 2018**
LKR (thousands)

INSTITUTE	RECURRENT	CAPITAL	TOTAL	PER CAPITA
Department of Technical Education and Training	1,959,816 (89%)	237,850 (11%)	2,197,666	68
National Apprentice and Industrial Training Authority	1,270,000 (86%)	200,000 (14%)	1,470,000	45
Vocational Training Authority	1,518,873 (88%)	200,000 (12%)	1,718,873	47
Ceylon–German Technical Training Institute	241,000 (77%)	70,000 (23%)	311,000	64
Ocean University	300,000 (61%)	190,000 (39%)	490,000	224
University of Vocational Technology	554,300 (53%)	487,000 (47%)	1,041,300	420
Total/average	**5,843,989 (81%)**	**1,384,850 (19%)**	**7,228,839**	**65**

Source: Original calculations for this publication based on State Ministry of Skills Development budget estimates and number of students in each institute.
Note: Shares of recurrent and capital spending are shown in parentheses. LKR = Sri Lanka rupees; TVET = technical and vocational education and training.

at CGTTI. In addition, Ocean University and UNIVOTEC provide longer National Vocational Qualification (NVQ) level 7 courses. Most training centers offer part-time courses for a fee; fee revenue can be used for operational activities.

Spending on vocational training by other ministries

The ministries responsible for policies and investments in major Sri Lankan industries sponsor their own skills development and vocational training activities. In 2021, total spending on TVET outside the SMSDVERI was approximately LKR 6.8 million, or 2.7 percent of public spending on TVET. Public TVET funding from other ministries fell 14 percent between 2018 and 2022 due to a 46 percent increase in recurrent spending and a 72 percent reduction in capital spending. A similar trend can be seen with an 11 percent reduction of total allocations and spending between 2018 and 2023 projected allocations.

Externally financed programs

The SSDP has been one of the largest TVET programs funded by foreign sources—the World Bank and the Asian Development Bank—accounting for nearly 84 percent in 2017, decreasing to 38 percent in 2020 (table 5.5). Major activities funded by the World Bank closed at the end of 2019, and the rest of the program was completed in June 2023.

COST-EFFECTIVENESS OF THE SKILLS SECTOR DEVELOPMENT PROGRAM

This section assesses the cost-effectiveness of the SSDP and analyzes the economic returns to investments made through the program over 2014–19.

Supply of skilled workers and efficiency of public TVET institutions

During the project period, TVET institutions supplied growing numbers of skilled workers relative to the baseline. However, it also saw efficiency fall in public TVET institutions, as measured by lower completion rates. The number of TVET graduates increased 20 percent, with spikes in 2014 and 2017 (figure 5.3), but the SSDP's original target—24 percent—was not met. In addition, the average completion rate for public TVET institutions fell from 75 percent in 2014 to 69 percent in 2019, while the private sector completion rate increased by half, from 51 to 75 percent, over the same period (figure 5.4). Due to the COVID-19 lockdown the number of students registered and graduated declined drastically in 2020.

Returns to TVET

Returns to TVET, controlling for education level and other factors, did not change and showed no significant difference before and after the SSDP

TABLE 5.5 **Externally financed TVET development programs funded through the Sri Lanka State Ministry of Skills Development, Vocational Education, Research and Innovations, 2017–23**
LKR (thousands)

SOURCE	PROGRAM	2017	2018	2019	2020	2021 (REVISED)	2022 (ESTIMATE)	2023 (FORECAST)
Australia	Skills for Inclusive Economic Growth	—	—	30,000	2,000	—	—	—
Austria	Upgrade of Katunayake Engineering Technology Institute	—	490,000	480,000	942,884	52,000	—	—
Germany (GIZ)	Vocational Training in the north and east of Sri Lanka	2,266	2,000	—	—	—	—	—
	Vocational Training in Sri Lanka	—	—	—	67,501	35,000	85,000	54,000
Korea, Rep.	Establishment of Colombo Vocational Training Center and Gampaha Technical College (EDCF of Exim Bank of Korea)	285,163	699,000	1,174,000	234,076	485,400	—	—
UNFPA	Comprehensive Reproductive Health Education	—	202	—	—	1,500	—	—
USAID	YouLead	—	—	45,000	4,387	5,000	85,000	44,000
World Bank and Asian Development Bank								
	Recurrent spending	243,134	80,000	77,000	56,671	60,000	—	—
	Capital spending	1,279,603	1,725,000	1,413,000	721,844	679,000	—	—
	Skills Sector Development Program (SSDP)	1,522,737	1,805,000	1,490,000	778,515	739,000	—	—
Total		**1,810,166**	**2,996,202**	**3,219,000**	**2,029,363**	**1,317,900**	**170,000**	**98,000**
Share of SSDP (%)		**84**	**60**	**46**	**38**	**56**	**—**	**—**

Sources: Ministry of Finance 2017, 2018, 2019, 2020, 2021.
Note: Costs associated with foreign loans are included. — = data not available; EDCF = Economic Development Cooperation Fund; LKR = Sri Lanka rupees; SSDP = Skills Sector Development Program; TVET = technical and vocational education and training; UNFPA = United Nations Population Fund; USAID = United States Agency for International Development.

FIGURE 5.3

Number of TVET graduates in Sri Lanka, 2012–19

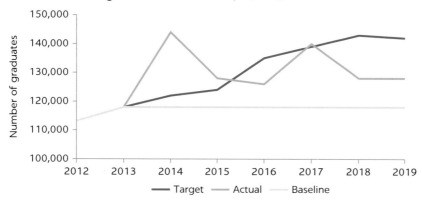

Source: World Bank 2020.
Note: TVET = technical and vocational education and training.

FIGURE 5.4

Enrollment and completion rates by public and private institutions in Sri Lanka, 2012–21

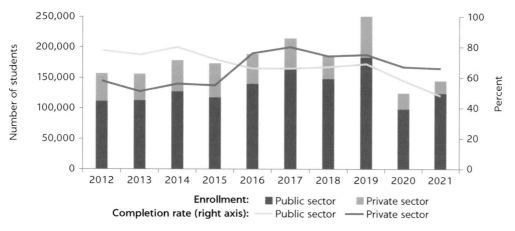

Sources: TVEC 2012, 2013, 2014, 2015, 2016, 2017, 2018, 2019, 2020, 2021.

started (DCS 2013, 2014, 2015, 2016, 2017). The only significant increase in returns occurred for students with university degrees, while a significant drop in returns hit primary graduates (figure 5.5). Among people ages 15–25 with education higher than primary and lower than university degree, TVET graduates earned, on average, 23 percent more than non-TVET graduates. There were no statistically significant changes before and after the SSDP started.

Meanwhile, the all-age group earnings ratio of TVET to non-TVET graduates in the same education group increased slightly from 1.39 in 2013–14 to 1.42 in 2015–17. This result indicates that the earnings gap between TVET and non-TVET graduates increases with age (or job experience), and this gap widened during the project years. The youth employment rate for this education group was 71 percent with TVET and 83 percent without it, and there was no difference before and after the SSDP.

FIGURE 5.5

Returns to education in Sri Lanka, 2013–17

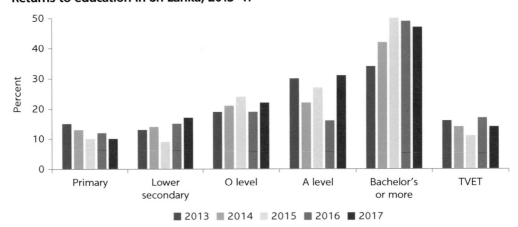

■ 2013 ■ 2014 ■ 2015 ■ 2016 ■ 2017

Source: World Bank 2020.
Note: Log of earnings regressed at each education level and age, age squared, and gender are included in the regression. TVET = technical and vocational education and training.

TABLE 5.6 **Cost-benefit analysis of the Skills Sector Development Program**

TOTAL BENEFIT (US$, MILLIONS)	TOTAL COST (US$, MILLIONS)	NET PRESENT VALUE (US$, MILLIONS)	INTERNAL RATE OF RETURN
296.6 (base) to 469.4 (high impact)	126.3	170.3 (base) to 343.1 (high impact)	10% (base) to 14% (high impact)

Source: Original calculations for this publication and World Bank 2020.
Note: Present value at beginning of the project in 2014.

Cost-benefit analysis of the Skills Sector Development Program

A cost-benefit analysis shows that the investment made in SSDP was economically sound. This analysis evaluates the cost-benefit of the SSDP using the DCS *Labour Force Survey* (various years) using target TVET graduates with a quality improvement assumption of a 1 percent increase in annual earnings as well as the actual number of TVET graduates during the project years and their labor market outcomes. The cost-benefit analysis largely relies on projections by project beneficiaries, their earnings profiles, and the project years covered.

To check its sensitivity to assumptions, the analysis was conducted with estimated benefits based on cohort-based, age-specific earning profiles and the five project years from 2014 to 2019. The analysis was conducted using actual project beneficiaries with base and high-impact scenarios. The base scenario assumes no lasting impact of the SSDP on TVET graduate trends after 2020. The high-impact scenario assumes that the SSDP's impact lasts five more years—in other words, the last-year impact of the SSDP on increased TVET graduates would last five years after the termination of funding. The analysis shows that the project generated an NPV of US$170.3 and an IRR of 10 percent during the project years (2014–19) with the base scenario. It confirms that the SSDP was an economically sound investment, with an NPV ranging between US$170.3 million (base) and US$343.1 million (high impact) and an IRR between 10 and 14 percent (table 5.6).

ASSESSING THE TVET FINANCING GAP

Public expenditure analysis and financial forecast in TVET

As a result of increasing economic uncertainty and unpredictable availability of adequate and timely government funding because of the 2022 economic crisis, the analysis in this section is based on historical trend, implications of the important policy change in 2018 that introduced the free TVET policy, and the financial forecast in the TVET sector derived from the per capita expenditures and historical enrollment trend.

Past data on TVET sector public expenditures and expenditure trends from items recorded in the budget documents of the SMSDVERI, and the financial implications of the free TVET policy serve as important guides for analyzing public expenditures and forecasting TVET spending in the future.

Expenditures in the TVET sector (table 5.7) mainly comprise recurrent and capital transfers to institutions and spending at the ministry level. Institution-level expenditure accounts for most of the spending in TVET: 93 percent of recurrent expenditures and 98 percent of capital expenditures. Until 2021, the government supported six public sector institutions: the VTA of Sri Lanka, NAITA, CGTTI, UNIVOTEC, Ocean University of Sri Lanka, and DTET. The 2022 budget estimates include two additional institutions: the Hardy Advanced Technological Institute and City University.

In 2018, Sri Lanka introduced the new policy of free TVET for all, which made enrollment in public institutions available to everyone free of charge. Prior to 2018, the institutions had received private revenue through tuition for operations and investments of the institutions. Following the introduction of the free TVET policy, through public expenditure, the government

TABLE 5.7 **Public expenditures in TVET (SMSDVERI) in Sri Lanka, 2017–22**
US$, nominal value

TYPE OF SPENDING	2017	2018	2019	2020	2021	2022 (ESTIMATE)
Expenditure to institutions						
Recurrent	4,988,539	5,864,732	6,050,000	6,092,151	7,146,800	7,021,600
Capital	776,107	1,383,711	1,319,000	402,439	1,044,200	1,280,000
Total	**5,764,646**	**7,248,443**	**7,369,000**	**6,494,590**	**8,191,000**	**8,301,600**
Expenditure at ministry level						
Recurrent	448,641	493,565	465,770	416,952	504,900	546,500
Capital	19,307	17,370	10,550	11,255	24,500	25,900
Total	**467,948**	**510,935**	**476,320**	**428,207**	**529,400**	**572,400**
Total expenditures						
Recurrent	5,437,180	6,358,297	6,515,770	6,509,103	7,651,700	7,568,100
Capital	795,414	1,401,081	1,329,550	413,694	1,068,700	1,305,900
Total	**6,232,594**	**7,759,378**	**7,845,320**	**6,922,797**	**8,720,400**	**8,874,000**
% of institutions—recurrent	92	92	93	94	93	93
% of institutions—capital	98	99	99	97	98	98
% of institutions—total	**92**	**93**	**94**	**94**	**94**	**94**

Source: Ministry of Finance Budget estimates 2018, 2019, 2020, 2021, 2022a, 2022b.
Note: Nominal value = the unadjusted rate or current price, without taking inflation or other factors into account as opposed to real values, where adjustments are made for general price level changes over time. SMSDVERI = State Ministry of Skills Development, Vocational Education, Research and Innovations; TVET = technical and vocational education and training.

tried to partially offset the financial deficits of the institutions since they were no longer raising private revenue. This made the per student expenditure (table 5.8) soar between 2017 and 2019. The trend shows both the recurrent and capital expenditures increased substantially from 2017 to 2018 and slightly decreased from 2018 to 2019 for all institutions except for DTET. Overall, in real terms, per student expenditure increased from 8 percent (VTA) to 664 percent (Ocean University) in just two years, excluding DTET. This has resulted in substantial fiscal pressure on the government coffers to finance the TVET sector.

Expenditure forecast for the TVET sector

Due to the dearth of financing data and the overall financial uncertainty in Sri Lanka, the analysis in this section is based on currently available unit cost (per capita expenditures) and the historical enrollment trend.

The expenditure/cost forecast is based on the unit cost (per capita expenditure in the skills development and education sector) and the total enrolment forecast for the TVET sector:

- The unit cost is calculated using the past three years' expenditures and the total enrollments between 2017 and 2019. Because of the negative impact of the COVID-19 pandemic on TVET enrollment, 2020 and 2021 information has not been used for the unit cost forecast.

TABLE 5.8 **Financing per student in TVET institutions in Sri Lanka, 2017–19**

	PER STUDENT EXPENDITURE (LKR)				% CHANGE		
	2017	2018	2019	TREND	2017–18	2018–19	2017–19
Vocational Training Authority							
Recurrent	40.11	43.99	43.49		10	−1	8
Capital	4.31	5.79	4.61		34	−20	7
Total	**44.43**	**49.78**	**48.11**		**12**	**−3**	**8**
National Apprentice and Industrial Training Authority							
Recurrent	30.61	41.70	40.01		36	−4	31
Capital	2.71	6.50	4.59		140	−29	69
Total	**33.32**	**48.20**	**44.61**		**45**	**−7**	**34**
Ceylon-German Technical Training Institute							
Recurrent	58.84	426.38	209.58		625	−51	256
Capital	23.45	123.85	64.16		428	−48	174
Total	**82.29**	**550.23**	**273.74**		**569**	**−50**	**233**
University of Vocational Technology							
Recurrent	167.93	190.24	186.02		13	−2	11
Capital	50.62	167.14	126.54		230	−24	150
Total	**218.55**	**357.38**	**312.56**		**64**	**−13**	**43**

Continued

TABLE 5.8, *continued*

	PER STUDENT EXPENDITURE (LKR)				% CHANGE		
	2017	2018	2019	TREND	2017–18	2018–19	2017–19
Ocean University							
Recurrent	432.83	522.93	2,844.83		21	444	557
Capital	102.97	331.19	1,250.00		222	277	1,114
Total	**535.80**	**854.11**	**4,094.83**		**59**	**379**	**664**
Department of Technical Education and Training							
Recurrent	50.62	61.10	44.71		21	−27	−12
Capital	7.76	7.49	8.51		−3	14	10
Total	**58.38**	**68.59**	**53.22**		**17**	**−22**	**−9**

Sources: Original calculations for this publication based on TVEC 2017, 2018, 2019; Ministry of Finance 2018, 2019, 2020.
Note: LKR = Sri Lanka rupees; TVET = technical and vocational education and training.

- Total enrollment for the next 10 years is projected based on the annual growth rate of 6.9 percent of total enrollment between 2012 and 2019 (table 5.9, panels a and b).

Base case scenario: Expenditure forecast and projections for the TVET sector (2022–32)

Assumptions

The base case scenario is based on total enrollment (public and private sector institutions), 6.9 percent annual growth rate from 2022 to 2032, and historical figures plus inflation to project expenditures for the next decade.

Caveats

Caveats are as follows:

- Expenditure data are available only until 2017.
- Enrollment numbers for 2020 are unclear due to COVID-19.
- No enrollment data are available for 2021.
- The budget for 2020 specifically is about the same as previous years. With declining enrollments due to the pandemic, the unit cost will likely increase sharply.

Methodology

There are two parts to the forecasting exercise:

1. *Estimating the unit cost based on data from 2017, 2018, and 2019*: The unit cost is calculated using the expenditures for the past three years and total enrollment between 2017 and 2019. Due to the negative impact of COVID-19 on TVET enrollment, the 2020 and 2021 data were not used for this forecast. Total enrollment for the next 10 years is estimated using an annual growth rate of 6.9 percent of total enrollment between 2012 and 2019. The enrollment projections from 2022 to 2032 are shown in figure 5.6.

2. *Estimating the entire budget* by factoring the recurrent and capital budget, excluding the estimated development partners' financing as shown in figure 5.7.

TABLE 5.9 **Expenditure projections for the TVET sector in Sri Lanka, 2022–32**

a. Constant 2022 LKR (thousands)

TYPE OF SPENDING	UNIT COST	2022	2023	2024	2025	2026	2027	2028	2029	2030	2031	2032
Operational												
Recurrent	23.7	5,943,606	6,354,485	6,793,768	7,263,419	7,765,536	8,302,364	8,876,303	9,489,919	10,145,953	10,847,339	11,597,211
Capital	5.0	1,253,281	1,339,919	1,432,547	1,531,579	1,637,456	1,750,653	1,871,675	2,001,063	2,139,396	2,287,291	2,445,411
Subtotal	28.7	7,196,887	7,694,405	8,226,316	8,794,998	9,402,992	10,053,017	10,747,978	11,490,982	12,285,349	13,134,630	14,042,622
Development												
Recurrent	0.8	191,285	204,508	218,646	233,761	249,920	267,197	285,669	305,417	326,530	349,103	373,236
Capital	15.1	3,788,104	4,049,974	4,329,947	4,629,275	4,949,295	5,291,437	5,657,232	6,048,314	6,466,432	6,913,454	7,391,378
Subtotal	15.9	3,979,389	4,254,482	4,548,593	4,863,035	5,199,215	5,558,635	5,942,901	6,353,731	6,792,962	7,262,557	7,764,614
Total	**44.6**	**11,176,276**	**11,948,887**	**12,774,909**	**13,658,033**	**14,602,207**	**15,611,652**	**16,690,879**	**17,844,713**	**19,078,311**	**20,397,187**	**21,807,236**
Foreign funding	3.7	918,331	981,815	1,049,688	1,122,252	1,199,833	1,282,777	1,371,455	1,466,263	1,567,625	1,675,995	1,791,855

b. Constant 2022 US$

TYPE OF SPENDING	UNIT COST	2022	2023	2024	2025	2026	2027	2028	2029	2030	2031	2032
Operational												
Recurrent	65	16,283,853	17,409,549	18,613,064	19,899,778	21,275,441	22,746,204	24,318,640	25,999,777	27,797,131	29,718,736	31,773,180
Capital	14	3,433,645	3,671,012	3,924,788	4,196,107	4,486,182	4,796,310	5,127,877	5,482,365	5,861,358	6,266,552	6,699,756
Subtotal	79	19,717,498	21,080,561	22,537,852	24,095,884	25,761,623	27,542,513	29,446,516	31,482,142	33,658,490	35,985,288	38,472,936
Development												
Recurrent	2	524,068	560,296	599,029	640,440	684,713	732,047	782,653	836,758	894,603	956,446	1,022,565
Capital	41	10,378,367	11,095,820	11,862,869	12,682,944	13,559,711	14,497,089	15,499,267	16,570,725	17,716,252	18,940,969	20,250,351
Subtotal	43	10,902,435	11,656,116	12,461,898	13,323,384	14,244,425	15,229,136	16,281,920	17,407,483	18,610,855	19,897,416	21,272,916
Total	**122**	**30,619,933**	**32,736,677**	**34,999,750**	**37,419,269**	**40,006,048**	**42,771,649**	**45,728,436**	**48,889,625**	**52,269,345**	**55,882,703**	**59,745,852**
Foreign funding	10	2,515,976	2,689,905	2,875,857	3,074,664	3,287,214	3,514,458	3,757,411	4,017,159	4,294,864	4,591,766	4,909,193

Note: 1 US$ = 365 LKR. LKR = Sri Lanka rupees; TVET = technical and vocational education and training.

FIGURE 5.6

Total TVET enrollments in Sri Lanka, historical trend and 2022–32 projections

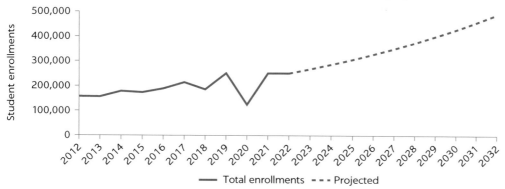

Source: Original calculations for this publication.
Note: TVET = technical and vocational education and training.

FIGURE 5.7

Budget forecast for the TVET sector in Sri Lanka for 2022–32, based on enrollment and unit cost

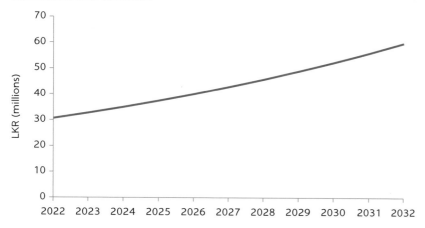

Source: Original calculations for this publication.
Note: LKR = Sri Lanka rupees; TVET = technical and vocational education and training.

Funding gap assessment

Government budget and development partners' support to the skills sector have been assessed according to the prevailing skills sector policies. Based on the ongoing financing for the skills sector, and projections, an attempt has been made to assess the financing gaps. This is the base case, all else held equal. The assessment has included the technical aspects of both grants and loans from development partners. On the financial side the following areas have been analyzed: grant-based donor support, loan-based donor support, and a gap analysis that allows government to make an informed decision about identifying the complementary areas for development partners' support.

Base case analysis

Using the base case assumptions explained above, both development and operational expenditure projections indicate an increase of 95 percent in 2032 over the 2022 expenditure to maintain the current state of services without discounting for inefficiencies and factoring the current runaway inflation in the country due to the 2022 economic crisis. Further, development partners' support (foreign funding) is also projected to increase by 95 percent over the 10-year period from 2022 to 2032. Teacher salaries constitute the largest proportion of recurrent expenditure.

The 2017 free TVET policy needs to be reviewed and a new policy instituted to ensure some cost recovery. Work-study will likely be a key feature of reskilling and upskilling in the future. This lends value to some level of cost recovery. Economies of scale and scope will need to be actively explored to rationalize TVET expenditures and improve systemic efficiencies. TVET instructors and teachers, lecturers, and workshop support staff will need to be fungible across related areas of specializations. For instance, instructors and teachers for electronics areas might need to also handle electrical technical education and technology-related training to impart digital skills. Further, policies such as multimodal training and blended learning will require additional investments and development expenditures. Commensurate teacher training will also be in demand, resulting in additional operational expenditure. Rationalization of financing for the TVET sector requires serious review.

Table 5.9 shows the estimated projections for the period 2022–32. In 2022 value, the unit cost of training one student was approximately LKR 44,600 (about US$122 in May 2022 exchange rate of US$1 = LKR 365). Development partners' financing constitutes only about 10 percent of the investment in training a student.

INTERNATIONAL EXPERIENCE

TVET financing in the Republic of Korea

The TVET sector in the Republic of Korea is financed through the Employment Insurance Fund (EIF). Workers/employees and employers pay a fee as a part of payroll tax. When determining the employment insurance fees, the Korea Worker's Compensation and Welfare Services assesses the fees based on digitized data and information across the workplace network managed by the Korea Employment Information Service. Currently, employers pay the insurance fee for vocational and competency development. The fee is 0.25 percent to 0.85 percent of base payroll, depending on the size of the business and the priority industries or national economic development policy; the fee for the unemployment benefit is shared by employees and employer (Korea Employment Information Service, n.d.).

Employment Insurance (EI) comprises two components: the unemployment benefit and the Vocational and Competency Development Plan (VCDP). The unemployment benefit is a passive safety net for the unemployed, whereas the VCDP is an active labor market policy tool to prevent unemployment and promote employment (Paik 2019).

EIF management is separate from the EI service management (implementation). The EIF is managed by financial experts. The Fund Investment Evaluation Committee regularly evaluates the EIF to assess the fund investment strategy and risk management (Employment Insurance Act). The EI service is managed by the Human Resources Development Service (HRD Korea) under the Ministry of Employment and Labor (figure 5.8).

FIGURE 5.8

TVET financing and management structure in the Republic of Korea

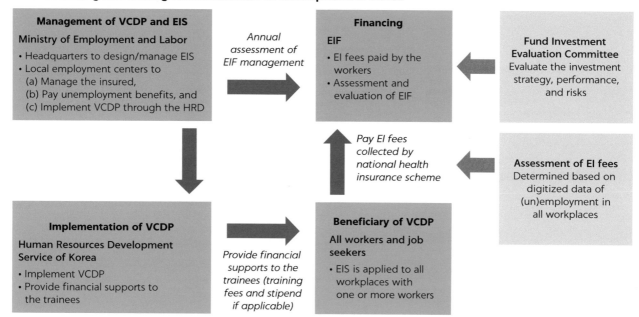

Source: Adapted based on the financing of TVET as described by Paik (2019).
Note: EI = Employment Insurance; EIF = Employment Insurance Fund; EIS = Employment Insurance System; HRD = Human Resources Development Service; TVET = technical and vocational education and training; VCDP = Vocational and Competency Development Plan.

Demand-driven programs: eVouchers and cost-sharing system in the VCDP

eVoucher

Potential beneficiaries of the VCDP include the workers in all workplaces and job seekers regardless of their EI payment history. The training program includes an eVoucher program for training programs in the future (figure 5.9), including on-the-job training, digital and innovative technology training, apprenticeship and national competency standards, and regional economy-specific training through regional employment support centers, among other programs. The eVoucher program is intended to provide the competency training for employees or job seekers for their current and future jobs. Eligibility is determined by HRD through online applications (HRD.go.kr), and the eligible student can register in any courses listed by the training providers (private and public) using the eVoucher. The eVoucher program is combined with a training subsidy and employment incentives.[3] The value of each eVoucher is about US$5,000 in training fees to be used within five years and a maximum of US$3,000 in one year. Students can use the voucher for any program(s) in public and/ or private training service institutes listed in the HRD network website (HRD-net).

Cost-sharing mechanism

The eVoucher pays a portion (45–85 percent) of training fees, and students pay the rest. The cost-sharing rate is determined by using the formula based on the past two years' average occupation-specific employment rate based on the

FIGURE 5.9

Process for accessing VCDP eVouchers for training programs in the Republic of Korea

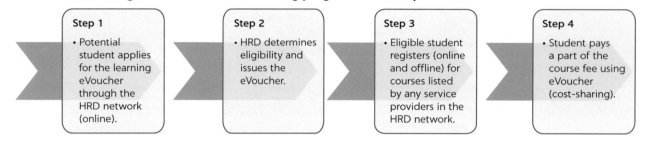

Source: Korea Employment Information Service (https://www.ei.go.kr).
Note: HRD = Human Resources Development Service; VCDP = Vocational and Competency Development Plan.

students' career plan and the students' eligibility score using age, income, and working status.[4] This mechanism takes both labor market demand and equity into consideration. It encourages eligible students to focus on high-performing, occupation-specific skills.

Performance-based establishment of national competency standard and training service market signaling in the Republic of Korea

National competency standard

The government of the Republic of Korea has put in place the National Competency Standard[5] (NCS) to systemize knowledge, skills, and attitudes required at work. The NCS is applied to all corporations for their human resource policy (employment, promotion, job skills statement, and so on); education and training institutes for development of training courses, materials, and instructors and teachers; and the qualifications center for assessment and evaluation methods. The NCS provides an objective basis to evaluate the performance of students and training institutes.

Training service market signaling[6]

Training service providers can register with the HRD.net if they are lawfully established.[7] The performance of the training service providers, using indicators such as employment rates and the pass rate of students with NCS certificates, is shared with potential students, and students can choose the provider based on their needs. On the HRD.net website, the training programs of high-performing institutes are promoted, and these courses are updated every day based on certain criteria such as courses focusing on 10 NCS occupations with high employment rates; greater than 70 percent employment rates; good or excellent-rated providers based on employment, facility, and student satisfaction (three years certification–rated as good quality or five years certification–rated as excellent quality); and courses starting within a month.

ANNEX 5A: DESCRIPTION OF PUBLIC TVET INSTITUTIONS AS OF 2020

TABLE 5A.1 **Public TVET institutions in Sri Lanka, 2020**

INSTITUTION	YEAR OF ESTABLISHMENT	LEVELS	DURATION	INSTITUTE STRUCTURE/ COMPOSITION	COURSES OFFERED
Department of Technical Education and Training	1893	Various levels including college degree and NVQ levels 5 and 6	3 months to 3 years	39 training centers (30 technical colleges in total with 9 regional colleges of technology)	Engineering technician, engineering craft, business studies, and general studies courses
National Apprentice and Industrial Training Authority	1990	Apprenticeship program; several craft courses and 4-year diploma courses, NVQ levels 3 and 4	6 months to 3 years	3 national training institutes, 25 district training centers, 5 regional training centers	Leading agency for the development of competency standards and assessment materials; offering crafts and engineering sciences
Vocational Training Authority	1995	Various levels including NVQ levels 3 and 4 and diploma courses	3 months to 1.5 years	Network of more than 186 small rural training centers throughout the country; 8 national vocational training institutes and 22 district vocational training centers	Craft courses; IT and industrial management
University of Vocational Technology	2008	NVQ level 7 and bachelor's degree programs	3 years	3 faculties including faculty of industrial technology, faculty of training technology, and faculty of vocational technology; and 6 university colleges offering NVQ levels 5 and 6	Construction technology, manufacturing technology, and information and communication technology; bachelor's of education (technology); vocational technology
Ceylon–German Technical Training Institute	1959	Various levels	3–4 years	—	Automobile engineering and related trades
Sri Lanka Institute of Printing	1984	Certificates and diploma programs	1.5 months to 2 years	—	Printing technology
Ocean University	2014	Various levels	10 days to 1 year	Formerly known as the National Institute of Fisheries and Nautical Engineering as the education and training arm of the Ministry of Fisheries and Aquatic Resources Development	Fisheries and nautical engineering

Sources: Databases and websites of the respective institutions; ADB 2017.
Note: — = not available; IT = information technology; NVQ = National Vocational Qualification; TVET = technical and vocational education and training.

NOTES

1. These are the Department of Technical Education and Training (DTET), National Apprentice and Industrial Training Authority (NAITA), Vocational Training Authority (VTA), Ceylon–German Technical Training Institute (CGTTI), Ocean University, University of Vocational Technology (UNIVOTEC, which includes university colleges), and Sri Lanka Institute of Printing (SLIOP). See annex 5A for descriptions of each.
2. For example, there are training institutes under the Ministry of Agriculture; Ministry of Urban Development and Housing; State Ministry of Foreign Employment Promotion and Market Diversification; State Ministry of Primary Health Care, Epidemics, and COVID Disease Control; and State Ministry of Rural Housing, Construction, and Building Material Industries.

3. Students who meet certain age and income criteria receive a monetary prize once they are successful in employment after the training.
4. The occupation- and skill-specific employment success rate is provided by the training providers and is based on the past two years' data.
5. Human Resources Development Service of Korea, National Competency Standards, https://www.ncs.go.kr.
6. Human Resources Development Service of Korea, HRD-Net, https://www.hrd.go.kr.
7. Current law sets criteria for the training institutes (space for students and capacity, online and offline) depending on the training category.

REFERENCES

ADB (Asian Development Bank). 2017. *Tracer Study for TVET Graduates' Employment in Sri Lanka*. Ministry of Skills Development and Vocational Training and Tertiary and Vocational Education Commission. Manila: ADB.

DCS (Department of Census and Statistics). 2013. *Sri Lanka Labour Force Survey Annual Report—2013*. Colombo.

DCS (Department of Census and Statistics). 2014. *Sri Lanka Labour Force Survey Annual Report—2014*. Colombo.

DCS (Department of Census and Statistics). 2015. *Sri Lanka Labour Force Survey Annual Report—2015*. Colombo.

DCS (Department of Census and Statistics). 2016. *Sri Lanka Labour Force Survey Annual Report—2016*. Colombo.

DCS (Department of Census and Statistics). 2017. *Sri Lanka Labour Force Survey Annual Report—2017*. Colombo.

Dundar, Halil, Benoît Millot, Yevgeniya Savchenko, Harsha Aturupane, and Tilkaratne A. Piyasiri. 2014. *Building the Skills for Economic Growth and Competitiveness in Sri Lanka*. Directions in Development. Washington, DC: World Bank. https://doi.org/10.1596/978-1-4648-0158-7.

Korea Employment Information Service. n.d. *Employment Insurance*. https://www.ei.go.kr/ei/eih/cm/hm/main.do.

MoF (Ministry of Finance). 2016. *Budget Estimates Fiscal Year 2016*. Volume II. Colombo: Democratic Socialist Republic of Sri Lanka.

MoF (Ministry of Finance). 2017. *Budget Estimates Fiscal Year 2017*. Volume II. Colombo: Democratic Socialist Republic of Sri Lanka.

MoF (Ministry of Finance). 2018. *Budget Estimates Fiscal Year 2018*. Volume II. Colombo: Democratic Socialist Republic of Sri Lanka.

MoF (Ministry of Finance). 2019. *Budget Estimates Fiscal Year 2019*. Volume II. Colombo: Democratic Socialist Republic of Sri Lanka.

MoF (Ministry of Finance). 2020. *Budget Estimates Fiscal Year 2020*. Volume II. Colombo: Democratic Socialist Republic of Sri Lanka.

MoF (Ministry of Finance). 2021. *Budget Estimates Fiscal Year 2021*. Volume II. Colombo: Democratic Socialist Republic of Sri Lanka.

MoF (Ministry of Finance). 2022a. *Budget Estimates Fiscal Year 2022*. Volume II. Colombo: Democratic Socialist Republic of Sri Lanka.

MoF (Ministry of Finance). 2022b. *Budget Estimates Fiscal Year 2022*. Volume III. Colombo: Democratic Socialist Republic of Sri Lanka.

MoF (Ministry of Finance). 2023. *Budget Estimates Fiscal Year 2023*. Colombo: Democratic Socialist Republic of Sri Lanka.

Paik, Sung Joon. 2019. "Financing TVET: A Comparative Analysis in Six Asian Countries—Korean Case Study." Agence Française de Développement (AFD) technical report No. 57. AFD, Paris.

TVEC (Tertiary and Vocational Education Commission). 2012. *Labour Market Information Bulletin*. Colombo.

TVEC (Tertiary and Vocational Education Commission). 2013. *Labour Market Information Bulletin.* Colombo.

TVEC (Tertiary and Vocational Education Commission). 2014. *Labour Market Information Bulletin.* Colombo.

TVEC (Tertiary and Vocational Education Commission). 2015. *Labour Market Information Bulletin.* Colombo.

TVEC (Tertiary and Vocational Education Commission). 2016. *Labour Market Information Bulletin.* Colombo.

TVEC (Tertiary and Vocational Education Commission). 2017. *Labour Market Information Bulletin.* Colombo.

TVEC (Tertiary and Vocational Education Commission). 2018. *Labour Market Information Bulletin.* Colombo

TVEC (Tertiary and Vocational Education Commission). 2019. *Labour Market Information Bulletin.* Colombo.

TVEC (Tertiary and Vocational Education Commission). 2020. *Labour Market Information Bulletin.* Colombo.

TVEC (Tertiary and Vocational Education Commission). 2021. *Labour Market Information Bulletin.* Colombo.

TVEC (Tertiary and Vocational Education Commission). 2022. *Labor Market Information Bulletin.* Colombo.

World Bank. 2020. "Implementation Completion and Results Report." Skills Development Project (ICR00005113). World Bank, Washington, DC.

6 Policy Recommendations

INTRODUCTION

Many young men graduating with O-level high school qualifications prefer to drive three-wheelers as an attractive alternative to signing up for technical and vocational education and training (TVET) programs. This is very telling about the TVET system. The TVET and skills development system needs to be reformed radically to improve access to quality and relevant technical and vocational training, and develop appropriate communication strategies for changing perceptions and the mindsets of parents, communities, and youth about TVET qualifications.

PRINCIPLES FOR TRANSFORMING THE TVET AND SKILLS ECOSYSTEM

Simplifying the skills ecosystem in Sri Lanka will require radical transformation, including introducing a revamped accreditation system for private sector institutions; providing incentives for consolidating small private sector institutions; consolidating public sector institutions to close small, inefficient ones; introducing centers of excellence; consolidating programs (closing unsubscribed programs); adding new 21st-century skills programs (such as stackable microcredentials in areas such as collaboration, creative problem solving, critical thinking, empathy, initiative, oral and written communication, intercultural awareness and fluency, and resilience) in public sector institutions to improve market relevance and quality; assessing the overall governance of the system; introducing new financing modalities; and doing a public expenditure review of the public skills development system. Six principles could guide the transformation of the skills development ecosystem and the articulation of a 21st-century skills strategy for Sri Lanka.

Principle 1: Selectivity

The skills sector is very large. Building resilience to crises such as the COVID-19 pandemic lockdowns that have negatively affected teaching and learning will require actions in the immediate and intermediate time frames. Access to skilling is constrained by the number of available places in classrooms. It is not possible to consider large-scale support to improve access due to some sectoral areas being highly resource intensive. Therefore, providing all the facilities for all the centers and equipping them with all the requirements is not possible.

Principle 2: Prioritization

Not all sectors will carry equal weight in the economy. The Government of Sri Lanka (GoSL) would need to identify the priority sectors for the economy for which skilling, reskilling, and upskilling would really be needed.

Principle 3: Blended teaching and learning

Toward fostering a hybrid or blended mode of teaching and learning, focus on putting in place a learning management system or an e-learning platform to facilitate skilling, reskilling, and upskilling through the approach of anywhere, anytime learning.

Principle 4: Relevance

Current industry demand outstrips the supply of relevant quality trained youth. This is linked to an appropriately skilled workforce with the ability to lead and respond to new labor markets.

Principle 5: Inclusion to build resilience

Skills development being a priority for the government, and gender being a binding constraint, skills development would need to be adjusted accordingly. Equal opportunity for quality and relevant skills development will be the guiding principle for targeting support. The target populations would need to include women and girls, people who are disabled, and marginalized or vulnerable populations.

Principle 6: Adaptation

Quality enhancements for blended teaching and learning adapted to a rationalized TVET and skills development infrastructure will be the driving force for transformation, specifically in the areas of instructor recruitment, training, performance evaluation, digital literacy and skills, and green skills and jobs.

- *Teacher training.* Review and upgrade teacher training standards in priority areas for the economy. Put in place a dynamic system to help instructors and teachers to reskill and upskill themselves. Review and assess the stock and flow of qualified instructors and teachers. Make use of visiting industry experts as teaching faculty outside of office hours and on weekends. Consider global knowledge exchange seminars to enhance local knowledge and expand beyond local perspectives.
- *Teacher recruitment.* Establish a performance-based system of pay for instructors and teachers through a new cadre of contractual instructors and teachers. Natural attrition is occurring among existing teachers, who currently have permanent jobs and draw a monthly salary without any performance appraisal

or promotion system, upskilling, or reskilling. Also, consider hiring young instructors who are able to grasp digital trends and apply new digital options for skilling, reskilling, and upskilling.

- *Large centers with enhanced facilities.* Rationalize institutions and programs to improve quality. At present, there are 600 public sector institutions and 700–800 private sector institutions. Centers of excellence in some provinces would help to improve the image of TVET.

- *Green infrastructure solutions.* Include the use of renewable energy solutions (solar, wind) and climate-resilient building materials in rehabilitating existing TVET infrastructure.

- *Coverage and access.* Adopt hybrid or blended teaching and learning modes and, where applicable and necessary, build the face-to-face service delivery mode to help increase the capacity of the TVET system to respond to growing demand.

- *Digitalization.* Digitalize systems, including by introducing e-teaching and e-learning materials and assessments. Address the digital divide from four dimensions: geographic/spatial, connectivity, affordability, and as it relates to marginalized and vulnerable populations.

- *Digital skills.* Develop programs for building the digital skills of instructors and teachers, trainers, tutors, assessors, and administrators and managers.

- *Skills bridges and ladders and skills identification.* Use career interest tests linked to O-level and A-level high school certification to assess students' areas of interest. Give attention to career paths for grade 9 students, the option and possibility for students to acquire NVQ-level credentials, career and success standards, career counseling, and guidance. Lend credence to the GoSL's Skills Passport. The Skills Passport includes details of NVQ certificates and the trade, number of years of work experience, and so on. Since it is more like a driver's license, workers can carry it with them. The Skills Passport is valid for five years. After that time period, the Skills Passport holder can reapply to get the validity period extended. Reskilling requirements have not yet been articulated and communicated. This would be an important area to address.

- *Curriculum and standards development.* Review the number of occupations for which NVQ-based standards have not yet been developed. Enhance capacity for curriculum assessment and change that currently takes three years per occupation. Put in place new approaches to curriculum assessments and standards setting. Modularize TVET to permit the stacking of credentials and adopt a qualifications-based approach to skilling. Of importance are also the inclusion of soft skills (teamwork, effective communication, self-presentation, problem solving, and so on) in the curriculum and English language skills to prepare an internationally competitive workforce. Mainstreamed English language curriculum would be a driving factor (Amarasekera 2019).

- *Fungible skills.* Create opportunities for developing fungible skills rather than specialized skills. Curricular reform should result in transforming skills.

- *District-wise assessment centers for awarding NVQs.* Assess the feasibility and establish, where possible, assessment centers in each district for the purpose of conducting competency-based assessments for the Tertiary and Vocational Education Commission (TVEC) to award NVQs in collaboration with the public, private, and nongovernmental organization TVET institutes. The proposed centers would be set up within the premises of existing public sector institutions operating under the line ministry in charge of vocational training. This measure is expected to expedite and facilitate the assessment process of the two pathways of obtaining NVQs (that is, competency-based training and the recognition of prior learning).

- *Recognition of prior learning (RPL)*. Use recognition systems to promote more inclusive and sustainable economic growth that benefits everyone. Sri Lanka has an RPL system in place and is seeking to better enforce it during the COVID-19 pandemic to address lost livelihoods. Building trust around the assessments offered through RPL is important to enforce the RPL system. More young graduates are entering the labor market. Further, Sri Lanka would benefit from assessing the outcome and impact of its RPL system to determine the effectiveness of the knowledge and skills certification provided under the system.

    The Sri Lankan RPL system has developed slowly over time. The following actions are recommended to increase access to and the quality of RPL:
    - Enhance awareness. The sector can only be developed by creating further awareness of RPL in the industry and schools. Some of the myths of RPL can be explained, and the number of workers opting for NVQ certification through RPL can be increased.
    - Encourage industry to get all workers certified through RPL.
    - Offer subsidized rates for RPL certification for those who are in need.
    - Develop more national competency standards to offer NVQ and RPL certificates and popularize RPL certification to enable offering RPL.
    - Map trade tests to RPL and popularize RPL. Develop competency standards for all trade tests for occupations with equivalency to permit RPL assessment.
    - Encourage further research to identify key success factors and minimize concerns, issues, and challenges.
    - Continue to develop innovative approaches to assessment and professional development of assessors to enhance quality.
    - Strengthen the quality assurance and monitoring of the RPL system to enhance NVQ obtained through RPL.
    - Review the fiduciary process relating to RPL and suggest simplified processes to encourage authorized agencies to offer NVQ through RPL.
- *Reskilling for returning migrants*. Introduce new certification options and upload credentials on the Skills Passport to help returning migrants take up new jobs and to foster the portability of knowledge and skills.
- *Entrepreneurship skills*. Promoting self-employment is a priority for the government. Include entrepreneurship skills in the curriculum to expand the opportunities for individuals to become entrepreneurs. This is especially needed for women who can enter the labor market through home-based work. With more women entering the labor market, they could productively contribute to the economy. This will likely also create additional job opportunities in the areas of child care and health care.
- *Communications for sensitization and mindset change regarding TVET*. Develop robust communication strategies to sensitize and change perceptions and the mindsets of parents, communities, and youth about technical education. A recent World Bank study (Sosale et al. 2023) found that mid-level skills predominantly help graduates remain in the labor market even during economic downturns, and they are critical for driving green growth.
- *Government research*. Identify Sri Lanka's competitive and comparative advantages as they relate to the national and global markets. The Department of Census and Statistics' Labour Force Survey is an annual survey of the national labor market and labor demand. In addition to this source, consider using

sources of global demand for skilled workers. This would help Sri Lanka to match the skilling, reskilling, and upskilling requirements of its workforce to also respond to the global marketplace. This is a vital space for investments not least because Sri Lanka has an aging population, but there is globally a need for health care and child care providers. In addition, TVEC and other institutions can be encouraged to conduct more research in the TVET sector.

• *Graduate tracer system.* Establish a dynamic graduate tracer system that captures qualifications and experience. There is no system in place to capture the dynamic nature of graduates and employment. The Skills Passport is a good option, but it needs to be improved and expanded.

• *Monitoring and evaluation system.* The TVET system lacks a credible management information system to monitor and evaluate the ecosystem, from access to relevant quality of TVET education to links with the labor market. Develop a viable and credible monitoring and evaluation system to facilitate dynamic measurement, assessment, adjustment, and reforms.

The objective of the financing gap assessment exercise was to better understand the current fiscal situation, articulate how best to use the existing resources, assess the capacity in the skills sector to utilize the resources for the intended purposes, determine the levels of development partners' ongoing funding for the skills sector, and identify the financing gaps and technical areas to be tackled during the skills decade (2021–30) for a One Plan approach.

Skills development must continue to be high on the government's agenda for Sri Lanka to become a "Smart Nation" with digitally skilled workers who possess job-ready soft and technical skills. The path to this would be through skills sector transformation, inclusion, and rapid recovery from the COVID-19 pandemic and the 2022 economic crisis, to build a resilient economy and a prepared nation.

Sri Lanka is recovering from the 2022 triple crisis (fuel, food, fiscal). In addition, the post-COVID-19 pandemic period has necessitated a review and analysis of the jobs and skills needed for the future of the economy. The government's new Technical and Vocational Education and Training Strategy for the period 2024–33 sets the direction for the future, includes key policy reforms, and aims to set up a road map as a response to and in anticipation of changes in the demand for jobs and skills in local, national, and global economies and labor markets. *Enhancing Skills in Sri Lanka for Inclusion, Recovery, and Resilience* sets out the analytical underpinnings and recommendations to inform the government's new 2024–33 TVET Strategy.

SUPPORT FOR SKILLS DEVELOPMENT

The government's policy and strategy strongly signal support for the skills development agenda. Sri Lanka aims to drive economic transformation with targets to increase the stock and flow of a skilled workforce; create employment opportunities; mobilize tax revenue; and increase annual export income, for inclusion, recovery, and resilience. Therefore, developing relevant skills and competencies to match the demands of a new economy job market is at the core of supporting the government's new vision for Sri Lanka to be transformed into a "Smart Nation." The strategy includes the following components:

• *Reviewing the TVET policy* and its strategic link to higher education levels and the labor market.

- *Improving access to TVET programs to enhance employability,* especially for women and people from socioeconomically disadvantaged backgrounds. Financial assistance programs for enrolling in TVET programs, including student stipends and vouchers, may be considered to improve uptake of TVET programs in areas of economic priority.
- *Providing reskilling opportunities* to upgrade the skills of the existing stock of workers through increased cooperation from industry and the private sector.
- *Raising the quality of TVET programs* through improvements to teaching–learning facilities, such as modern equipment and materials, for practical learning in classrooms; upgrading curricula with industry inputs; and increasing teaching strength through recruitment of qualified instructors and instructors' and teachers' professional development opportunities.
- *Fostering digital skills acquisition* by developing a country action plan and creating ready-to-deploy tools for a digital skills agenda: preparation of a terms of reference and composition of the government teams; developing a methodological guidebook for an action plan and templates, including strategies, prework tools, and connecting information on connectivity; a digital skills demand study for the provinces; a planning tool for generating cost simulations; and a web-based costing tool for detailed cost estimates, projections, and evaluations. Guidance on curricula for information and communication technologies (ICT) will be a critical element (Ranatunga 2020).
- *Reorienting and introducing new programs to enhance employability.* Programs that impart both cognitive and noncognitive skills will be critical. Competencies would include personal initiative training, entrepreneurship, soft skills training such as self-presentation, oral and written communication, preparing a winning CV, public speaking, English language and mathematics training, and computing skills through boot camps. In addition, socioemotional skills have now assumed greater importance in the post-COVID-19 environment. Therefore, the application of problem solving, resilience, achievement motivation, control, teamwork, initiative, confidence, and ethics or *practice* skills will be important, especially in the informal and formal sectors. Finally, of critical importance are career guidance programs to guide and counsel students to make informed career choices.
- *Enhancing governance and accountability* by improving coordination among the various providers across the skills delivery system; strengthening and widening quality assurance mechanisms across all providers; accelerating the implementation of the National Vocational Qualification (NVQ) framework or the Sri Lanka Qualifications Framework (SLQF); reviewing and upgrading teacher career progression and human resource incentives; providing TVET agencies and centers more decision-making autonomy and utilization of performance-based financing with accountability mechanisms; and regularly conducting labor market surveys and widely disseminating the information.
- *Strengthening center management plans.* The management plans created by centers could be further strengthened by developing a stronger learning management and monitoring and evaluation system.
- *Deepening private sector involvement* by expanding existing training programs and initiating new ones in priority economic sectors with industry partnership; strengthening representation in TVET management to provide industry-specific knowledge and skills demands; promoting industry

partnerships in curricula review and development; and expanding official apprenticeship programs and skills certification in partnership with the private sector.

- *Fostering entrepreneurship* to enhance labor market opportunities for self-employment and wage employment specifically to address recovery and resilience in the post–COVID-19 pandemic "new normal" environment to build back better, encouraging entrepreneurship and job creation through the options of competitive innovation matching grants or similar instruments for start-ups in a transparent manner, working in collaboration with chambers of commerce and the Chamber of Small and Medium Enterprises.
- *Broadening the governance of skills development by harnessing the chambers of commerce and sector skills and/or employment councils* to improve the relevance of skills for the existing stock of employees and the future flow of trained youth.
- *Improving the social perception of TVET* through awareness-building and mass communication events to increase the social value of TVET among students, parents, and communities.

A three-pronged approach would be necessary to assess gaps in technical areas and financing. First, the government needs to undertake an annual needs assessment of the labor market to determine priority sectors for the economy. Second, the skills development system needs to be flexible and compatible (through governance and institutional measures) and equipped to address emerging labor market needs. Finally, the financing for skills development needs to be pegged to addressing efficiency, sufficiency, and effectiveness. The policy of free TVET education needs to be seriously reviewed to avoid deadweight loss to the economy.

The development of skills needs to include digital skills to enable people whose jobs and livelihoods have been adversely affected by the COVID-19 pandemic to find employment in the new economic environment. To ensure greater inclusion and productive employment, four considerations would be warranted:

- The reskilling and upskilling of Sri Lankan expatriates who are returning to the country (as a result of COVID-19) to better integrate them into the job market;
- Skills development for women to enhance their employability and labor-market participation;
- Skills development for youth to promote self-employment; and
- Preparation of a flow of well-trained semiprofessionals for the global labor market.

Overall, skills development needs to be demand-led with the active participation of employers, the private sector, chambers of commerce, and the sector skills councils in both shaping the content of the skills areas as well as in imparting the skills through enterprise-based or on-the-job training.

STRATEGY FOR SKILLS DEVELOPMENT

The government's strategy for the development of 21st-century skills could be threefold.

Supporting fast recovery and building skilled workers in priority sectors

A rapid livelihood assessment of the impact of the COVID-19 crisis in Sri Lanka would be important to inform the areas and depth of skills development required toward developing and offering flexible learning modules focusing on priority sectors to support rebuilding the workforce for economic recovery in the areas of manufacturing, services, agriculture and fisheries, and government-identified priority sectors. The modules developed could range from improving productivity through broadening and enhancing the quality of export-oriented products, safer and hygienic tourism, modern farming methods, fishing and preservation methods, and enhancing income-earning options. The modules could be delivered through flexible learning and multimodal media (radio, television, face-to-face, online) to support the reskilling of the current workforce in the formal and informal sectors, and youth to obtain suitable technical and vocational qualifications at a later stage.

Investing in the informal sector

This element requires enhancing the skills of informal sector workers to improve productivity with options for enterprise-based training, skilling, and reskilling in a priority sector, and developing modules in entrepreneurship, promoting young entrepreneurs, and gradually formalizing the work environment.

Strengthening programs for the skilling, reskilling, and upskilling of citizens

It is critical for government to ensure targeted assistance for the vulnerable segments of the population such as single women, people with special needs, and the elderly to help them pursue various skills development programs, engage in lifelong learning, and contribute through increased productivity to fuel growth commensurate with Sri Lanka's aspiration to become a full-fledged middle-income country. TVET needs modular programs to help with lifelong learning and skills development. Specifically, employees and employers should be given options for stacking skills, building theoretical and practical expertise over time. Facilitating the acquisition of microcredentials (short, focused credentials for skills in demand)and of stackable microcredentials to provide pathways for students to acquire certificates or to pursue full degree programs will enhance opportunities for lifelong learning. Making TVET skills more flexible, credible, and stackable is essential to bridge gaps in livelihoods and skills.

REFERENCES

Amarasekera, C. L. 2019. "Background Review of English Language Curriculum in Sri Lanka." World Bank commissioned study for the Skills Sector Transformation for Inclusion, Recovery, and Resilience program, World Bank, Colombo.

Ministry of Education, Department of Skills Development. 2023. "Technical and Vocational Education and Training Strategy 2024–2033." Colombo.

Ranatunga, R. V. S. P. K. 2020. "Background Review of Information and Communication Technologies Curriculum in Sri Lanka." World Bank commissioned study for the Skills Sector Transformation for Inclusion, Recovery, and Resilience program, World Bank, Colombo.

Sosale, Shobhana, Graham Mark Harrison, Namrata Tognatta, Shiro Nakata, and Priyal Mukesh Gala. 2023. *Engendering Access to STEM Education and Careers in South Asia. South Asia Development Forum*. Washington, DC: World Bank. doi:10.1596/978-1-4648-1966-7.